Teaching *The Wire*

Teaching *The Wire*

Frameworks, Theories and Strategies for the Classroom

Edited by Tia Sherèe Gaynor
and Jocelyn DeVance Taliaferro

McFarland & Company, Inc., Publishers
Jefferson, North Carolina

ISBN (print) 978-0-7864-9390-6
ISBN (ebook) 978-1-4766-2576-8

LIBRARY OF CONGRESS CATALOGUING DATA ARE AVAILABLE

British Library cataloguing data are available

Front cover images © 2016 iStock

Printed in the United States of America

McFarland & Company, Inc., Publishers
  Box 611, Jefferson, North Carolina 28640
    www.mcfarlandpub.com

This book is for all the stars, in all the skies,
in all of the universe.—Tia

I dedicate this book to my husband, Earl Warren.
Thank you for watching *The Wire*. Every. Single. Time.
I had to teach the course and three additional times
to edit this book and write my chapter.
You are indeed a helpmate.—Jocelyn

Acknowledgments

The editors would like to thank the following individuals who without their contributions, counsel, encouragement, and support this book would not have been written:

Karen Bullock, Marc Fudge and Antonio Johnson

Table of Contents

Acknowledgments   vi

Introduction   1
    TIA SHERÈE GAYNOR *and* JOCELYN DEVANCE TALIAFERRO

The Clash of Aristocratic and Bourgeois Virtues in *The Wire*   5
    GUS P. GRADINGER *and* BART J. WILSON

"You gonna look out for me?" Intersectionality, Young Black   24
    Male Giftedness and Cultural Competency Using *The Wire*
    HEATHER CHERIE MOORE

"Cause they're not learning for our world; they're learning   40
    for theirs": A Critical Race Theory and Phenomenological
    Variant of Ecological Systems Theory Analysis of Season 4
    of *The Wire*
    HANNAH CARSON BAGGETT, CRYSTAL G. SIMMONS,
    SHARONDA R. EGGLETON *and* JESSICA T. DECUIR-GUNBY

Schooling You on the Domains of Power in *The Wire*   63
    TIA SHERÈE GAYNOR *and* BRANDI BLESSETT

From Sentimentalism to Grief: Pedagogies of Humanization   80
    in *Waiting for "Superman"* and *The Wire*
    MARK STERN

"Omar listening": Queer Theory, Gender Play and *The Wire*   98
    JASON P. VEST

What Then? The Cultural Forum of *The Wire*   116
    JOE ALLEN *and* CHRISTOPHER S. TOENES

It's All in the Game: How NOT to Teach *The Wire* in   132
    Predominantly White Institutions (PWI)
        PEGGY JONES

"Soft Eyes": Pragmatic Considerations and Strategies for   146
    Teaching *The Wire*
        JOCELYN DEVANCE TALIAFERRO

About the Contributors   169

Index   173

Introduction

TIA SHERÈE GAYNOR *and*
JOCELYN DEVANCE TALIAFERRO

At the advent of higher education, theory knowledge was the basis of knowledge in the halls of academia. The most prestigious and elite institutions of higher education in the United States provided instruction in liberal studies, not focusing on practical knowledge until the late 1800s with the land grant institution movement (Geiger, 2014). Only then did practical knowledge become of high value in U.S. higher education. Today, practical knowledge and applicability are the focus of many academic classes, in fact entire programs. Increasingly, students want to know that what they are learning has real-world relevance and application during and after college. As professors, in public administration and social work, respectively, we are acutely aware of the need for practical knowledge. It is imperative that our students are able to access the bridge that connects their theoretical knowledge to the activities, environments, and situations that they routinely face once in the "field." It is not, however, just students of social science that require this conceptual bridge. All students, whether they are studying engineering, philosophy, biology, business, or dance, need to understand the world that informs their academic studies and society at large.

In our quest to identify resources that construct this bridge and provide students with context, we discovered a mutual appreciation for the way that HBO's critically acclaimed television series *The Wire* provides a glimpse of the complexities of real world grand challenges. It was at this point that we each (independent of the knowledge of the other's work) began using *The Wire* to teach. We were not alone. Universities across the globe use *The Wire* to teach students in wide ranging programs (the authors included in this volume demonstrate this). Some of these programs are the expected ones—public administration and policy, social work, criminal justice, sociology—but others are far more surprising—religion, literary studies, law, and history. The popularity and seamless integration of *The Wire* in higher education is evidenced by the existence of conferences focusing on the show, journal articles and dedicated journal symposia, as well several books examining the show through varied academic perspectives.

The Wire strengthens student learning by exposing students to material in a way that no academic source would be able to (Wilson & Chaddha, 2010). Students are gripped by the realistic nature of the show. Some students even become invested to the point of frustration, grief, and anger to name just a few emotions experienced as they share the "lived experiences" of the characters. Students often relay their enjoyment of the show in class, holding lively discussions about the plot lines and characters, as well as the critical evaluation of U.S. society and organizations. The show tactically illuminates the notion that the United States and its institutions are full of ambiguity, complexity, and moral and ethical dilemmas. The show uses multiple contexts, including informal economies, schools, gang hierarchies, municipal government, arguing that oftentimes formal and informal institutions may not be all that different.

The purpose of this book is therefore, twofold. First, the text seeks to explore the usefulness and challenges of using *The Wire* in university and college classrooms and explores paralleled connections between the show (as a proxy for practice) and theory. Secondly, the authors discuss how the show can be (and has been) used to teach issues such as leadership, gender expression, sexuality, education, cultural competency, democracy, policy, and myriad other discourses and narratives.

The Wire is as timeless as the issues portrayed in the show. First airing in 2002, the show remains relevant 15 years later. The characters—D'Angelo, McNulty, Herc, Michael, Randy, Carver, Kima, Prez, and of course Omar, to name a few—can all be found in communities across the United States. The stories, challenges, and triumphs are familiar and hold some truth (in one way or another) to the experiences of community residents across the country. *The Wire*, in some way, speaks to everyone's truth.

Readers of this book will learn essential elements of teaching *The Wire* and gain a clear understanding of its effectiveness in meeting course objectives. Gradinger and Wilson present their freshman seminar course, *Humanomics*. This course uses *The Wire* to understand the bourgeois ethics of the marketplace by combining an economic inquiry into the inclination to exchange with the cultural interpretation of the human condition. Ultimately, this essay, through its nuanced discussion of *The Wire* and the bourgeois ethics of the marketplace, challenges the notion that the humanities and economics are distinct courses of study.

Moore explores the importance of cultural competency in higher education and expands upon normative definitions of intelligence. She uses *The Wire*, specifically Season Four, to demonstrate how select characters' behaviors contest normative conceptions of intelligence.

Following this discussion, Baggett, Simmons, Eggleton, and DeCuir-Gunby continue the focus on education in their exploration of the ways race and racism impact the social and economic policies that influence the adolescents' environment inside and outside of school as portrayed in Season Four. Authors analyze the schooling and developmental experiences of four of the adolescent characters through two distinct frameworks—Critical Race Theory and Phenomenological Variant of Ecological Systems Theory—consequently, illustrating how *The Wire* can be used to elucidate the various racialized contextual factors that affect student development in schools.

Gaynor and Blessett continue the discussion of Critical Race Theory, but incorporate the domains-of-power framework to illustrate the ways power, in *The Wire*, is exercised to create or resist inequity. In this regard, the authors argue *The Wire* can aid educators in helping their students discover answers to questions like: what role does structural, cultural, or interpersonal factors have in contributing to systems that result in disproportionate outcomes? How do structures, institutions, and processes perpetuate the widespread marginalization of historically disenfranchised groups? Why does it take a critical tipping point before society is concerned with the lived realities of people of color?

Stern uses his experiences in the classroom to engage the documentary *Waiting for "Superman"* in conversation with *The Wire*. Ultimately, he uses the show and documentary to illustrate how media structures influence pedagogical and political responses to public education and to help answer questions students have on the future of public education in the United States.

Vest focuses on two primary characters of the show—Omar Little and Shakima Greggs—to illustrate how *The Wire* can be used as a tool to teach fundamental concepts of queer theory. Here the author uses *The Wire* to provide graduate and undergraduate students with a more sophisticated understanding of heteronormativity, the social construction of gender roles, the onscreen portrayal of gay and lesbian people, and the formulation of femininity and masculinity.

Allen and Toenes ask students to consider the impact *The Wire* has on American culture. The authors, through their experiences teaching and supporting courses that debate *The Wire*'s cultural significance, use the show to examine topics including income inequality, drug sentencing laws, poverty, and a wealth of other pressing issues. Ultimately, they posit that *The Wire*, as a pedagogical tool, presents students with an avenue to increase their awareness of and solutions to the many challenges facing U.S. cities.

Jones uses her experiences using *The Wire* in the classroom to offer insight for how to teach the show, particularly at Predominantly White Institutions. Jones argues that, for students, recognizing the humanity of the characters is vital to its impact on knowledge and intellectual development. The essay is grounded within an ideology that *The Wire* must be taught in a way that does not increase racial stereotyping, essentializing, or epistemologies of ignorance.

Finally, Taliaferro offers pragmatic considerations for using *The Wire* in course instruction. Taliaferro uses her own and other faculty members' experiences to discuss some of the salient pragmatic issues in creating and teaching a class using *The Wire*. In this discussion, she explores methods to engage student discussions, teaching in both online and traditional face-to-face formats, creating work activities and exams, and the shows ability to be effective over time.

Each essay included herein explores the pedagogical impacts and considerations of using all or portions of *The Wire* in higher education courses. The reader will quickly find that each author is passionate about not just the show, but its unique ability to offer insight, critique, knowledge, and exposure in ways more traditional texts and learning tools could ever do. We hope that you enjoy reading this text as much as we enjoyed creating it!

REFERENCES

Geiger, R. (2014). *The history of American higher education: Learning and culture from the founding to World War II*. Princeton: Princeton University Press.
Wilson, W.J., and A. Chaddha. (2010 September 12). Why we're teaching "the wire" at Harvard. *The Washington Post*.

The Clash of Aristocratic and Bourgeois Virtues in *The Wire*

Gus P. Gradinger *and* Bart J. Wilson

The Course of Inquiry

Humanomics: Exchange and the Human Condition is a freshman seminar course, which explores specific lines of inquiry: What makes a rich nation rich? What makes a good person good? And what do these questions have to do with one another? These questions cannot be answered simply nor completely, yet through them, the course examines the history of humanity as a history of poverty until approximately 1800 when something changed, something that triggered exponential growth in world gross domestic product (GDP) per capita, a shift from poverty to prosperity that continues to this day. Combining an economic inquiry into the human propensity to exchange with the cultural interpretation of the human condition, the three texts of the course are Matt Ridley's *The Rational Optimist*, Deirdre McCloskey's *The Bourgeois Virtues: Ethics for an Age of Commerce* and HBO's *The Wire*.

The texts are not taught, so much as they are learned through close reading, thought-provoking questions, and inspired discussions. For each class session students bring two cogent questions of their own. These questions are not to be easily answered, but rather, discussed, explored and expanded. Forming the basis of a professor-led, but student-guided discussion, where each student is expected to contribute and the questions, not a syllabus, determine the direction of the course. This course structure engages and inspires first-year college students who have no exposure to a humanistic science of economics.

Ridley sets the stage for the inquiry by explaining that *Homo sapiens* is the only species in the history of the planet to trade one thing for another for mutual gain. For at least 100,000 years, the archeological record indicates, humans have been trading. Seashells and obsidian have been found far from their origins, too far for individuals to travel there and back. Yet world GDP per capita remained stagnant at approximately $3/day until economic growth first took off in England around 1800 (McCloskey, 2006; Ridley, 2010; see Figure 1). Why England and why around 1800? What changed, McCloskey argues, first in 17th century Netherlands and then in 18th century England, was a shift in ethical systems. Since the advent of the city-state, an aristo-cratic/warrior class ruled while a priestly class advised and a peasant class toiled. The up valuation of commerce introduced a new social class and with it a new system of ethics, one that was distinctly bourgeois. Whereas honor, loyalty, courage, and justice grounded the rules of aristocratic society; and duty, faith, fortitude, and fairness, the rules of peasant society; the new bour-geois ethic was rooted in reliability, sociability, enterprise, and responsibility. Instead of assuming that capitalism is evil incarnate, McCloskey confronts her readers with the bold claim that exchange through markets has enriched us and continues to enrich us, both materially and ethically. Not only is being a businessperson not antithetical to being ethical, but engaging in commerce "nourishes lives of virtue" (McCloskey, 2006, p. 4).

Humanomics uses the classes of systematized ethics in *The Bourgeois*

Figure 1. World GDP per capita.

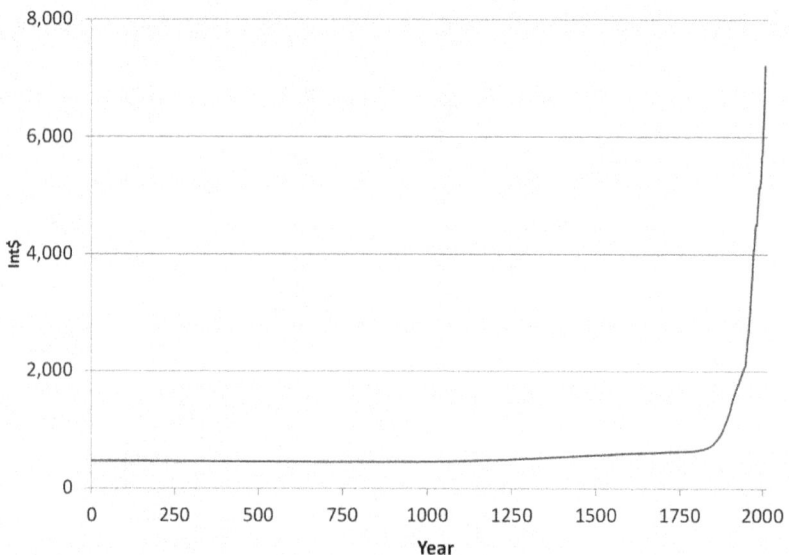

Source: Quandl, 2014

Virtues to understand the characters and the story of *The Wire* to understand the bourgeois ethics of the marketplace. Because the distribution and sale of narcotics is illegal, the drug economy of West Baltimore is organized by its own rules and order, "the game." In a sense, the streets of Baltimore are a pre–1700 aristocratic society, achieving order through honor, demanding loyalty of subordinates, and administering its own brand of justice. The world of David Simon's *The Wire* provides a case study in understanding these two ethical systems, and the conflict in shifting from an aristocratic cosmos to a bourgeois cosmos. In this essay we will explain the insights that the authors, student and professor, synthesized from a concurrent reading, viewing, and discussion of these two very different texts. Our essay will challenge, as the course does, the perception of the humanities and economics as distinct courses of study.

West Baltimore: A Pre–1700 Aristocratic Society

West Baltimore's streets in *The Wire* are wracked by violence, poverty, and rivalries. The killing, the stealing, and the lying are all written off as being part of "the game." Why can't a simple transaction, money for dope, be just that, a voluntary transaction for mutual gain? Detective Jimmy McNulty first plants this idea in our humanistic heads when he asks D'Angelo Barksdale, a gangster with a conscience, "Why can't you just sell the shit and walk away?" (Simon, 2002a). Bodie Brauddus, after D'Angelo relays the question to him, answers, "Because they dope fiends," (Simon, 2002b). This answer is not sufficient for us. Just because the dealers do not have to treat their customers well to keep them coming back, does not mean they cannot nor should not.

At the outset it is important to note that the demand for drugs is omnipresent and someone will find a way to meet the demand. Even prison inmates find a way to get their fix. The virtues of the drug trade are certainly tainted and controversial, but it is not this course's goal to evaluate the morality of buying and selling narcotics. The course works within the framework that when viewed as a voluntary transaction between two parties, the drug trade can be seen as acceptable, if not moral. What we want to understand is the difference in ethical systems present in both *The Wire*'s West Baltimore drug economy in the 2000s and the world economy around 1800, aristocratic and bourgeois, and the challenge in transitioning from the broad poverty maintenance of the former system to the wealth-creating potential of the latter. The story of *The Wire* provides a rich case study in this clash.

"The game" is good to the Barksdale organization. They make money, have power, and receive loyalty and respect; an aristocrat's dream. Unfortunately, aristocrats' dreams tend to not be progressive for society at large, which the 110 dead bodies over five seasons attest to.[1] So, what is Baltimore waiting for? Overthrow the king! Take the city back! Oh, if only it were so simple. You see, in West Baltimore, "the King stay the King" (Simon, 2002b).

The King of West Baltimore is Avon Barksdale, third generation drug kingpin. Barksdale, incentivized by power and governed by honor, embodies the character of drug royalty. Every decision is final. As the king, he is never challenged by his lieutenants and leaves no room for them to challenge him. Always in control of the conversation, Avon never shies away from his power or the respect that comes along with it. He does not show weakness, because an aristocrat must not. This is no façade; Avon Barksdale is royalty through and through. He does not know anything else. How could he? He was groomed to be King of the corners.

D'Angelo Barksdale, the nephew of Avon, lays out the hierarchical setup of the Barksdale organization in a chess lesson given to Wallace, Poot, and Bodie, three young Westside dealers. The King is obvious, Avon. His queen is Russell "Stringer" Bell, the "go get shit done piece." The rooks are the drug stashes. They move side to side across the projects. The pawns are the dealers. There are lots of them but individually they are not particularly important. If one or two pawns get taken early in the game the King is not concerned, but a strong frontline is essential to any organization. The game of chess, like the game of drugs, is able to keep the pawns interested and motivated by changing a pawn who makes his way across the entire board into a queen. This caveat may keep pawns interested, but it certainly does not help them. Pawns who try to make it to the other side are usually harmed quickly. And their attempted advancement certainly does not help the organization as a whole. The very idea of having more power is too much for the pawns to handle. It takes them over, consumes them, until they act on it. In David Simon's world, a pawn stepping out of place must be punished. This is seen when Orlando, whose only job is to be a clean name for Avon's liquor license, wants to buy and sell his own package (i.e., drug shipment). He oversteps his role as a pawn and shortly thereafter is removed from the board.

A hierarchy never goes unchallenged. It will always have an enemy, much like a chessboard will never have just one side. Proposition Joe, oversees the drug trade in East Baltimore. The eastside crews are constantly fighting with those from the west, whether it is for territory, product, or pride. This fighting comes off as part of "the game," a necessary evil. We, as humanomists, even in a world of drugs, do not see evil as necessary, but rather, as counterproductive. How can either side grow if they are locked in an endless chess battle with an endless supply of pawns being groomed by the same street corners on which they will likely die? Simple, end the battle. Not through force, not through fighting, but through persuasion, sweet bourgeois persuasion.

Simon's Baltimore is stuck in the 1700s. It is stagnant, while the world around it is growing exponentially. The show is quick to comment on the isolation of Baltimore from the rest of the country. Detective McNulty even goes so far as to say of our country's leaders, "The only way any of these guys would even find West Baltimore is if, I don't know, Air Force One crash lands on to Monroe Street" (Simon, 2004e). Baltimore seems to have been left behind while the rest of the country thrives, but the young dealers do not know anything else. Bodie who proves to be an ambitious and effective pawn within the Barksdale organization did not even realize that radio stations would change once outside of Baltimore.

Very few characters in the show are bothered by the isolation. In fact, most are completely oblivious to it. Even if the dealers do not realize it, West Baltimore has not changed like the rest of the world has changed, from a world governed by an aristocratic ethical system to one that is bourgeois.

An aristocratic ethic is not necessarily an immoral one. There is much merit to be had in honor, courage, and loyalty, particularly in a time of war. A peasant's ethic is also moral. There is certainly dignity in a peasant's service. It is not that these ethical systems are wrong; it is that they are not well tailored to promote peace and wealth-creating trade; they are not made for the modern world. As McCloskey (1994) puts it, "We are all bourgeois now. The ideals of nationalism or socialism do not suit our lives. Those of the townspeople, the bourgeoisie, do" (p. 3). An aristocracy, a hierarchy, is not well suited to prosperity for the masses with each aspiring warrior trying to climb up the hierarchal pyramid on the shoulders of those below him or her. The aristocrat attempts to take as large a chunk of this pyramid as possible.

The bourgeois world of business also has structure. There are fewer at the top than bottom, but those at the top are not trying to forcibly take more of the pyramid, they are trying to increase the size and scope of the pyramid through voluntary exchange, through peaceful persuasion. This point is not easily communicated and often ill-received. Students were quick to point to the greed and corruption that makes up the caricature of a modern-day businessperson. Greed and corruption surely exist within a bourgeois world, but they stand as outliers, as opposed to their role as the foundation of an aristocratic world. To further the understanding of this point, students participate in a series of software-based economic experiments that simulate market transactions. Those who act virtuously and with trust prosper, while those who act with greed eventually fail. Although simplified and on a very compressed timeline, the model provides students with a concrete understanding of the necessity of virtue in business.

Historical Context of a Shift from Aristocratic to Bourgeois Ethics

McCloskey contends that between 1600 and 1848 the attitude toward the bourgeoisie changed, and dramatically so. While there are precursors in the Hanseatic League and the northern Italian cities of Venice, Florence, and Genoa, it was in Holland where the shift first took hold following the revolt against Phillip II of Spain in the late 16th century. The result of one of the first successful secessions in Europe was not only an early republic in the modern era, but a republic whose aristocratic families had been so decimated that a king could not emerge to replenish the aristocracy and return a monarch to the throne. Without a perpetual reinforcement of heroic warrior values, the Dutch began to practice the bourgeois virtues increasingly more to support its global shipping industry abroad and its shopkeepers at home (McCloskey, 2016). McCloskey further argues that the British by 1700, following the Dutch monarchy of William and Mary, had evidently adopted Dutch institutions of commerce and the businesslike ethic that accompanies them. The British, with a decentralized tradition of common law, became bourgeois.

While McCloskey (2016) supports her case for an ethical shift by documenting how a new concept of honesty of the bourgeoisie emerged in the language of literature and science to supplant the old aristocratic standard of honor and courage, there is no visible trace of any tension at the level of individual people when an upstart system of ethics emerges to challenge the status quo. We use the narrative of *The Wire* to explore that clash of values to help students more deeply understand the difficult transition for the world to adopt a bourgeois system of ethics and the implications thereof for creating prosperity.

Opportunity in West Baltimore

Transitioning from an aristocratic to a bourgeois society is by no means a simple or quick process. The stars must align just so, or the powerful kings and queens will simply use their position and control to halt any changes in their path. For the residents of West Baltimore and the humanomists of Chapman University, the stars began to fall into place at the conclusion of Season 1. Avon Barksdale, the great King, is headed to prison, leaving his kingdom in the trusted hands of his second in command, Russell "Stringer" Bell.

Bell, although childhood friends with him, is not like Avon Barksdale. He lives his life with a different set of virtues, a different code. This code diminishes the importance of loyalty, honor, and power and instead promotes responsibility, enterprise, and reliability. Stringer Bell longs for a life as a part of the bourgeoisie, as a legitimate businessman. Kings, never a merchant, have always ruled West Baltimore. Kings turned West Baltimore into a battleground. Kings sanctioned killing over a drug deal. A merchant, however, would turn West Baltimore into a marketplace. A businessman, maybe Stringer Bell, would find a way to increase profits and prosperity while decreasing dead bodies (and attention from police).

Stringer shows himself as bourgeois throughout the series. His day-to-day running of the operation's money laundering fronts is just the beginning. He is not satisfied with the front organizations operating like fronts; he wants them to operate like legitimate businesses. He even goes so far as to relay a lesson about price elasticity of demand, learned in his economics course at the local community college, to two young members of the Barksdale crew who treat the copy shop as nothing more than a corner. This will not be the last time that Stringer calls upon his education in economics to change "the game."

With Avon in prison, Season 2 is our first look at a Stringer Bell–led drug organization. In the opening episode, Bodie and Shamrock make a drug run, and Stringer's caution and meticulousness becomes instantly evident. The drugs are nowhere to be found in the car they picked up. Stringer knows the mileage of the car at the start of the run and what it should be at the end. He hassles the two young dealers about being three tenths of a mile long, but eventually reveals he knows they did nothing wrong because he was having them followed the entire time. Stringer's caution keeps the young, often-reckless, dealers in check with a personalized lesson on the importance of details.

The drugs missing from the car are our first indication of Stringer's major problem: getting product. When Avon receives a relatively short prison sentence, his suppliers worry that he may have cooperated with police. This prompts them to cut ties with the Barksdale organization. Stringer does his best to work with the product he has. He uses marketing tactics, such as changing the name of the dope, using different colored vials, and even creating artificial competition between his own dealers.

These strategies are discussed at organizational meetings where even lower-level dealers have a chance to speak their minds, in accordance with Robert's Rules of Order. Under Avon, these meetings would be out of the question. Avon Barksdale does not want advice from young, uninformed peddlers. He would never stoop to their level. Stringer, though, will stoop. He will ask and listen to advice from those below him because he would not want his own pride to get in the way of improvement. He is willing to admit he does not know all and acknowledges that valuable information can be obtained simply through conversation. This information helps him make overarching organizational decisions. McCloskey (1994) explains, "The aristocrat never stoops; the peasant stoops silently to harvest the grain or to run the machine; the bourgeois stoops metaphorically to make his will quite clear, and to know the will and reason of the other" (p. 184). Stringer, not Avon, will stoop. Consider Stringer's "40-Degree Day" lecture to Sapper, a soldier who is not as adept with his mind as he may or may not be with his handgun. Stringer equates his performance with a 40-degree day, a day that nobody will complain about, but nobody will be excited about either. In this instance, Stringer does all he can to put his sentiments into terms the rank and file will understand.

The supply problem is one of the first times we see Avon and Stringer split on an issue. Although he is in prison, Avon is still well connected and talks often enough with Stringer to have a major influence on the direction of the organization. Avon's solution to the problem is an aristocratic one. He uses connections in New York to hire some muscle to take territory back that has been encroached on by dealers who have actual product. He plans on using his reputation and prison connections to find a supplier down the road. Meanwhile, Stringer is working out his own solution, one that is bourgeois. Instead of wasting lives and money trying to hold on to territory without any product, Stringer is actually willing to concede territory.[2] He crosses town and works out a deal with Proposition Joe, exchanging three of his best corners for a product connection.

This simple trade, product for territory, is the unique characteristic of the bourgeoisie. To enter into contract is to enter into trust. It incentivizes both parties to make good on their end of the deal, because as long as they do, both parties win. Stringer has territory and needs product. Joe has product and needs territory. They each give up a little of their surplus, and both are better off for it. Everybody wins, except the territory-driven Avon, of course.

Stringer draws the interest and the attention of a class of humanomists looking for the good in drug business, but he is by no means perfect. After executing this deal, he does not have the courage to relay it to Avon and make him call off Brother Mouzone, the hired muscle from New York. Avon is stubborn and territorial, but Stringer still is influential enough to persuade Avon and yet Stringer fails to muster the courage to rise to the occasion. Instead, Stringer's initial instinct is to use his enterprising skills to construct a workaround. Trying to both avoid the wrath of Omar, a noble but dangerous warrior-robber, and ensure the elimination of Brother Mouzone, Stringer tells Omar that it was Brother Mouzone who murdered and tortured his boyfriend, Brandon. The plan backfires when the two killers realize they have been crossed.

Stringer's questionable decision making does not end there. His decision to have D'Angelo Barksdale, Avon's kin and one of the show's most decent characters, killed in prison is certainly worth examining. The decision is made solely by Stringer; Avon knows nothing of the plan. Avon could never have made that decision. To Avon, much like a stereotypical aristocrat, family is the most important thing. After all, the family name is where aristocrats derive their power, so great lengths are often taken to preserve their name and reputation. Stringer's decision is certainly heartbreaking for viewers, but it is not necessarily stupid. D'Angelo is a loose end with lots of time left in prison to rethink his loyalties. Even if it is, in fact, the right organizational decision, Avon would have never followed through. The love of family comes first and honor on the street comes second.

The rules of the drug game are a code of engagement. To be good at "the game" is to instinctively rely on that honor code. Stringer Bell, however, instinctively relies on a prudent code of conduct. This is most evident when he gives two pawns the order to kill Omar on a Sunday morning, while he is with his grandmother en route to church. As long as anyone in 'the game" has been around, there has been a strict rule of no killing on Sundays. To the practical-minded, there is killing all the time. Why is Sunday different? How is killing somebody on a Monday more honorable? It is not as if Stringer has never heard of the Sunday truce; it is that Stringer's first instinct is not to play by the principles of honor when in the heat of the moment. Stringer plays "the game" with a bourgeois impulse.

Again, Stringer Bell is clearly not perfect. But we are not looking for perfect. We are looking to understand how a bourgeois ethic creates value, in both senses of the word (McCloskey, 2006). Stringer is not a good guy, and as seen by his failures in real estate development, he may not make a good legitimate businessman either. But he is a businessman. He is thrifty and he is modest (compare his Camry sedan to Avon's luxury SUV) and he has the foresightedness to remake "the game" in West Baltimore when the opportunity presents itself.

Two Different Systems of Virtues

McCloskey organizes the virtues by four social classes: Aristocrat, Bourgeois, Peasant, and Priest. As she stresses, these are "stereotypes, not always, I repeat, sociological facts" (McCloskey, 2006, p. 349). We humanomists use the schema to identify and analyze character types. Whereas Avon Barksdale, Omar Little, and Brother Mouzone are stereotypical aristocrats, who exude a pride of being and whose core patrician virtues include honor, loyalty, courage, magnanimity, justice, temperance, and love. Stringer Bell and Proposition Joe are stereotypical bourgeoisie, who display a pride of accomplishment, and whose corresponding mercantilistic virtues are reliability, sociability, enterprise, consideration, responsibility, thrift, and affection (McCloskey, 2006, p. 348).[3]

To reiterate, neither we nor McCloskey view goodness as a trait of only the bourgeoisie. Each of the four classes are ethical classes, meaning that if a peasant lived by all the virtues within his or her class, he or she would be a good and moral peasant. The same is true for priests and aristocrats. None of the classes are inherently better, in a moral sense, than any others. This is not our focus. Instead, we focus on the results and consequences of living virtuously according to the ethics within the class, especially those of the aristocracy and bourgeoisie. Living bourgeois means living as part of the free market, a market where persuasion, not power, is key. Stringer lives within the bourgeois class and Avon in that of the aristocrat. This is the driving force between their different views of the world. The ethical differences between an aristocrat and a bourgeois are certainly present in the plot, but the separation becomes apparent with a close analysis of the show's rich dialogue.

The Wire makes for the perfect case study because there is so much to work with in the show, even focusing on this very specific aspect of the series—the clash of virtues. To examine the clash, much of the helpful dialogue comes from conversations between Avon and Stringer. Tension is present in the clash and is certainly present in their dialogue. Consider their prison conversations, especially regarding product and territory. Stringer wants a smooth operation based on the merit of the product, but Avon will not be denied his corners. Stringer pleads his case, telling Avon, "No flexing, no threats. This is a good thing" (Simon, 2004a). Avon, stubborn as ever responds, "Yeah, but we gonna need some good corners, close to downtown. Everybody watchin' us on this…. Wanna see if we weak or real." The war-averse Stringer suggests, "If we can do without the bodies we should." The lifelong friends seem to be split past a point of return. Stringer will not get behind a war effort unless absolutely necessary, and Avon does not want to cooperate with a rival tribe, which he sees as capitulation. Avon wants to conquer. Stringer's look when Avon tells him, "I'll be home before it's cold" (Simon, 2004a) says it all. He knows he and Avon will not be able to work well together. The good of the aristocracy is not the good of the bourgeoisie. Avon may not have had the same foresight.

Once released from prison, however, Avon quickly becomes aware and sensitive to the ethical differences between Stringer and himself. This is evident when Avon comes along for one of Stringer's real estate development meetings. He is out of his element. He is a king, yes, but he has always been a king of the projects; his reach never extended to the types that Stringer is in business with. When one of the developers suggests that they will need to increase the budget because of a miscalculation on their part, Avon is confused: "You messed up; you take the hit," he preaches. He does not understand that, "Cost overruns are the nature of the business" (Simon, 2004c). Later in the episode, Avon is again angry at the lack of territorial control his interim CEO has retained. After Stringer suggests buying corners back from other crews, a frustrated Avon asks, "Since when do we buy corners? We take corners." Stringer tries to explain the new workings of the world to the tradition-based Avon: "Eastside, Westside ready to get together. We past that run and gun shit man.... We can run more than corners, B, period. Run this goddam city" (Simon, 2004c), which receives nothing more than a semi-sarcastic, "Like businessmen?" response from Avon. Soon after, we are rewarded with one of the most relevant statements of the entire series from Avon, "I'm not some suit wearing businessman like you. I'm just a gangster I suppose, and I want my corners" (Simon, 2004c). As with Stringer and the Sunday truce, Avon's exclamation illustrates an ethical gap. He is a gangster, an aristocratic warrior, and even if new ways would lead to prosperity, he wants things to stay the same. He wants his power to stand alone. He does not want people outside of his organization, his tribe, to succeed. He wants his corners.

Avon fundamentally views "the game" as win *or* lose. Different crews taking from each other, whether it be bodies, money, drugs, or corners. One group wins and the other loses. Stringer recognizes this: "I'm thinking this is the worst part of the game. Best we do is break out even" (Simon, 2002c). After trying to find a way around the violence and bodies, Stringer finally has. He finds a scenario that benefits almost everybody involved. Trading territory for Proposition Joe's package sparks a mini revolution. Baltimore's drug crews, ready for much needed change, band together instead of fighting, to form the New Day Co-Op. Every crew involved with the Co-Op gives money toward a bulk, wholesale drug shipment under the expectations that there will be no fighting for territory or thievery amongst the participating crews. This is not a win-lose proposition. It is a win-win-win-win-win-lose proposition, as McCloskey would say. The supplier of the drugs gets to move a bigger shipment and achieve high sales volume. The wholesale price means that the drugs are cheaper for the drug crews. These lower prices lead to a product with more bang for the customer's buck. The dealers are in much less danger from formerly rival crews. And the police do not have as many homicides on their hands. But, Avon loses his corners. This is a sacrifice that everyone in the New Day Co-op but Avon is fine with making.

Virtues of Commerce in Hamsterdam

Stringer Bell and the New Day Co-Op are not the only ones working to revolutionize "the game." When asked how he was going to diminish the crime rates in his Eastern District, Major Bunny Colvin answers, "I thought I might legalize drugs" (Simon, 2004b). With six months left until retirement and little to lose, Major Colvin develops what fondly becomes known as "Hamsterdam." Hamsterdam—a contained and monitored safe zone where police will look the other way at drug consumption and distribution—piques a humanomist's curiosity. Not because of the legality of drugs, but because of a competitive market for drugs.

When the first batch of dealers arrives to their new safe haven, their facial expressions express a sense of excitement and confusion; they look like they are getting a glimpse into a whole new world. Turns out, they are. With the police maintaining the rules and order, Hamsterdam quickly becomes a bustling market. Dealers and users are free to come, go, sell and use as they see fit; and in return they consent to police supervision and a promise to avoid violence. This promise may seem optimistic for crews of drug dealers and hundreds of addicts, but through the power of voluntary exchange, it is actually quite feasible. The dealers and addicts both know how beneficial Hamsterdam is. If one crew breaks the rules, it could ruin it for everybody. Instead of fighting each other, they are actually depending on each other to be good, fair, and honest. We see only one murder in the entire lifespan of Hamsterdam, but it is not handled like a murder on the streets. Knowing what is at stake, the opportunity to stay in Hamsterdam, a crew leader actually convinces the shooter, a young dealer, to turn himself in to police. On the streets, this would never happen. Witnesses would not cooperate and a killer would once again escape justice.

To please the police is not the only reason violence decreases, however. Before Stringer Bell and Bunny Colvin's efforts to revolutionize and modernize, customers purchased from the dealer who was closest, the one who controlled the local territory and likely the local muscle. In Hamsterdam, the users choose based on product quality and customer service. That is right, customer service. As opposed to dealers treating fiends like "junkyard dogs," dealers must now treat each potential buyer as a valued customer. Those who do not will quickly begin to lose business and profits. Why go to a rude, unhelpful dealer when another who greatly appreciates your business is standing just ten feet away? Avoiding violence and conflict is not only ethically good, it is good for business.

Virtue cultivates commerce. That is hardly contentious. But does it go the other way? Does commerce cultivate virtue? Consider Dee Dee, an anxious young white woman rolling into Hamersterdam in a car with District of Columbia license plates. When she approaches a dealer, he pleasantly asks his customer how she is doing. Unsure whether this open market is for real or not, she responds, "No offense, but can we just get the eight ball?" What is the dealer's reply? "Alright, alright, just being social" (Simon, 2004d).

Whereas loyalty to one's own people is an aristocratic virtue, sociability to those personally unknown to us is the corresponding virtue of the bourgeoisie. McCloskey (2006) illustrates how commerce opaquely fosters virtue with an (autobiographical) example. Note how well the final sentence fits this scene in Hamsterdam (p. 4):

> A little farmers' market opens before 6:00 a.m. on a summer Saturday at Polk and Dearborn in Chicago. As a woman walking her dog passes the earliest dealer setting up his stall, the woman and the dealer exchange pleasantries about the early bird and the worm. The two people here are enacting a script of citizenly courtesies and of encouragement for prudence and enterprise and good relations between seller and buyer. Some hours later the woman feels impelled to buy $1.50 worth of tomatoes from him. But that's not the point. The market was an occasion for virtue, an expression of solidarity across gender, social class, ethnicity.

We are all bourgeois, but we need the liberty to foster its ethic. Exchange through markets enriches us materially and ethically.

Hamsterdam is not perfect. A walk through it at night is frightening. It is filled with dangerous criminals and unstable persons, not to mention a whole lot of drugs. But it is *better*. *Better* than drug dealers being on corners, disturbing families and civilians who are not involved in the game. *Better* than crews killing each other for territory. *Better* for the police who do not have to chase participants of a victimless crime. Crime is down, murder is down, and profits are up.

Stringer Bell pushes West Baltimore to the edge of becoming bourgeois, to the brink of peace and prosperity, but it is not enough. In David Simon's world it rarely ever is. The longstanding institutions of West Baltimore once again prevail over the individuals attempting to change them. Drugs go back to where they "belong"—the corners—and dealers turn back to violence, all when we are just getting our hopes up.

Greek Tragedy or Moral Failing?

The Wire is not a series for those in search of happy endings. Each season ends and nothing really changes. Sure, characters get shuffled around and move up and down the ranks, but West Baltimore stays the same, "always." The institutions rule and the individual is powerless. David Simon describes *The Wire* as a postmodern Greek tragedy.[4] The fates of the characters are determined by the drug economy. Their agency is stripped from them. They are mere pieces on a chessboard. To challenge the institution of "the game" is to fly too close to the sun. Similarly, Read (2009) interprets *The Wire* as an allegory of capitalism and Stringer Bell as a tragic character caught between "the semi-feudal loyalties of the drug trade and the ruthless world of capital, until the contradictions between the two eventually kill him" (p. 122). But did institutions and contradictions kill Stringer Bell? With a consequentialist lens we can take the series as a whole and conclude as Simon and Read do. Stringer Bell is shot dead in his own real estate investment.

But sometime around 1800, humanity challenged the gods and defied its tragic fate. As Figure 1 starkly indicates, the modern (and coterminous postmodern) world is a different one from the millennia that preceded it. *Homo sapiens* lives longer, healthier, and less violent lives than just 200 years ago (Ridley, 2010). Something changed, and if it was the ethical system by which we live that changed, some people along the way inevitably challenged the aristocratic status quo while adhering to a different ethical framework. If those challengers did not succeed, then we have, or at least the 75 percent who no longer live in abject poverty have. *Because 200 years ago everyone lived in abject poverty.*

So let us consider the decisions and virtues of the tragic characters within the story itself to understand why the embourgeoisfication does not take hold. But first, cue Avon: "Are you talking about a fucking do over? That's not how the game is played" (Simon, 2002d). Well, Avon may be right, but that will not stop us from exploring what could have been. Perhaps Stringer Bell is not a virtuous enough member of the bourgeoisie. Perhaps Hamsterdam is rushed into existence. Perhaps Marlo Stanfield prevents the change. In a world as complex as David Simon's West Baltimore, it is likely a combination of all three. But let us take a closer look.

Our class interpretation of the story is that Stringer's vices led to his downfall. He does not live within the rules of "the game," and he pays dearly for it. Stringer tries to use "the game" as a gateway to a life as a legitimate businessman. He wants to own things in his own name and not to have to worry about attention from police. He comes close, with close being the recurring theme of the series. He is even able to hand McNulty a B&B Enterprises business card. Although he looks and sounds the part, Stringer is not ready for business in the political world. He naïvely expects the politics of business to be played ethically and by bourgeois rules. While trying to secure a deal for a downtown redevelopment plan, Stringer is swindled by State Senator Clay Davis, a corrupt aristocrat. The story is clear: Stringer is trying to straddle the line between a legitimate businessman and a drug lord. But the straddling does not kill Stringer. Stringer makes choices.

As Avon harshly puts it, "You know the difference between me and you? I bleed red and you bleed green. I look at you these days, String, you know what I see? I see a man without a country. Not hard enough for this right here and maybe, just maybe, not smart enough for them out there" (Simon, 2004d). Avon does not give Stringer enough credit for his "hardness," but he may just be right about Stringer as a businessman. Maybe Stringer was trying to be something he is not, control something he cannot. He dresses well, has a chic apartment, and could tell you what you need to know about economics, from market saturation to elasticity of demand, but at his core is Stringer too much of a gangster?

Not long before he is killed in prison, D'Angelo gives a rag tag book club his analysis of Jay Gatsby astutely observing that "'cause he wasn't willing to get real with the story, that shit caught up to him" (Simon, 2003). Can the same be said of Stringer? If so, he may have never been able to fulfill the role of a merchant in polished shoes instead of a knight in shining armor. Stringer even foreshadows his own inability to revolutionize "the game" when he tells D'Angelo, "This shit right here, D, it's forever" (Simon, 2002b).

Stringer's *forever* is not very long. Brother Mouzone and Omar, after realizing Stringer has crossed them, band together to take him out. First, the honorable thing for Brother Mouzone to do is to get the king's consent. After Avon reluctantly passes judgment from the barber's chair, accepting that this is Stringer's fate for scheming without honor, Brother Mouzone and Omar corner and kill Stringer in the very building he is developing. Why is Brother Mouzone a problem for Stringer? Because, as we have already noted, Stringer lacks the courage early on to stand up to Avon and have him call off his muscle. Stringer has the audacity to put a hit on a state senator but not the bravery to stand up to an imprisoned Avon and explain that product not muscle is their fundamental problem. Stringer fails to exercise the virtue of courage, and this moral failing, not an institution nor a contradiction, costs him his life.

Avon may have consented to ending Stringer's life, but Bell likewise contributes to Avon's demise. When police raid the safe house that serves as the organization's wartime headquarters, Avon reads the search warrant only to learn that the informant who gave him up is none other than his lifelong friend and right hand man. Bell had gone to the police after the New Day Co-Op gave him an ultimatum: deal with Avon or leave the Co-Op. The difference in how Avon and Stringer cross each other is telling of the two characters' systems of ethics. Avon gives Bell a soldier's death, while Bell takes the route of carefully negotiating a deal with the police that causes the least damage and leaves Avon alive.

Avon Barksdale's virtues and vices are quintessentially aristocratic and, as such, in conflict with those of his queen, Stringer Bell. Stringer is a businessman in a world of warriors. While most are playing the game for respect and honor, Stringer is playing for money and ultimately to be a legitimate bourgeois outside "the game." The longtime friends and partners' conflicting ethics and individual vices inevitably lead to the demise of both, as well as the entire Barksdale organization. Their differences cannot be resolved because one cannot use the ethical rules of one system of virtues to demonstrate the right course of action to someone who relies on another system. There is an ethical gap that separates aristocratic and bourgeois virtues, which Avon concisely summarizes to Stringer as "I bleed red, you bleed green." The conflict first between Avon and Stringer and then between Marlo Stanfield and the New Day Co-op illustrate the great difficulty for wealth-creating bourgeois virtues to supplant aristocratic and peasant virtues as the world's standard ethical system. *For as long as Stringer argues within the aristocratic system of virtues, he can never convince Avon to abandon it.* Stringer would have been well served to read Adam Smith's first great book, *The Theory of Moral Sentiments*, as part of his economics education, for he would have learned that samurai swords are incompatible with the *Wealth of Nations*.

Even in a Stringer Bell–less Baltimore, Bunny Colvin's crazy idea almost works. Not everybody participates in the experiment. Enter Marlo Stanfield, the young, hardheaded dealer whose only motivation is to become king. Marlo is ruthless. Human lives, even his own, mean nothing compared to the glory of taking the crown. Recognizing his dangerous nature, the New Day Co-Op tries to deal with him (how bourgeois of them), but the stubborn Stanfield will not budge. He will not trade power and control for profits and peace. The Co-Op eventually finds an agreeable solution: leave Marlo his territory and let him run his operation how he wants, have him buy into the product package, and not war over turf. The bourgeois-natured Co-Op recognizes that nobody is gaining from warring with Marlo, so they find a way to coexist, to compromise. Hamsterdam makes this easier for them. Marlo can have all the corners he wants and the Co-Op crews will still be able to thrive, and do so in a virtuous and bustling marketplace. Persuasion, not power.

This solution is shot dead in the water when Hamsterdam falls. With no central market for drugs left, territory is quickly put back at a premium. The crews have to spread back out across Baltimore, warring as they go. There is no more chance to coexist with the aristocrats. The clash is back because the broader world of Baltimore, the voters and the politicians, is not bourgeois enough to decriminalize voluntary transactions. There will always be somebody who wants to be king, somebody who is motivated only by power, but Hamsterdam, for a time, gave Baltimore the ability to marginalize the aristocrats, for the virtues of merchants to supplant those of warrior-kings.

The Baltimore of *The Wire* is at a tipping point. It may seem crazy to place so much weight on such a specific point, the clash of virtues, especially in a television series with so much depth and so many different perspectives, but this clash and overcoming it is, as McCloskey (2011) argues, the crucial catalyst for the growth and development of the world. This worldwide growth in prosperity is not guaranteed or even expected. Just look at what the people of West Baltimore were up against. For this to happen all over the world is nothing short of a miracle. Even if David Simon and the writers of *The Wire* did not intend to capture this, the show provides a rich setting to view and analyze a world on the verge of change, an aristocratically-controlled world ready to become bourgeois. The people of West Baltimore are ready to end the seemingly un-endable, multi-front war against the police, the Eastside, and themselves.

Capturing the next king is not enough, as the plot of *The Wire* makes abundantly clear. Something bigger is necessary. David Simon sharply fingers local government and democratic politics as the institutions responsible for choking off an emerging merchant-dominated drug game. Any illegal market under relentless siege by the police, in art or reality, cannot prosper, materially or ethically, and so for *The Wire* to be authentically good art qua art, Colvin and his bourgeois experiment must be fated to fail. Colvin's Greek tragedy, then, is on us. Legalizing marijuana is slowly becoming a part of a state-by-state conversation on drug policy, but eight balls ... they are still taboo. *And that failure in courage to discuss the drug economy with bourgeois dignity and liberty is our moral failing.*

The take-home lesson from *The Wire*, however, should not be that the natural urban world is similarly fated to fail. Great art fosters social change, and if a change in ideas, a change in ethics, made the prosperity of the modern world possible, then *The Wire* as great art can be a catalyst for what the natural world needs—a broader application of the bourgeois ethic, politically, economically, and socially. Read McCloskey's *The Bourgeois Virtues*, watch HBO's *The Wire*, and then *discuss* them concurrently to learn why and how.

Acknowledgments

We thank Deirdre McCloskey, Jan Osborn, and the 2012 IFREE Summer Scholars and the Fall 2012 students in Humanomics at Chapman University for stimulating conversations on virtues, commerce, and *The Wire*. We also heartily thank Taylor Jaworski, Erik Kimbrough, and Jan Osborn for comments and careful readings which substantially improved the exposition and argument of the essay.

NOTES

1. *The Wire* Deaths (last accessed June 14, 2014): http://thewiredeaths.tumblr.com/.
2. For Stringer, of course, the decision to risk lives is pure cost-benefit analysis. More bodies mean more attention from the police and hence more costs.
3. Even though our focus is on the Aristocrat and Bourgeois ethical systems, two other characters squarely fit into the Peasant and Priest classes. Frank Sobotka

is a stereotypical peasant, who projects a pride of service and whose corresponding plebian virtues are duty, faith, fortitude, benevolence, fairness, frugality, and charity. Lester Freamon is an artistic, intellectual priest who exudes a pride of creation; his corresponding virtues are integrity, professionalism, imagination, sympathy, accuracy, discipline, and agape (McCloskey, 2006, p. 348).

4. Nick Hornby interview with David Simon, *The Believer*, August 2007 (last accessed June 4, 2014): http://www.believermag.com/issues/200708/?read=interview_simon.

REFERENCES

Kostroff, Noble, N. (Producer). (2008). *The wire. The complete series*. New York: HBO Video.

McCloskey, Deirdre N. (2006). *The bourgeois virtues: Ethics for an age of commerce*. Chicago: University of Chicago Press.

McCloskey, Deirdre N. (2011). *Bourgeois dignity: Why economics can't explain the modern world*. Chicago: University of Chicago Press.

McCloskey, Deirdre N. (2016). *Bourgeois equality: How ideas, not capital or institutions, enriched the world*. Chicago: University of Chicago Press.

McCloskey, Donald. (1994). Bourgeois virtue. *American Scholar* 63(2): 177–191.

Quandl. (2014). *World GDP since AD 1*. [Data] Retrieved from http://www.quandl.com/MADDISON/WORLDGDP-World-GDP-since-AD-1.

Read, Jason. (2009). Stringer Bell's lament: Violence and legitimacy in contemporary capitalism. In C.W. Marshall and Tiffany Potter (Eds.), *The wire: Urban decay and American television*. New York: Bloomsbury Academic.

Ridley, Matt. (2010). *The rational optimist: How prosperity evolves*. New York: Harper.

Simon, D. (Writer), Simon, D., & Burns, E. (Story), & Johnson, C. (Director). (2002a, June 9). The detail [Television series episode]. In Simon, D. (Producer), *The wire*. Baltimore, MD: Blown Deadline Productions & Home Box Office.

Simon, D. (Writer), Simon, D., & Burns, E. (Story), & Medak, P. (Director). (2002b, June 16). The buys [Television series episode]. In Simon, D. (Producer), *The wire*. Baltimore, MD: Blown Deadline Productions & Home Box Office.

Simon, D. (Writer), Simon, D., & Burns, E. (Story), & Muzio, G. (Director). (2002c July 28). Lessons [Television series episode]. In Simon, D. (Producer), *The wire*. Baltimore, MD: Blown Deadline Productions & Home Box Office.

Simon, D. (Writer), Simon, D., & Burns, E. (Story), & Manchevski, M. (Director). (2002d, August 4). Game day [Television series episode]. In Simon, D. (Producer), *The wire*. Baltimore, MD: Blown Deadline Productions & Home Box Office.

Simon, D. (Writer), Simon, D., & Burns, E. (Story), & Shill, S. (Director). (2003, July 6). All prologue [Television series episode]. In Simon, D. (Producer), *The wire*. Baltimore, MD: Blown Deadline Productions & Home Box Office.

Simon, D. (Writer), Simon, D., & Burns, E. (Story), & Shill, S. (Director). (2004a, September 27). All due respect [Television series episode]. In Simon, D. (Producer), *The wire*. Baltimore, MD: Blown Deadline Productions & Home Box Office.

Simon, D. (Writer), Simon, D., & Burns, E. (Story), & Bailey, R. (Director). (2004b, October 2). Dead soldiers [Television series episode]. In Simon, D. (Producer), *The wire*. Baltimore, MD: Blown Deadline Productions & Home Box Office.

Simon, D. (Writer), Simon, D., & Burns, E. (Story), & Libman, L. (Director). (2004c,

October 31). Homecoming [Television series episode]. In Simon, D. (Producer), *The wire*. Baltimore, MD: Blown Deadline Productions & Home Box Office.

Simon, D. (Writer), Simon, D., & Burns, E. (Story), & Holland, A. (Director). (2004d, November 14). Moral midgetry [Television series episode]. In Simon, D. (Producer), *The wire*. Baltimore, MD: Blown Deadline Productions & Home Box Office.

Simon, D. (Writer), Simon, D., & Burns, E. (Story), & Zakrzewski, A. (Director). (2004e, November 21). Slapstick [Television series episode]. In Simon, D. (Producer), *The wire*. Baltimore, MD: Blown Deadline Productions & Home Box Office.

"You gonna look out for me?"
Intersectionality, Young Black Male Giftedness and Cultural Competency Using The Wire

HEATHER CHERIE MOORE

Throughout the United States, pre-service teachers enroll in courses that prepare them to teach in classrooms with diverse learners. Most coursework in these programs prepare undergraduates to teach in their specific subject area of specialization. However, there should be more commitment to critical media literacy and cross-cultural competency in education programs. It is important to train teachers to be sound organizers and empathetic global citizens, but it is equally important for teachers to recognize the cultural diversity among their students. Pre-service teachers should understand how popular culture influences U.S. perspectives on race, culture, and academic achievement. Yet there is limited pre-service coursework that shows college students the role that media plays in educating the public about Black and brown students. The vast amount of visual media and popular culture that could be regularly shown as part of the primary curricula in college classrooms, especially given their treatments of the failures of American public education, is constantly growing.

Television series like *The Wire* top that aforementioned list, particularly the fourth season of the series that depicts the multifaceted experiences of four young Black male students in Baltimore. *The Wire* presents a reality to viewers that cannot be easily dismissed. The show even challenges common understanding of "the police procedural" challenging the mainstream viewer to consider police departments as repressive state apparatuses and reconsider their views of individuals involved in illegal drug activity (Althusser, 1971; McMillan, 2009). The television series becomes all the more powerful when adolescents become part of the plotline. The inclusion of gripping characters like Michael Lee, Duquan Weems, and Randy Wagstaff (all under the age of

18) present the sad reality that youth are not safe from the racist, classist, and heavily gendered practices in the United States.

Some colleges and universities in the United States offer students courses that explore cultural competency. Including *The Wire* and specifically emphasizing characters like Michael Lee, Randy Wagstaff, and Duquan Weems in these courses may help students develop cultural competency skills. More importantly, a course on *The Wire* would challenge prevailing views of Black male youth in working class communities as destructive, criminal, and innately inferior—all concepts that have become the "master narrative" of Black males since their introduction on American soil (Ikemoto, 2000).

Furthermore, incorporating *The Wire* into college classrooms would emphasize the personal narratives of and provide insight, for those less familiar, into the lives of young African American men like Michael, Randy and Duquan. The show challenges the "at-risk" classification that has become commonplace in American educational scholarship and its assessment of Black male student achievement patterns. While, generally, Black male students are largely deemed to be at-risk, their experiences, character traits, and ability to survive despite (insurmountable) odds should be read as a form of giftedness. Such a reading of Black male youth may be shocking for readers considering the high rates of homicide, poverty, and school drop outs in predominantly Black and urban communities. But such a policy-oriented perspective would add complexity to an assessment of *The Wire* and encourage academics to produce "thick description" and a thorough analysis of West Baltimore, Edward Tilghman Middle School, and of Black male students themselves (Geertz, 1973). The discussion of both popular culture and the cultural backgrounds of historically othered groups will show cultural diversity that "challenges the belief that students of color are deficient" (Gay, 2010, pp. 15, 13). A course integrating these ideals and concepts would not only equip students with the tools to assess current scholarship, but also radically shift student perspectives about historically othered groups.

This essay speaks strongly, although not exclusively, to instructors in college classrooms and argues that *The Wire*'s fourth season (and an analysis of three Black male youth in particular) would serve as a useful teaching tool. Arguments included throughout demonstrate the importance of media literacy in interdisciplinary programs that teach scholarship on race, gender, and intersectionality. Scholars in the academy should reconsider the perspectives of young Black males of color and examine the giftedness inherent in their informal educational experiences. Central to this argument are the broad representations of giftedness as displayed by three characters in *The Wire*—Michael Lee, Duquan Weems, and Randy Wagstaff. Special emphasis is given to the narratives of these three characters as they were left to make sense of their surroundings in a rocky urban landscape.

Michael, Duquan, and Randy exhibit non-conventional giftedness in the midst of despair. More specifically, these three Black male youth represent diverse definitions of giftedness in leadership, cognitive intellectualism, and entrepreneurship. As the main argument presented relies on the idea that Black male students are the quintessential at-risk group, this discussion begins with a brief scholarly overview of the term at-risk, followed by an examination of the governmental policies and educational initiatives that helped define Black males by such terminology. The experiences of Black male students in *The Wire* are then examined with a subsequent discussion of how they each represent different elements of giftedness. The essay concludes with specific pedagogical tools and activities that can be used to teach a course on *The Wire* which will help promote cultural competency in college classrooms.

History of At-Risk Terminology and New Readings of Black Male Students

The term at-risk has been part of educational, sociological, and psychological disciplines since the passage of Brown vs. Board of Education (1954). As mainstream educators in public schools sought ways to educate Black children in predominantly White schools, academics identified so-called "cognitive" and intellectual distinctions between Black and White children. The following terms have been used to classify at-risk youth: culturally deprived, educationally deficient, culturally deficient, socially disadvantaged, intellectually deprived, disadvantaged, and at-risk (Havighurst, 1965; Pallas, Natriello, & McDill, 1990). During the 1960s, two terms became synonymous with discussions of low-performing students in America's schools. "Socially disadvantaged" youth were described by scholars like Robert Havighurst (1965) as young people who were both handicapped in "the task of growing up to lead a competent and satisfying life in American society" and who were deprived of a good intellectual start in life (p. 40). These perspectives argued that students who fall into this category are less likely to become successful in their adult lives due to a "disadvantaged" start during childhood. The term "culturally deprived" suggests the cultural backgrounds of Black students were the reason for their low performance in the American public school system. In Kenneth Clark's (1989) *Dark Ghetto*, he identified culturally deprived students as those whose families were unable to provide the necessary resources for their children in order to prepare them for their academic success. Clark (1989) argued that the "culturally deprived child" was a "pupil whose home does not have books and at home discourse lacks the stimulation needed for academic achievement" (p. 126). Additionally, cultural deprivation assigns blame to the families who failed to fully participate in American mass culture as a means to prepare their children for an emphasis on middle class values in school settings (Havighurst, 1965, p. 44).

By the 1970s, there was a shift in the ideology on student experiences and potential student success. During this period, scholars argued that students' experiences in the classroom are directly related to the structure of society outside of the school setting (Baratz & Baratz, 1970; Bowles & Gintis, 1976). As a result, scholars determined that students of color, particularly those who were part of impoverished communities, were not "culturally deficit" but were simply "culturally different" (Baratz & Baratz, 1970). Instead of arguing that these underserved students were in a problematic position because of their socio-cultural backgrounds, these scholars contend that these students' educational needs are not being met within the classroom setting.

After the publication of *A Nation At-Risk* (United States, 1983), school leaders began to question the effectiveness of core coursework in U.S. public schools and created tracking procedures in order to identify students who were performing below grade level. Tracking, an educational term that defines achievement based upon specific coursework for students, has become a common indicator of whether a student is deemed high achieving or below average (Sadker & Zittleman, 2007). According to educational policy researcher Jeannie Oakes, the students who would remain part of the lower echelon of society would be placed in vocational courses that would lead students to menial or low wage employment, while other students were "tracked" into advanced coursework that prepared them for college-level academics (Oakes, 2005). The racial and socioeconomic makeup of academic "tracks" mimicked other forms of division outside the classroom setting. By the late 1980s and 1990s, Black students (particularly African American males) became the group most likely to be recommended for special education programming (a lower educational track). Black male students were so disproportionately represented in special needs classrooms that they outnumbered their presence in the general school population (Pitre, 2009). For special needs students, especially Black males, who are identified early in their K–12 education, this classification follows them throughout their educational careers and negatively impacts their experiences outside the school environment.

These historic moments in education have created the image of Black male students as the quintessential at-risk group in American public school and in society writ large. The No Child Left Behind Act (2001) illuminated the fact that Black male students have consistently underperformed in comparison to their peer groups. While standardized tests do not consider the diverse ways that students learn, they are widely used to determine students' intellectual capabilities. Black male students who attend public schools across the nation have exponentially higher drop-out rates in comparison to their White male counterparts (Balfanz, Legters, West, & Weber, 2007). Outside of formal educational settings, it was widely accepted that Black male youth were an "endangered species" destined for failure, premature death, or a life of incarceration (Gibbs 1988). Black males have the highest homicide rate for youth between the ages of 15 to 24 and are more likely to be unemployed or working menial jobs (Noguera, 1996; Barconey & Pitre, 2009).

Although Black male students have become defined by the at-risk status largely imposed upon them, *The Wire* in the classroom would provide context to this status and examine the (fictional) personal narratives of Black male youth to critically assess their experiences both inside and outside the school setting. While most Black male students do not possess the dominant cultural capital in mainstream society and school settings, they do, however, have a set of character traits, creativity, and leadership qualities that could render them gifted under current, normative definitions. Teaching *The Wire* would elucidate this perspective. Although characters like Michael Lee, Duquan Weems and Randy Wagstaff would initially be perceived as "at-risk" for high school incompletion, there are facets of their characters that, if properly identified, would render them gifted by mainstream standards. The succeeding section describes and presents a radicalized assessment of these characters and argues that they, too, should be considered gifted based upon their leadership, cognitive intellectualism, and entrepreneurship skills.

Revisiting Black Male Youth and Considering Giftedness in The Wire

Gifted in Perpetual Leadership: Michael Lee

Besides the fact that Michael Lee is a poor young Black male in West Baltimore, there are other more substantial aspects of his identity that influence the decisions he makes regarding his family, friends, and future occupation. Although Michael Lee's involvement in Marlo Stanfield's West Baltimore organization serves as the primary focus of the fourth season, there are other dimensions of Michael's "possible self" that broadens his character. The possible selves theory, a concept coined by Daphna Osyerman (1995), argued that various components of an identity should define an individual. The identity that is created is largely dependent upon the survival mechanisms formed in response to specific social contexts where people reside (Frazier, 2012; Osyerman, Gant & Ager, 1995). Michael's possible selves are created in response to his lack of a true childhood and the weight of responsibilities imposed upon him as an eighth grader. His primary responsibility is to protect and provide for his youngest sibling as a pseudo father figure, but Michael is also observant, cautious, sensitive, and a natural born leader.

Michael Lee's responses to significant life events altered his future and presented him as a natural born leader in both his immediate peer group and in his neighborhood. Unlike his peers, Michael was one of few youth who did not accept "handouts" from nonconventional leaders in his neighborhood. In one of the most pivotal scenes from the series, Marlo Stanfield, a well-known drug dealer (and Michael's future employer), rode around a West Baltimore neighborhood to give money to children for "new school clothes" (Burns, Mills & Moore, 2006, "Soft Eyes"). When one of Marlo's workers offered Michael money, he declined (Burns, Mills & Moore, 2006, "Soft Eyes"). To an outsider who has had limited engagement with the show, this could be seen as a moment where an individual simply turns down an offer. However, in Michael's case he has established himself as a leader, being more observant and conscious of his surroundings than most individuals in his age group. As a result of his refusal of the monetary donation, Marlo became more intrigued by Michael, his fearlessness, and independence. Leadership skills are a key component of various definitions of giftedness used to identify gifted and talented students. In 1972, the United States Office of Education defined gifted students as individuals with "outstanding abilities" including "leadership abilities" (Harris & Ford, 1991, p. 6). When considered inside the social context of West Baltimore and the neighborhoods where youth like Michael reside, he can be seen as gifted based upon his desire to stand apart from his peers to walk boldly and confidently into his manhood at a young age.

When Michael was exposed to a school curriculum that was more reflective of his own community, he excelled in the formal educational setting. Extensive scholarship in the field of Education supports the inclusion of culturally relevant pedagogy (i.e., the deliberate decision to incorporate the histories and perspectives of historically marginalized groups into the curriculum) and has been the basis of many conversations regarding race, equity, and teacher education (Banks 2001; DeCuir-Guncy, Taliaferro & Greenfield, 2009; Hillard, 2000; King, 1993). Discourse on culturally relevant pedagogy distances itself from the current trend towards high-stakes standardized testing as the measurement of a student's academic success (Hillard, 2000). Once teachers at the fictional Edward Tilghman Middle School taught material that was "culturally congruent" to the students' backgrounds, teachers and administrators found that the students from West Baltimore were invested in the learning they received in the classroom.

Michael was one of the students in his mathematics class most eager to learn skills that helped him survive outside of school. During a lesson where the students were taught the intricacies of probability through dice, Michael was an active participant and was one of few youth who remembered the formulas and techniques from previous classes. He was a student leader who helped his peers understand probability due to its applicability to their local communities. As a boxer at a local gym, Michael was also eager to learn information about his physical attributes that would help him be successful in his newfound extracurricular passion. In one mathematics class, the students learned how to record various body measurements (e.g., height and wingspan). Michael, who was praised by the head of the boxing gym for his size and agility, measured his wingspan (a physical feature that is undoubtedly important in that particular sport) (Burns & Zakrzewski, 2006, "Know Your Place"). His teacher, who was well aware of his interest in boxing, proclaimed, "You say you like to box huh? You must have some kind of reach" (Burns & Zakrzewski, 2006, "Know Your Place"). Once Michael was exposed to academic material and pedagogical strategies that connected to his informal education, he became one of the more participatory students inside the classroom. Most notably, he became invested in the education that he received because the material was aligned with skills necessary to survive in his West Baltimore community. Michael's intellect and his commitment to student leadership amongst his peers in the classroom is in stark contrast with the perceived perspective of at-risk students of color who are reared in working class communities riddled with crime, violence, and inferior social institutions.

Michael's character traits and the diversity apparent in his total "self" can be viewed as gifted if viewers reconsider his actions based upon his social context. As the son of a drug addict, Michael could easily be viewed as gifted based upon his ability to survive despite the insurmountable odds stacked against him. Michael's giftedness, like his "possible selves," is entirely context specific. Most teachers and administrators inaccurately identify youth as gifted based upon their high performance on standardized tests and a competitive IQ (Harris & Ford, 1991). But Michael's ability to survive and provide for his family and friends makes him gifted in his own right. By dismissing his adolescence in lieu of a father figure and leadership role while simultaneously acquiescing to the demands of his Baltimore neighborhood makes him both a survivor and a gifted youth.

Cognitive Giftedness and Pragmatic Intellectualism: Duquan Weems

Of the four boys featured in the fourth season of *The Wire*, Duquan Weems' character fits inside the traditional definitions of giftedness. While most of his peers were interested in fighting, the pursuit of young women, and acquiring material goods, Duquan was an observant, recluse intellectual who learned about the idiosyncrasies of life through hands on experimentation. But Weems would undoubtedly be considered gifted based upon his "general intellectual ability" and his "specific academic aptitude" (Bonner, 2000, p. 644). Weems' character was often seen conducting micro-level research in his West Baltimore community. Specifically, Duquan's immediate and extended family were the victims of the illegal drug trade prominent in his neighborhood. As a result, Duquan rarely had the basic necessities vital to his survival both inside and outside his home environment. He seemed to find solace in the individualized assessment of his neighborhood. In select scenes, Duquan's giftedness as a true intellectual shines through.

While Duquan's giftedness was not a trait featured most in the fourth season of the show, there were several moments throughout the season which provided a glimpse into his attention to detail and intellectual capabilities. At the onset of the season, the audience is introduced to Michael, Duquan, and Randy in popular areas of their neighborhood. Some of the main characters decide to catch pigeons in order to make a profit from one of the local drug dealers (Simon & Chappelle, 2006, "Boys of Summer"). But after the bird flies away, Duquan told his peers that they were not the homing pigeons they were seeking due to the absence of a tag. Due to Duquan's own individualized research he possessed important knowledge that his peers failed to consider. As an outcast in his community and at his school (because of his family's social standing and his poor hygiene), his perspective was rarely considered. Yet it is evident that he possessed the skills and tools necessary to be considered gifted by many conventional definitions. In one of the most poignant episodes of the season entitled "Home Rooms," Duquan finds a broken fan on the sidewalk while en route to school. Throughout the first day of school, Duquan is seen playing with the fan and ultimately fixes the device (Burns & Mann, 2006, "Home Rooms"). Duquan's giftedness, in this instance, is most obvious: he restored a previously shattered fan to working condition with limited tools or outside assistance. Duquan was also sensitive to the needs of his peers who shared similar life experiences. Not only did Duquan understand the pain of a bullied classmate, he also saw the need to comfort them in a chaotic classroom setting. Lastly, because of Duquan's pragmatic intellectualism, he became one of few students allowed to use the computer in the mathematics classroom as an assistant to the teacher, Mr. Pryzbylewski (Prez) (Burns & Zakrzewski, 2006, "Know Your Place"). He was one of few youth in the season who had a strong connection to his formal education.

Part of Duquan's investment in formal education was due to his relationship with his homeroom and mathematics teacher, Roland Pryzbylewski. Mr. Pryzbylewski gave him access to a school shower before the start of the day, provided him with new clothing at the beginning of each school day, and even shared his lunch with him on a daily basis (Burns & Attias, 2006, "Margin of Error"). Through Mr. Pryzbylewski's culturally relevant pedagogical strategies, Duquan was empowered socially, intellectually, and emotionally (Ladson-Billings, 2009, p. 20). And as a new teacher, Prez was committed to a pedagogical method in his classroom that was a direct reflection of his students' West Baltimore neighborhood. Pryzbylewski's commitment to culturally relevant instruction and the holistic development of his students helped Duquan see his junior high school as a safe space where he was supported.

Paradoxical Entrepreneurship: Randy Wagstaff

Randy Wagstaff's character exemplified paradoxical entrepreneurship inside his community and in the school setting. As a product of the foster care system in Baltimore, Randy sought out various forms of employment and micro-level entrepreneurship in order to support himself. Although his then foster mother, Ms. Anna, invested in Randy and his development as a young man, Randy desired to make additional, independent income. His commitment to non-conventional forms of employment as an eighth grader was a direct reflection of communities largely populated with working class people of color. Randy was one of few young Black males in his West Baltimore neighborhood who failed to participate in the illegal drug arena, but he appreciated the security and power that came with having access to material possessions. For young men in communities like West Baltimore (as depicted in *The Wire*), "money is the primary marker of individual success, not how one acquires money" (hooks, 2004, p. 18). Randy acquired his money through the re-sale of bulk candy throughout his neighborhood and in his school during various lunch periods. He was not only committed to making money but was also interested in giving community residents quality merchandise at a discounted price, much less than the cost at local convenient stores (Simon & Chappelle, 2006, "Boys of Summer"). Randy used the mathematical techniques from his classroom instruction on probability to make a profit in a local dice game in his neighborhood (Burns & Zakrzewski, 2006, "Know Your Place"). He also participated in the Tommy Carcetti mayoral campaign, posting flyers around his community in a last minute attempt to secure votes on Election Day (Burns & Attias, 2006, "Margin of Error"). Not only was Randy committed to entrepreneurship and making an income, he also challenged the normative values in his community through non-conventional honesty.

His character actively challenged the "status quo" of "no snitching" in his community using honesty and an overall commitment to truth. As a young African American male growing up in an urban area plagued by various social ills, Randy attempted to navigate the complex spaces inside his community. One of the most intricate codes of conduct in this community is based upon one's interaction with residents in your community and outsiders across various social institutions. In communities where individuals are required to abide by certain rules for survival, it is difficult for anyone (especially a child) to challenge the dominant code of conduct. These rules become institutions in and of themselves and create a set of values that are difficult to change. Like critical theorist bell hooks argued, "a culture of domination necessarily promotes addiction to lying and denial" (1994, p. 28). A culture of snitching in communities full of historically marginalized groups promotes a similar culture of domination. But in season four of *The Wire*, Randy's character, a paradoxical entrepreneur, directly challenged this common conduct. Randy's character should be viewed as gifted due to his commitment to challenging the normative values which instilled fear in his home environment. Undoubtedly, some leaders took advantage of Randy's honesty and used it as a controlling mechanism to satisfy their own interests (i.e., Marcia Donnelly, vice principal at Edward Tilghman Middle School) (Burns & Attias, 2006, "Margin of Error"). Yet Randy's desire to tell the truth in various situations showed his desire to separate himself from the negative inner workings of his community of origin. Instead of being complacent and abiding by the unwritten code in his community, he was compelled to live life on his own terms.

Future Considerations: Teaching Cultural Competency Using The Wire in Undergraduate Classrooms

The Wire is a visual text that would be extremely useful for undergraduate students in colleges across the country. The countless numbers of undergraduate courses nationwide, which use *The Wire* as their primary source text, supports this claim (Swansburg 2010; Cannon 2011; Heyboer 2013). Using *The Wire* in the classroom as a teaching tool and discursive visual text allows students the opportunity to see a first-hand glimpse into the lives of fictional characters situated in realistic circumstances. While some students may question the authenticity of a fictional television series, others may be introduced to a reality that radically alters their perspective on race, class, and educational access. This television series would be a useful tool to teach urban life and social institutions in general, and more specifically, would challenge the master narrative of Black male students prominent in mainstream popular culture. This show would move beyond discussions of diversity by encouraging cultural competency at the college level. Scholars like James Banks (1994) have argued that understanding certain social groups is "a gradual and developmental process ... the stages should not be viewed as strictly sequential and linear" (as cited in McAllister & Irvine, 2000, p. 13). Shows like *The Wire* would support Banks' claims. Instead of watching a short movie that presents a limited glimpse into the narratives of othered groups, *The Wire*'s fourth season provides a more complex image of the lives of Black male students in a 21st century context. Instead of simply discussing the cultural backgrounds of historically marginalized groups, it allows students the opportunity to deeply analyze the intricacies of Black urban life from the eyes of children. The preceding "future considerations" portion of this final section presents micro-level, course related examples for educators interested in teaching Black male student experiences in the fourth season of this series. In addition to examining the narratives of the Black male students featured in the fourth season of the show, scholars are encouraged to consider including other important concepts in a course on this series. The following set of recommendations is not exhaustive but allows the reader to see ways to incorporate different pedagogical methods for diverse undergraduate learners.

Provide a Sound Theoretical Framework Prior to Introducing *The Wire*

Prior to introducing *The Wire* to students, there should be a lengthy discussion of various theories, tropes, and scholarly concepts that would provide a foundational framework for analyzing the show. The television series engages with various concepts and realities for historically marginalized groups that may be unclear to White, wealthy and otherwise privileged students. For instance, how would an instructor teach about "snitching" and vigilante justice in urban areas? Most importantly how would an instructor engage various perspectives on the aforementioned terms and accurately explain their deep connection to Black working class communities? For White and wealthy students who entrust various social institutions (e.g., police department) to support their interests and protect their communities, they may have difficulty understanding why some Black and brown people have problems trusting law enforcement agencies and officers. By exposing students to both the complexities of urban life and the history of at-risk categorizations that are placed upon Black male students, it will allow them to see the intricacies and the failures of social institutions that are supposed to help society. Scholars like bell hooks (2004) and her discussion of "gangsta culture" may provide insight into some of the realities for Black urban residents.

College students may not understand the "acting White" phenomenon that may explain why some Black students have difficulty finding value in the pursuit of formal education. The controversial discussion of John Ogbu and Signithia Fordham's (1986) "acting White" and the educational experiences of involuntary African Americans (or Africans whose ancestors were brought to the Western world through conquest or domination) could shed light into why some students have issues with their formal education. In order to challenge commonly accepted terms used to describe historically othered groups, undergraduate students must be well aware of the state of current academic scholarship that describes Black male student achievement. It would also help students question whether at-risk terminology can be accurately used to describe the diverse experiences of the Black male students we see in *The Wire*. Without a discussion of academic scholarship that deals directly with the experiences of Black male youth, a course including *The Wire* would be significantly less effective.

Screen Documentaries About Baltimore

Undoubtedly some students may have difficulty understanding why a television series is the primary text in a college course. Students may question the authenticity of a show like *The Wire* and ask if this series is a true representation of life in Baltimore for historically othered groups. In order to show some of the realities for some Black male youth in *The Wire*, a screening of various documentaries would help support the television show's credibility all the while showing everyday examples of life for Black working class residents. While there are several documentaries to choose from, *The Boys of Baraka* (Ewing & Grady, 2005) documentary is a compelling narrative about Black male youth in Baltimore. The film showed the complex educational experiences of Black public school students. Yet once this group was taken out of Baltimore and educated in Kenya and isolated from their home environments, these young Black males became academically successful and devoted their undivided attention to their education. This documentary would actively challenge the images of education in *The Wire* and question whether Black male youth would have more educational opportunities if they were educated outside Baltimore. Overall, showing undergraduate students documentaries that present an image of Baltimore that is both similar and different from *The Wire* will add complexity to the primary curricula used in a potential course on the series.

Use Board Games and Hands-on Activities to Teach About Choices and Chance

Prior to introducing students to *The Wire*, teachers should consider nonconventional course materials to teach the realities for residents in West Baltimore. For some White and wealthy students who have been able to use various resources to their advantage, they may wholeheartedly believe in a unidimensional perspective of myriad social institutions. To teach these students about the realities that some Black working and underclass people may experience, instructors may choose to employ the "board game" method. While board games are usually used for recreational purposes, they can be used in a class using *The Wire* to explain the lack of control that these Black male youth have on their choices and their futures. For instance, how would Michael's life be different if he was recommended to the "Corner Kids" specialized program and became Bunny's adopted son? This possible plot alteration could be best illustrated using a game of Monopoly. In this common American game, every person is given the opportunity to choose a figure as their prominent gaming piece and "roll the dice" to see where they will land on the board. It does not matter about the social standing of the individual rolling the dice, the amount of education, or even where the person is positioned in juxtaposition to their competitors. It is simply based upon how you roll the dice. This could be compared to the Black male youth in the television series. Depending upon the "roll of the dice," "card," or "hand" you are dealt will determine how you will move forward in your life. For some students who are visual learners it may be easier for them to understand "chance" based upon everyday games that may depict life roles.

Examine Hip-hop Lyrics from Urban Artists

Rap music is the most popular music genre in the world. Most undergraduate students have had some exposure to the music through their personal enjoyment or interactions with individuals in their immediate peer group. But most students are not aware of the origins of this genre as an art form created by African American and Latino working class residents. Teachers who are interested in exposing students to the realities of hip-hop and how it can relate to some of the images we see in *The Wire* could ask students to examine the lyrics from popular hip hop artists who discuss urban life. For instance, in rapper Jay-Z's song "Where I'm From," he described his experiences growing up in his Brooklyn neighborhood. Undergraduate students inside of a classroom could analyze how his narrative relates to the visual images seen in *The Wire*. Furthermore, Jay-Z's chronicle could provide a first-hand account to students who have limited knowledge of the intricacies of the inner-city. For many people who actively consume hip-hop they may be unaware of the realities that some urban people of color face even though they may sing (or rap) along with the lyrics to their favorite rap tracks. But when rap songs are coupled with the visual imagery from *The Wire*, this activity would help to make stronger connections for students unfamiliar with urban life.

Final Reflections

On the surface, these narratives present the image of Black male youth who fit the status quo. For the most part, they are located on the outskirts of mainstream society in the inner city, a place that is discussed and regularly commodified in the media. Yet a renewed reading of these Black male youth as gifted would encourage undergraduate students (and college instructors) to consider these Black male youth as more than drug dealers, homeless youth, and victims of the foster care system. Such an analysis examines the complexities of their realities and looks for examples of their giftedness in the midst of despair.

The experiences that Black male students have in working and underclass communities prepare them for the uncertainty of the future. While their White peers may have access to a wealth of resources, an excess of material possessions, and the stability of a nuclear household, giftedness is conceptualized in a broader sense because of these Black male youth's multifaceted backgrounds. This is a common finding that could be discussed in various college classrooms and could teach cultural competency from a unique perspective. While some courses in the field of Education use examples of qualitative research as their primary source texts, a viewing of *The Wire* would present a fictional (yet realistic) portrayal of why cultural competency in college classrooms is a necessity. A deep engagement with this series would help develop well-rounded undergraduate students who will actively question racism and classism. This series challenges the bootstrap model of social mobility and makes the argument that these youth are simply trying their best to survive in an urban community full of various social ills. College students' exposure to youth from *The Wire* who have no control over their futures or the families they were born into may reconsider the perspective that all people located on the margins of society can transcend their surroundings and pull themselves out of their dire circumstances. In addition, this context specific reading of Black male students as gifted broadens our understandings of this group as both students and as the quintessential at-risk group.

REFERENCES

Althusser, L. (1971). *Lenin and philosophy and other essays.* New York: Monthly Review Press.
Balfanz, R., N. Legters, T. West, and L. Weber. (2007). Are NCLB's measures, incentives, and improvement strategies the right ones for the nation's low performing high schools? *American Educational Research Journal, 44,* 559–593.
Banks, J. (2001). Citizenship education and diversity: Implications for teacher education. *Journal of Teacher Education, 52,* 5–16.
Baratz, J., and S. Baratz. (1970). Early childhood intervention: The social science base of institutional racism. *Harvard Educational Review, 40,* 29–50.

Barconey, M., and A. Pitre (2009). African American males in urban schools. In A. Pitre, E. Pitre, R. Ray and T. Hilton-Pitre (Eds.), *Educating African American students: Foundations, curriculum, and experiences* (95–105). Lantham, MD: Rowman & Littlefield.

Bonner, F. (2000). *Academically Gifted African American Male College Students.* Santa Barbara, CA: Praeger.

Bowles, S., and H. Gintis. (1976). *Schooling in CAPITALIST America: Educational reform and the contradictions of economic life.* London: Routledge.

Burns, E. (Writer), and D. Attias (Director). (2006). Margin of Error [television series episode]. In D. Simon (Executive Producer), *The Wire*, New York: Home Box Office.

Burns, E. (Writer), and S. Mann (Director). (2006). Home Rooms [television series episode]. In D. Simon (Executive Producer), *The Wire*, New York: Home Box Office.

Burns, E. (Writer), and A. Zakrzewski (Director). (2006). "Know Your Place" [television series episode]. In D. Simon (Executive Producer), *The Wire*, New York: Home Box Office.

Burns, E., Mills, D. (Writer), and C. Moore (Director). (2006). Soft Eyes [television series episode]. In D. Simon (Executive Producer), *The Wire*, New York: Home Box Office.

Cannon, H. (2011). New course uses HBO's "the wire" to examine urban America. *UVA Today.* Retrieved from http://news.virginia.edu/content/new-course-uses-hbos-wire-examine-urban-america.

Clark, K. (1989). *Dark ghetto: Dilemmas of social power.* Hanover, NH: Wesleyan University Press.

DeCuir-Gunby, J., J. DeVance Taliaferro, and D. Greenfield. (2009). *Educators' Perspectives on Culturally Relevant Programs for Academic Success: The American Excellence Association. Education and Urban Society,* 42(2), 182–204. http://dx.doi.org/10.1177/0013124509349874.

Ewing, H., and R. Grady (Producer), and H. Ewing, R. Grady (Director). (2005). *The Boys of Baraka* [Documentary]. USA: Loki Films.

Fordham, S. and J. Ogbu. (1986). Black students' school success: Coping with the burden of "acting White." *Urban Review, 18,* 176–206.

Frazier, A. (2012). The Possible selves of high-ability African males attending a residential high school for highly able youth. *Journal for the Education of the Gifted, 35,* 366–390.

Gay, G. (2010). *Culturally responsive teaching: Theory, research, and practice* (2nd ed.). New York: Teachers College Press.

Geertz, C. (1973). Thick description: Toward an interpretive theory of culture. In C. Geertz (Ed.), *The interpretation of cultures: Selected essays* (3–30). New York: Basic Books.

Gibbs, J. (1988). Young black males in America: Endangered, embittered, and embattled. In J. Gibbs, A. Brunswick, M. Connor, R. Dembo, T. Larson, R. Reed and B. Solomon (Eds.), *Young black and male in America: An endangered species* (1–36). Westport: Auburn House.

Harris, J., and D. Ford. (1990). Identifying and nurturing the promise of gifted black American children. *The Journal of Negro Education, 60,* 3–18.

Havighurst, R. (1965). Who are the socially disadvantaged? *Journal of Negro Education, 34,* 39–46.

Heyboer, K. (2013). Rutgers offers course on HBO's "the wire." Retrieved from http://www.nj.com/education/2013/12/rutgers_offers_course_on_hbos.html.

Hillard, A. (2000). Excellence in education versus high-stakes standardized testing. *Journal of Teacher Education, 51*, 293–304.

hooks, b. (1994). *Teaching to transgress: Education as the practice of freedom.* London: Routledge.

Ikemoto, L. (2000). Traces of the master narrative in the African American/Korean American conflict: How we constructed "Los Angeles." In R. Delgado and J. Stefancic (Eds.), *Critical Race Theory: The Cutting Edge* (302–312). Philadelphia: Temple University Press.

King, S.H. (1993). The limited presence of African American teachers. *Review of Educational Research, 63*, 115–149.

Ladson-Billings, G. (2009). *The dreamkeepers: Successful teachers of African American children.* San Francisco: Jossey-Bass.

McAllister, G., & Irvine, J. (2000). Cross cultural competency and multicultural teacher education. *Review of Educational Research, 70*, 3–24.

McMillan, A. (2009). Heroism, institutions, and the police procedural. In C.W. Marshall and Tiffany Potter (Eds.), *The Wire: Urban decay and American television* (50–63). New York: Continuum.

No Child Left Behind Act of 2001, 20 U.S.C. § 6319 (2008).

Noguera, P. (1996). Responding to the crisis confronting California's black male youth: Providing support without further marginalization. *The Journal of Negro Education, 65*, 219–236.

Oakes, J. (2005). *Keeping track: How schools structure inequality* (2nd ed.). New Haven: Yale University Press.

Osyerman, D., L. Gant,and J. Ager. (1995). A socially contextualized model of African American identity: Possible selves and school persistence. *Journal of Personality and Social Psychology, 69*, 1216–1232.

Pallas, A., G. Natriello, and E. McDill. (1990). *Schooling disadvantaged children: Racing against catastrophe.* New York: Teachers College Press.

Pitre, E. (2009). Overrepresentation of African American males in special education: An examination of the referral process in the K-12 public school setting. In A. Pitre, E. Pitre, R. Ray and T. Hilton-Pitre (Eds.), *Educating African American students: Foundations, curriculum, and experiences* (79–92). Lantham, MD: Rowman & Littlefield.

Sadker, D., and K. Zittleman. (2007). *The teachers, schools, and society.* Boston: McGraw-Hill.

Simon, D. (Writer), and J. Chappelle (Director). (2006). Boys of Summer [television series episode]. In D. Simon (Executive Producer), *The Wire.* New York: Home Box Office.

Swansburg, J. (2010). More college courses on HBO's "the wire." *Slate.* Retrieved from http://www.slate.com/blogs/browbeat/2010/03/31/more_college_courses_on_hbo_s_the_wire.html.

United States Department of Education, National Commission on Excellence in Education. (1983). *A nation at risk: the imperative for educational reform: A report to the Nation and the Secretary of Education.* Washington, D.C.: Retrieved from http://www2.ed.gov/pubs.NatAtRisk/index.html.

"Cause they're not learning for our world; they're learning for theirs"

A Critical Race Theory and Phenomenological Variant of Ecological Systems Theory Analysis of Season 4 of The Wire

HANNAH CARSON BAGGETT,
CRYSTAL G. SIMMONS, SHARONDA R. EGGLETON,
and JESSICA T. DeCUIR-GUNBY

Educational researchers have long studied the ways in which schools, teachers, and students are functions of larger societal systems (e.g., Anyon, 1980; Kozol, 1991; Howard, 2008; Tyack, 2003). In Season Four of *The Wire*, David Simon and co-creators delve into an educational system nested in a broken community. As Heather Moore described in the previous chapter, the episodes in this season present viewers with an explicit look into the lived realities of four, Black, adolescent males: Namond, Michael, Randy, and Duquan. During Season Four, Namond is a middle school student whose father is an imprisoned drug dealer and whose mother is dependent on the income associated with the sale of drugs. In some ways, Namond is more privileged than his peers in the neighborhood because of his father's association with the Barksdale drug organization, who are partially responsible for the drug trade in West Baltimore. Michael is a self-sufficient, independent, middle school student who is the primary caregiver of his little brother. He is viewed as a leader amongst his peers—a trait that is also admired by Marlo Stanfield, a competing drug lord in the neighborhood. In Season Four, the viewers observe Michael's metamorphosis from an innocent adolescent to an emerging violent criminal. Randy is a middle school student, raised in foster homes, who is prone to mischievous acts both in school and out. His propensity for honesty garners his reputation as a "snitch." Duquan is a shy, somewhat withdrawn middle school student whose family's drug abuse severely impacts his livelihood. These four characters, over the course of the season, experience poverty, crime, drug use, and both positive and negative school experiences.

In addition, viewers are presented with a complex look at the power associated with various adult "role" models in these adolescents' lives, both in school and the community. These relationships foster resiliency and productive student outcomes in some of the adolescents, but draw others into the street economies of the community. The viewers are also exposed to the social infrastructures (i.e., foster care, "street politics," and the local public schools) that directly impact the lives of these characters as they navigate through adolescence.

For educators and education researchers, ecological models are often a starting point for examination of the complex relationships between and among systems, student development, and outcomes. Many current models postulate that one's interactions within a particular environment and society influence his or her development (Bronfenbrenner, 1994; Spencer, 2006). The characters in *The Wire* underscore a need to apply ecological models to educational outcomes in order to recognize how systemic issues influence the interplay among the various systems and individuals within. In this way, *The Wire* serves as an excellent and informative text for educators, researchers, and education policy makers to examine and critique the racialized, hegemonic power structures that not only perpetuate the status quo in education, but in society. While educators may sometimes have limited power to affect change on the systems at work outside of the school building, using *The Wire* as a case study can lead teachers and policy makers to a deeper understanding of both the students in their future classrooms and schools, and the ways that teachers can potentially foster student development. This essay explores the ways race and racism impact the social and economic policies that influence the adolescents' environment inside and outside of school in Season Four. The schooling and developmental experiences of each of the four adolescent characters are analyzed through the lens of particular frameworks which focus on racialized contexts and experiences. The ways in which Season Four can be used to initiate conversations between and among teacher educators, preservice and practicing educators, and policy makers are provided.

Theoretical Frameworks

This discussion of Season Four of *The Wire* as a text for preservice and practicing educators and education policy makers is framed by Critical Race Theory (CRT) and Phenomenological Variant of Ecological Systems Theory

(PVEST). Critical Race Theory was developed by legal scholars Derrick Bell, Alan Freeman, and Richard Delgado during the mid–'70s as a response to the failure of the legal system to adequately address the effects of race and racism in the United States. Critical Race theorists usually cite five main tenets (Delgado & Stefancic, 2012). First, a basic premise includes the centrality and intersectionality of race and racism, which posits that *racism is ordinary*; experiences with racism are an everyday, lived reality for people of color (Bell, 1992); and Whites enjoy certain privileges due solely to the color of their skin (Harris, 1993). In addition, the intersectionality of multiple statuses and identities may lead to multiple forms of oppression (e.g., being racially Black and female, Crenshaw, 1989). Next, *race is viewed as a social construction* (Omi & Winant, 1994), and racial categories are manipulated by society, as needed, to preserve the status quo. Due to this desire to preserve the status quo, Critical Race Theory is also premised on the idea of *interest convergence*: change to the status quo only comes about when White mainstream society serves to gain from it (Bell, 1980). This leads Critical Race theorists to *critique liberalism* and its ideals, such as colorblindness and meritocracy. CRT scholars argue that this critique is necessary since the gradual, incremental changes that result from liberal ideologies and policies tend to be subsumed by the larger, hegemonic structures in place in U.S. society (Bonilla-Silva, 2002; Gotanda, 1991; Solórzano & Yosso, 2002), thus securing the permanence of racism and White supremacy. Finally, *storytelling* is an important part of Critical Race Theory (Bell, 1992; Delgado, 1992). Critical Race scholars, in their work, focus on and emphasize voices that have been traditionally and historically marginalized.

Critical Race Theory, as a framework, has expanded into other disciplines, including education. Critical Race theorists in education center social inequality and school inequity on several main ideas: (1) ethnoracial status (Frederickson, 2002) continues to be a significant factor in determining inequity at institutional and classroom levels, due to the permanence of racism and White supremacy in education, (2) whiteness is a form of property (Harris, 1993) the dominant cultural capital in schools (Ladson-Billings & Tate, 1995), and (3) this intersection of race and property creates an analytic tool through which we can understand social and school inequity (DeCuir & Dixson, 2004). Schools perpetuate societal inequities in a systematic way, and these inequities are intricately linked to perceptions about ethnoracial status, such as deficit thinking, low expectations, and stereotyping (Ladson-Billings & Tate, 1995). Critical Race theorists in education view the public school system as a primary mode of transmission of racist ideology and practices (Harrell, 1999) and educational policies as mechanisms by which White supremacy is maintained (Gillborn, 2005). Critical Race scholars in education also reject underlying assumptions in the education system such as objectivity, meritocracy, equal opportunity, and color/gender blindness (DeCuir & Dixson, 2004; Solórzano, 1998; Yosso, 2002). Finally, Critical Race theorists assert that schools have the potential to empower students who are marginalized, if effective teachers and resources are in place (Howard, 2008; Ladson-Billings, 1994). However, the research on teacher preparation indicates that White teachers are not adequately prepared to meet the needs of diverse learners (e.g., Sleeter, 2001). During Season Four, the lived experiences of the adolescents are impacted by the institutionalized racism they experience in all spheres of their lives. The intersection of their racial and gender identities contributes to the difficulties they face, and the liberal ideologies in which the school system is rooted contribute to their marginalization.

The second framework applied to the student outcomes seen in *The Wire* is the Phenomenological Variant of Ecological Systems Theory (Spencer, Dupree, & Hartman, 1997; Spencer, 2006), which helps educators and education policy makers to understand the developmental trajectories of the four African American, male adolescents. This theory examines both historical and contemporary impacts of social policy and context on the development of adolescents of color. PVEST is used to analyze the ways in which some characters develop coping mechanisms that lead to productive developmental outcomes.

Inherent in models of human development is the notion that all individuals are vulnerable in some way. Risk factors exist that have the potential to cause stress. Some specific examples of risk factors for adolescents include "socioeconomic conditions, such as living in poverty, and imposed expectations based on race, immigration status, unstable family economic status, and gender stereotypes" (Spencer, 2006, p. 847). At school, as in broader macro contexts, risk factors can also include perceived racial discrimination (and discrimination attributed to other identity statuses, such as gender expression and sexual orientation, or the intersection of identity statuses that differ from White, cis-gendered normative statues) by peers, teachers, or administrators (e.g., Almeida, Johnson, Corliss, Molnar & Azrael, 2009; Neblett, Smalls, Ford, Nguyen, & Sellers, 2006; Wong, Eccles, & Sameroff, 2003). Developmental theories also point to protective factors that exist, which have the potential to offset or 'buffer' the stress induced by encounters with risk factors and contexts. Some examples of protective factors are "privilege group membership, a particular cultural socialization history, skin color, facial features, body type, intellectual superiority, attractiveness, economic stability, well-educated parents and protective extended family networks, emotionally available and caring adults" (Spencer, 2006, p. 847). Many of these protective factors, such as skin color and body type, are those physical characteristics that have been normalized by dominant culture as desirable or preferred. Furthermore, racial socialization messages from parents and family members, and racial or ethnic identity have been theorized to be important buffers. Indeed, much empirical research has been conducted to test racial identity as a moderator in positive developmental outcomes (e.g., Garcìa Coll, et al., 1996; Neblett et al., 2006; Sellers, Linder, Martin, & Lewis, 2006).

However, despite the presence of protective factors, some contexts and risks create a "net stress" effect that an adolescent must manage. To do so, adolescents develop coping mechanisms, some of which are adaptive, and others that are not. Examples of adaptive strategies are school engagement, avoiding risk-taking behavior, and economic self-sufficiency (Spencer, 2006). Some examples of maladaptive coping strategies include "staying away from home or other sources of support, using drugs ... becoming committed to negative peer models" (Spencer, 2006, p. 850), school disengagement, and poor academic outcomes. Depending on the desirability of the results achieved after implementation of these coping mechanisms (Spencer, Dupree, & Hartmann, 1997), and the response or appraisals of others (Bandura, 1978), adolescents may repeatedly engage in maladaptive strategies, which have the potential to lead to non-productive developmental outcomes.

Some have argued that risk environments profoundly affect African American adolescents in general (e.g., Kochman, 1994), and that African American male adolescents are particularly vulnerable (e.g., Cunningham & Spencer, 1996) because of negative societal messages and scripts regarding stereotypes of Black males, experiences with racial discrimination, and macrosystems that impose low expectations for positive outcomes. As such, the PVEST framework differs from previous ecological systems models (e.g., Bronfenbrenner, 1994) in that it accounts for risk and protective factors related to the individual, and also both the racialized historical and social contexts in which individuals develop and form identities. In this model, racial discrimination is viewed as a primary risk factor, "which increases the net vulnerability for youth of color and may result in adverse consequences if youth do not develop appropriate coping strategies and support skills" (Spencer, 2006 as cited in Seaton, et al., 2011, p. 1850) and focuses on the ways that racial identity can buffer this risk factor. PVEST also integrates Critical Race Theory by considering the ways in which race and the pervasiveness of racism affect adolescent development at macro and micro levels. Spencer (2006) explains:

> in the social sciences and child development literatures, the unequal conditions and historical circumstances that diverse youth have inherited, grown up with, and psychologically developed in response to are, for the most part, inadequately considered or totally ignored [p. 834].

Indeed, the racialized, inequitable systems in which adolescents live and grow are often overlooked in developmental theories and in educational research. Too often, poor developmental outcomes are localized to the individual, and adolescent behavior is pathologized. PVEST, by contrast, centers racialized contexts as *responsible* for creating factors that place adolescents of color "at risk." As such, in order to explore the ways in which the adolescents in Season Four develop, cope, and form identities, it is necessary to acknowledge the racialized contexts in which they are situated. Acknowledging these contexts and their impacts on the characters' development, although fictitious, can provide an understanding of the pervasiveness of racism and the real and deleterious impact it has on youth of color, especially when their resources are scarce.

An Analysis of Season Four of The Wire Using the PVEST Model Within a CRT Framework

Critical Race Theory explicitly acknowledges the role of race and racism in shaping and influencing historical and contemporary social policies and laws that impact the environments of students of color (Ladson-Billings & Tate, 1995). Particularly, in Season Four of *The Wire* school inequities impact the contexts of the adolescents in the story. This complex context includes embedded risk and protective factors that shape and inform the experiences of each of the four adolescents. When situated within a Critical Race framework, it becomes apparent that racialized institutional policies and practices affect, and ultimately impact the four adolescents in various ways. The following section details the educational inequalities in Season Four.

Educational Inequities

In Season Four, there are explicit instances of educational inequities, such as the lack of technology, up-to-date textbooks, or class materials. Since public schools are largely funded by local tax bases, schools located in low socio-economic neighborhoods and communities are often poorly funded and under-resourced (e.g., Anyon, 1997). Despite the passage of The Fair Housing Act of 1968, which was created to prohibit housing discrimination based on race, neighborhoods continue to be racially segregated due to covert instances of racial bias in the housing sector (DeCuir-Gunby & Taliaferro, 2013; Fischer & Massey, 2004). As a consequence of housing discrimination, people of color are not only limited to residential opportunities, but they also experience inequities in employment, wealth, health, and education (Fischer & Massey, 2004; Pager & Shepherd, 2008). From a CRT and PVEST perspective, housing discrimination thus provides evidence of structural and institutional forces that restrict opportunities and resources based on race. As such, the underfunded school portrayed in Season Four is intrinsically related to historical housing discrimination and economic depression in the neighboring communities.

Furthermore, the viewers also see the failure of the school system to support and meet the needs of students of color. For instance, truancy officers are hired to gather students from the neighborhood in order for the school to meet their attendance quota and receive federal funds. Viewers are thus shown a picture of a community where students appear to find the street more appealing than school. One could hypothesize that this is, in part, attributed to the failure of the school to provide a challenging and rigorous school curriculum and culturally relevant teachers (Ladson-Billings, 1995), which in turn hinders and stifles student engagement and learning. For example, at the beginning of the school semester the teaching style of Mr. Pyrzbylewski "Prez"—the boys' math teacher—reflected a lack of attention to student interest and the cultural capital his students brought to the classroom. However, after developing relationships with Randy and Duquan, Prez developed an understanding of the importance of making content relevant. African American males' experiences in school can have a negative impact on their academic outcomes (Noguera, 2008). Howard (2013) attributed these negative experiences to classroom teaching and practices.

> Many of the challenges that confront Black males in education go beyond their communities and their social class status and are directly located in classrooms, the lack of racial awareness and cultural ignorance among school personnel, apathetic teacher attitudes, and poor-quality instruction that they receive, be it in urban, rural, or suburban schools [pp. 61–62].

To understand the racialized experiences of African American adolescents in schools and in other contexts, it is important to examine how other aspects of their identity impact their lived experiences. The intersectionality among being African American (race), male (gender), and poor (SES) is a central theme in Season Four. Intersectionality examines how multiple identities in conjunction with race (e.g., gender, class, and sexuality) are interrelated in a system of oppression and discrimination (Crenshaw, 1989; Howard, 2013). According to Howard and Reynolds (2013):

> The intersections of race, class, and gender have manifested themselves in a multitude of complex and harmful ways within the U.S. that have profoundly influenced the manner in which Black males experience schools and society. This intersectionality is rarely examined and, as a result, opportunities to authentically capture the breadth and depth of Black males are missed, and efforts to capture their stories and reform schools are misinformed and misguided [p. 234].

Viewers come to understand how each of these intersecting identities provides insight into the varying experiences that exist within groups as it relates to oppression and discrimination (Howard & Reynolds, 2013). Specifically, each character in *The Wire* experiences different outcomes. For example, all of the adolescents lived in poverty and predominantly single-parent homes. However, they each coped and responded differently to these contexts: Michael and

Duquan ultimately fall victim to the crime and drug use of the neighborhood; Randy remains a ward of the state and is placed in a group home; and Namond is adopted by a middle-class African American family and experiences positive academic outcomes, a rare outcome for youth in his situation.

Developmental Processes in *The Wire*

PVEST, as a model which differs from its precursors, encourages the adoption of a developmental perspective when working with adolescents of color. As Spencer (2006) explains, "theorizing about youth of color frequently *underexamines* developmental processes and *overemphasizes* risk factors and unproductive stage-specific outcomes (e.g., early pregnancy, disproportionate incarceration rates, school failure, and aggression)" (p. 838). While the four adolescents in Season Four may seem to share the same contexts, their outcomes are disparate. PVEST, and its focus on both risk and protective factors, and the "experiences of risk and protection in context" (p. 849), allows viewers to explore the ways in which some students develop adaptive coping mechanisms and productive outcomes (i.e., resiliency), while others do not. This allows for a more nuanced view of individual experiences within a group membership. Since a majority of preservice and practicing educators and education policy makers are White (Zumwalt & Craig, 2005) and may stereotype students of color (King, 1991; Sleeter, 2008), a more detailed view of differing outcomes among a particular group of students (e.g., African American) can help combat essentialist, monolithic views of student groups, as well as help to combat deficit perspectives and stereotypes. In order for classrooms to be positioned as sites of success and critical engagement for students of color, ecological systems frameworks like PVEST are needed in education courses to expose teacher candidates and researchers to the complex processes of adolescent development as situated in their racialized contexts. Specifically, PVEST (Spencer, 2006), which integrates historical and contemporary contexts and ethno-racial identity into developmental trajectories, is beneficial in helping educators and researchers to understand that students may have qualitatively different schooling (and lived) experiences depending on their ethnoracial status, but that within ethnoracial groups, student experiences may differ as well.

In addition, using *The Wire* as a "mapping" tool for analyzing adolescent development could provide insight into the ways in which students experience school. Ecological systems theories are used as seminal adolescent developmental models in many education courses. Educators' conceptions of adolescent development are critical to both understanding the lived experiences of their students and to implementing effective, responsive pedagogical practices. Indeed, even using the word "adolescent" when discussing students has the potential to reframe educators' perspectives; this shift could represent a move away from viewing students as lacking or "deficient," to seeing them as individuals that are not yet fully formed and are "developing" (Lesko, 1996; 2001).

In conjunction with tracking the individual characters' trajectories in Season Four, an exploration of the broader, racialized contexts of education and politics may underscore the ways in which students are affected by larger systems. Indeed, an overarching goal of using *The Wire* as a text for preservice and practicing educators and policymakers is to eschew the deficit thinking that often comes with students in difficult circumstances and/or the individual blaming that tends to occur when students fail. For instance, preservice and practicing teachers often hold misconceptions about parents who "don't care" and students who are "at risk" without critically analyzing their beliefs about students and their families. These misconceptions reflect a fundamental misunderstanding of the ways in which the practices of both institutions and individual teachers have historically contributed to the marginalization of certain student groups (King, 1991). However, teacher educators can use Season Four as a conduit to discuss the origin of risks and contexts (historical and contemporary racialized practices and policies that impact students of color); to identify risks and protective factors related to characters and contexts; and to assess coping strategies as either adaptive or maladaptive, while considering the stress that prompted them to emerge.

Risk and Protective Factors

As they develop, adolescents cycle through risks, protections, contexts, and corresponding challenges and support. Risk factors for adolescents are numerous and varied, and can lead to negative developmental outcomes if they are not mitigated (Werner, 1993). Risk factors that contribute to stress, specifically in African American adolescent developmental processes, include discrimination (Wong, Eccles & Sameroff, 2003), increased likelihood of poverty and its damaging effects (McLoyd, 1990), and particular negative perceptions about African American boys (Ladson-Billings, 1994). These risk factors are present throughout the contexts seen over the course of Season Four, and viewers see how the combination of low socio-economic status and inadequate caregiving contributes to the adolescents' vulnerability. For example, Michael's mother is addicted to drugs and has a live-in boyfriend who viewers may assume sexually assaulted Michael and possibly his brother. Michael's mother sells their groceries for drugs, which leaves the family without food. Duquan's mother is also addicted to drugs, and he is not provided the very basic necessities, such as clean clothes, food, or stable living conditions.

As they progress during adolescence, the four characters in Season Four grapple with development of racial and gender identities (Erikson, 1968). In this formative stage of identity development, socialization practices and efforts from parents and peers can lead to positive or negative outcomes. Consequently, the impact of poverty on the family structure and parent-child interaction for these four African American adolescents creates periods of stress and confusion (Conger & Conger, 2007; McLoyd, 1990). Potts, Wickrama, Simons, Cutrona, Gibbons, Simons, and Conger (2015) added, "as children enter adolescence they may be more vulnerable to developing emotional (internalizing) problems in response to economic (or any other) stressor" (p. 234). This was the case for Michael, Duquan, and Namond as they have to deal with the economic hardships and stressors experienced by their parents. These various risks, however, are not independent of context, and are not innate to the families and individuals themselves (Spencer, 2006); instead, these risk factors have been created by the overarching racialized structures in which the adolescents and their communities are situated (Milner, 2013), and have introduced stress for the adolescents and their development.

Within the developmental context, protective factors may help to mitigate the effects of risk (Spencer, 2006). For example, Namond is more privileged than the other adolescents with respect to the relative economic stability of his mother compared to the family structures of the other adolescents. Also, because of his father's previous "street" association, Namond is granted a greater level of respect in the "street" community. This level of respect gives Namond a sense of pride and self-esteem. Research shows that having high self-esteem serves as a protective factor against depression and other maladaptive behaviors (Blocker & Copeland, 1994; Cowen, Wyman, Work, Kim, Fagen, & Magnus, 1997; Li, Nussbaum, & Richards, 2007). Randy has the strongest support system in that he is with a foster family and has relationships with law enforcement in the community. Duquan has supportive relationships with school personnel who frequently provide him with clothes and resources. These extended family and kinship networks within the schools and community provided both Randy and Duquan support to counteract potential risks and negative outcomes (Li et al., 2007; Taylor, Casten, & Flickinger, 1993). When analyzing developmental trajectories of students of color, protective factors are often overlooked (Spencer, 2006). As such, it should be noted that buffers exist for White students *and* students of color to help reduce the tendency to focus on and pathologize risk factors and nonproductive outcomes for adolescents of color.

Coping Mechanisms

When the challenges they experience begin to outweigh the supports provided for them, adolescents must develop coping strategies in order to offset a portion of the stress that has been introduced. While coping mechanisms alleviate stress for adolescents, they may be either adaptive or mal-adaptive. Using Season Four may help preservice and practicing educators and education policy makers gain insight into the potential causes of seem-ingly negative student behaviors in schools and classrooms; specifically, these behaviors, which may not be congruent with school contexts, may actually be coping mechanisms to mitigate the stress caused by risks and contexts outside of school. While this does not excuse negative behavior, nor should it prompt educators to lower expectations, it does grant an opportunity to potentially identify the root of a perceived misbehavior and work with stu-dents to develop adaptive coping strategies.

For example, Randy leaves class frequently to sell candy in the cafeteria. This behavior may be viewed as maladaptive within the school context because consistent absences will likely lead to poor academic outcomes; how-ever, his actions are a clear means of coping and avoiding the alternative, which is selling drugs. As a means of coping when he is at home with his mother, Namond stays in his room and plays video games to escape the con-sequences that come with being a player in "the game." This behavior again may be perceived as maladaptive in that it may lead to decreased academic engagement or withdrawal from peer or family relationships. However, this is Namond's response to the pressure asserted by his mother to be more active in selling drugs. In addition, Michael exhibits maladaptive coping responses to the stress created by the reintroduction of the man who abused him. He begins to fear for his brother's (and his own) safety and makes the decision to leave the household and join the ranks of a powerful street drug organi-zation. Michael's attempt to remove his brother from a destructive home life is laudable, and he is additionally able to provide support for Duquan who is left homeless after his family is evicted. As Spencer (2006) explained, "in response to decreased time and attention from parents and the need for ado-lescents to take on more familial responsibilities, youth may engage in more risk taking behavior (a maladaptive response) or seek more support through greater interaction with extended kin (e.g., grandparents) and non-kin adults (e.g., school counselor, teacher, or religious leader)" (p. 850). In this case, Michael engages in more risk-taking behavior (i.e., selling drugs) in his attempt to financially provide for his brother and Duquan in their new envi-ronment. This example is especially poignant in light of the public and polit-ical rhetoric about "single mothers" and "single parent households" and family structures that are usually framed as related to negative outcomes for students. In this situation, the introduction of the male figure into the household actu-ally creates a more stressful environment and Michael responds to the pres-sure created by this stressful context by engaging in a stage-specific coping mechanism that can be viewed as maladaptive.

By contrast, "positive coping skills are important life-course acquisitions because they provide psychological protection and stability across time and place." (Spencer, 2006, p. 837). Coping strategies are especially important to analyze because they are repeated and begin to "yield emergent identities" (p. 850). A coping strategy that most of the adolescents employ is that they seek stable friends and/or adult caregivers to replace the unstable family structures in their lives. Creating connections with peers, and finding secure networks of both peers and adults, is a critical part of adolescent development, and may be particularly important for students of color (Boykin & Toms, 1985; Tatum, 1997). For example, Duquan finds a pseudo-family in his three friends, Randy, Namond and Michael. It is through this family structure that Duquan obtains support, shelter, and protection.

Furthermore, several adult characters in *The Wire* attempt to create environments that facilitate school and community engagement of the adolescents. Prez builds trust with the students through pedagogical strategies that allow him to get to know his students and their lives. Specifically, he creates lesson plans that incorporate dice games that students frequently play outside of school, which give the students in his class a way of connecting with him and their peers in the classroom. This implementation of culturally relevant pedagogy (Ladson-Billing, 1995) leads to increased student engagement with the curricular content in his classroom. By building on his students' interests, he finds ways to connect broad mathematical concepts with students' lives and gives them opportunities to be academically successful in ways that extend beyond traditional problem sets and pen-and-paper learning. Thus, his students eventually find a sense of stability and connectedness in the classroom that they continue to seek once they have experienced it.

Another stable adult figure that Namond connects with is Bunny Colvin. As previously discussed, Namond lives in the shadows of his father's legacy. However, Namond is given opportunities to display his leadership skills and to articulate his experiences and emotions during the course of his participation in a University of Maryland research focus group. Throughout the sessions, Namond's self-perceptions begin to change and he sees potential alternative roles for himself that no longer include selling drugs. During this time of development, he is supported by Colvin, a former Major in the Baltimore City Police Department, who becomes a paternal figure to Namond. It is through this process and the nurturing relationship that Namond ends his role as a "corner boy" and embraces the opportunity to go back into "gen pop" with his classmates.

Finally, Dennis "Cutty" Wise's boxing gym provides a safe space for the adolescents as a means to avoid the streets and occupy their time after school. While Michael is the only student who fully takes advantage of his training, Cutty, who was formerly incarcerated for drug dealing, establishes the gym as a refuge for the adolescents because he knows the dangers of the "street" from his experience in the neighborhood. These trusting relationships and safe spaces allow the characters to feel protected and supported; in turn, they are able to maintain their roles as adolescents instead of being forced to assume adult responsibilities that may not be congruent to their actual stages of development.

Outcomes

As a result of the interplay among risks and protections in context, adolescents experience both productive and nonproductive outcomes during the course of their development. Spencer (2006) outlined some examples of non-productive outcomes for student development, including "school dropout, poor school performance, illegal means of earning income, poor health, incarceration, and teenage or out-of-wedlock child bearing" (p. 850). In contrast, productive outcomes include, "school engagement, positive family relationships, adequate employment preparation, staying out of jail, and low levels of high-risk behavior" (p. 850). In Season Four, the viewers see a variety of nonproductive and productive outcomes through the narrative of various characters. For example, Michael ultimately joins "the game" and begins to sell drugs, and Duquan drops out of school (and ultimately begins to use drugs in Season Five). Namond becomes more academically engaged and participates in extracurricular activities. Randy, on the other hand, is placed in a group home and begins to exhibit aggressive behavior (also seen in Season Five). When decontextualized from their environments and the risks associated with them, these outcomes are localized to individual, seemingly innate characteristics about each adolescent. However, when the external contexts that create these risks are deconstructed and viewed from a Critical Race perspective, viewers see how the development of these students is affected by racialized policies and practices.

While educators and policy makers may not have the power to "fix" social infrastructure problems, they do have agency: they can work actively to facilitate productive student outcomes. Analyzing the development of the four characters in Season Four can lead educators and education policy makers to engage in discussions about the importance of students' sense of self, self-perceptions, and peer perceptions as buffers and protective factors as identities develop. Season Four can also prompt discussions about the gendered experience that is presented in the four adolescent characters, such as hypermasculinity; teachers' perceptions about their students at the intersection of race and gender; and the ways in which the characters in *The Wire* may evoke and reify stereotypes of African American youth, and how educators can unpack, debunk, reject stereotypes about adolescents of color by acknowledging both racial group membership and individual developmental characteristics. In addition, preservice and practicing educators and education policy makers can extend these discussions to brainstorm the ways in which their own school policies, classrooms, and practices may privilege or marginalize certain student groups. To further localize these discussions, education stakeholders could draft (and ultimately) implement both school practices and community programs that may help foster positive coping mechanisms in their student population.

Conclusions

This essay has provided several examples of the ways in which *The Wire* can be used to illustrate the various racialized contextual factors that affect student development. Educators and policymakers must recognize that schools do not operate in a vacuum; likewise, student failure in school cannot be wholly localized to the student or the extracurricular context in which the student lives. *The Wire* includes insight into the ways in which schools operate as part of a larger societal system, and how students are affected by multiple systemic factors, including institutionalized racism. In addition, Season Four emphasizes the ways in which teachers must connect not only with their students, but with their communities and their caregivers. Even with sound educational programming, there are societal forces at work that have the potential to jeopardize life trajectories and positive developmental outcomes for students of color. *The Wire*, although fictitious, illustrates this reality. Viewed from a Critical Race perspective, *The Wire* illuminates the racialized systems and contexts that impact varying facets of students' lives, both in and out of school. By viewing *The Wire* in conjunction with application of a model of adolescent development, it becomes apparent that students' developmental trajectories are nuanced and complex, and that teachers, mentors, and adult caregivers can lead students to cultivate positive coping skills that may lead to productive outcomes, even in high risk environments.

As a final commentary, it should be noted that when using *The Wire* as a text, White educators and policy makers should be challenged to apply developmental models to White students as well. As Spencer (2006) noted, when referring to "diverse" youth, attention is paid to non–Whites. This conceptual error reinforces the pathologization of adolescents of color, and continues to perpetuate the misconception that White adolescent development is the norm. Instead, "the term *diverse youth* ... [is used] *to include both European-American (Caucasian) and* [Asian, Hispanic, African American and Native American] *AHAANA (frequently marginalized) youth* [emphasis in the original]" (Spencer, 2006, p. 833).

Appendix A

Themes by Episode

Episode	Parental Involvement	Peer Relationships	Community Programs	Economic System	Physical/Implied Sexual Abuse	Substance Abuse
1: Boys of Summer		The viewer is introduced to relationships among Namond, Michael, Randy, and Dukie.			Duquan is "jumped" by boys in the neighborhood.	
2: Soft Eyes	Namond's mother buys him school clothes so that he can be "fly," despite the fact they wear uniforms. Michael takes care of the daily needs of his brother.					

Episode	Parental Involvement	Peer Relationships	Community Programs	Economic System	Physical/Implied Sexual Abuse	Substance Abuse
3: Home Rooms					A violent incident between two girls occurs in Prez's classroom.	
4: Refugees	Bubbles becomes Rashad's primary caregiver.	Randy "snitches" on another student to prevent the principal from calling his foster mother.	The boys spend time at Cutty's boxing gym. Researchers from University of Maryland begin searching for schools to conduct their study. Community truancy officers round up students so schools can receive federal funding.		Michael expresses discomfort when alone with Cutty in the car.	Michael's mom is on drugs.

Episode	Parental Involvement	Peer Relationships	Community Programs	Economic System	Physical/Implied Sexual Abuse	Substance Abuse
5: Alliances		Duquan and Randy inform Mr. Prez as to why Michael cannot attend detention in an attempt to prevent him from further punishment				Prez is informed that Duquan's parents sell his clothes for drugs.
6: Margin of Error	Carver speaks to Ms. Anna about Randy's "involvement" in the murder of Lex. Namond's mother insists that he step up and be the "man of the house" by selling drugs to provide for the family.		University of Maryland initiates grant program for "problem students."			
7: Unto Others			Class begins for the University of		Namond is jumped by rival drug dealers	

Episode	Parental Involvement	Peer Relationships	Community Programs	Economic System	Physical/Implied Sexual Abuse	Substance Abuse
			Maryland grant program.		for selling on "their" corner.	The father of Michael's younger brother returns to the household. Michael is uncomfortable and becomes more protective of his brother.
8: Corner Boys		Namond buys all the boys Chinese food and tells Duquan he can get whatever he wants.			Michael's mother sells the family food stamp card for drugs. Michael maintains control over the food stamp card, giving his mom an allowance.	
9: Know Your Place					Carver, a "Narco," warns Namond about selling drugs.	
10: Misgivings	Namond's mother leaves him with the police after he is picked up on the streets. Namond eventually stays the night with Bunny Colvin.				Michael has his younger brother's father killed.	

Episode	Parental Involvement	Peer Relationships	Community Programs	Economic System	Physical/Implied Sexual Abuse	Substance Abuse
11: A New Day					Randy is "jumped" and constantly harassed at school because of his reputation as a "snitch."	
12: That's Got His Own	Namond's mother leaves him with the police after he is picked up on the streets. He eventually stays the night with Bunny Colvin.	Randy is further bullied over accusations of being a "snitch." After school, he is harassed by several boys and Michael helps him fight.		Duquan's family is evicted and Michael offers him a place to live.		
13: Final Grades	Namond lives with Bunny Colvin. Randy returns to foster care.				Michael commits his first murder.	

REFERENCES

Almeida, J., R.M. Johnson, H.L. Corliss, B.E. Molnar, and D. Azrael. (2009). Emotional distress among LGBT youth: The Influence of perceived discrimination based on sexual orientation. *Journal of Youth and Adolescence, 38*(7), 1001–1014.

Anyon, J. (1980). Social class and the hidden curriculum of work. *Journal of Education, 162*, 67–92.

Anyon, J. (1997). *Ghetto schooling: A political economy of urban educational reform.* New York: Teachers College Press.

Bandura, A. (1978). Reflections on self-efficacy. *Advances in Behaviour Research and Therapy, 1*(4), 237–269.

Bell, D.A. (1980). *Brown v. board of education* and the interest-convergence dilemma. *Harvard Law Review, 93*, 518.

Bell, D.A. (1992). Racial realism. *Connecticut Law Review, 24*, 363.

Blocker, R.S. and E.P. Copeland. (1994). Determinants of resilience in high stressed youth. *High School Journal, 77*, 286–293.

Bonilla-Silva, E. (2002). The linguistics of colorblind racism: How to talk nasty about blacks without sounding racist. *Critical Sociology, 28*(1–2), 41–64.

Boykin, A., and F. Toms. (1985). African American child socialization: A conceptual framework. In H. McAdoo & J. McAdoo (Eds.), *African American children: Social, educational, and parental environments* (pp. 31–51). Thousand Oaks, CA: Sage.

Bronfenbrenner, U. (1994). Ecological models of human development. *International Encyclopedia of Education,* Vol. 3, 2nd Ed. Oxford: Elsevier.

Conger, R.D., K.J. Conger, and M.J. Martin. (2010). Socioeconomic status, family process, and individual development. *Journal of Marriage and Family, 72*(3), 685–704.

Cowen, E.L, P.A. Wyman, W.C. Work, J.Y. Kim, D.B. Fagen, and K.B. Magnus. (1997). Follow-up of young stress-affected and stress-resilient urban children. *Development and Psychopathology, 9*, 566–577.

Crenshaw, K. (1989). Demarginalizing the intersection of race and sex: A black feminist critique of antidiscrimination doctrine, feminist theory and antiracist politics. *University of Chicago Legal Forum, 140*, 139–167.

Cunningham, M., and M.B. Spencer. (1996). The black male experiences measure. *Handbook of tests and measurements for black populations.* Hampton: Cobb & Henry Publishers.

DeCuir, J.T., and A.D. Dixson. (2004). "So when it comes out, they aren't that surprised that it is there": Using critical race theory as a tool of analysis of race and racism in education. *Educational Researcher, 33*(5), 26–31.

DeCuir-Gunby, J.R., and J.D. Taliaferro. (2013). The impact of school resegregation on the racial identity development of African American students: The example of Wake County. In J.K. Donnor and A.D. Dixson (Eds.), *The Resegregation of School: Education and Race in the 21st Century* (pp. 139–163). New York: Routledge.

Delgado, R. (1992). Rodrigo's chronicle. *Yale Law Review, 101*, 1357–1383.

Delgado, R., and J. Stefancic. (2012). *Critical race theory: An introduction* (2nd ed.). New York: New York University Press.

Erikson, E. (1968). *Youth: Identity and crisis.* New York: W.W. Norton.

Fischer, M.J., and D.S. Massey. (2004). The ecology of racial discrimination. *City & Community, 3*(3), 221–241.

Fredrickson, G. (2002). *Racism: A short history.* Princeton: Princeton University Press.

Garcia Coll, C., G. Lamberty, R. Jenkins, H.P. McAdoo, K. Crnic, B.H. Wasik, andH.V. Garcia. (1996). An integrative model for the study of developmental competencies in minority children. *Child Development, 67,* 1891–1914.

Gillborn, D. (2005). Educational policy as an act of white supremacy: Whiteness, critical race theory and education reform. *Journal of Educational Policy, 20*(4), 485–505.

Gotanda, N. (1991). A critique of "Our constitution is color-blind." *Stanford Law Review, 44,* 1–68.

Harrell, C.J.P. (1999). *Manichean psychology: Racism and the minds of people of African descent.* Washington, D.C.: Howard University Press.

Harris, C. (1993). Whiteness as property. *Harvard Law Review, 106*(8), 1707–1791.

Howard, T.C. (2008). Who really cares? The disenfranchisement of African American males in preK-12 schools: A critical race theory perspective. *Teachers College Record, 110*(5), 954–985.

Howard, T.C. (2013). How does it feel to be a problem? Black male students, schools, and learning in enhancing the knowledge base to disrupt deficit frameworks. *Review of Research in Education, 37*(1), 54–86.

Howard, T.C., and R. Reynolds. (2013). Examining black male identity through a raced, classed, and gendered lens: Critical race theory and the intersectionality of the black male experience. In M. Lynn, and A.D. Dixson (Eds.). (2013). *Handbook of critical race theory in education* (pp. 232–247). Routledge.

King, J.E. (1991). Dysconscious racism: Ideology, identity, and the miseducation of teachers. *Journal of Negro Education, 60*(2), 133–146.

Kochman, T.J. (1992). The relationship between environmental characteristics and the psychological functioning of African American youth. Unpublished honors thesis. Emory University, Atlanta, GA.

Kozol, J. (1991). *Savage inequalities: Children in America's schools.* New York: Crown.

Ladson-Billings, G. (1994). *The dreamkeepers: Successful teachers of African American children.* San Francisco: Jossey-Bass.

Ladson-Billings, G. (1995). But that's just good teaching! The case for culturally relevant pedagogy. *Theory into Practice, 34*(3), 159–165.

Ladson-Billings, G., and W.F. Tate, IV. (1995). Toward a critical race theory of education. *Teachers College Record, 97*(1), 47–68.

Lesko, N. (1996). Past, present, and future conceptions of adolescence. *Educational Theory, 46*(4), 453–72.

Lesko, N. (2001). *Act your age!: A cultural construction of adolescence.* New York: Routledge.

Li, S.T., K.M. Nussbaum, and M.H. Richards. (2007). Risk and protective factors for urban African-American youth. *American Journal of Community Psychology 39,* 21–35.

McLoyd, V.C. (1990). The impact of economic hardship on Black families and children: Psychological distress, parenting, and socioemotional development. *Child Development, 61*(2), 311–346.

Milner, R.H. (2013). Analyzing poverty, learning, and teaching through a critical race theory lens. *Review of Research in Education, 37*(1), 1–53.

Neblett, E.W., C.P. Smalls, K.R. Ford, H.X. Nguyen, and R.M. Sellers. (2006). Racial socialization and racial identity: African American parents' messages about race as precursors to identity. *Journal of Youth and Adolescence, 38,* 189–203.

Noguera, P. (2008). "Joaquin's dilemma: understanding the link between racial identity and school related behaviors." In Michael Sadowski (Ed), *Adolescents at school:*

PERSPECTIVES on youth, identity, and education (2nd ed.) (pp. 23–50). Cambridge, MA: Harvard Education Press.

Omi, M., and H. Winant. (1994). *Racial formation in the United States: From the 1960s to the 1990s.* New York: Routledge.

Pager, D., and H. Shepherd. (2008). The sociology of discrimination: Racial discrimination in employment, housing, credit, and consumer markets. *Annual Review of Sociology, 34,* 181.

Potts, M.A., K.A.S. Wickrama, L.G. Simons, C. Cutrona, F.X. Gibbons, R.L. Simons, and R. Conger. (2015). An extension and moderational analysis of the family stress model focusing on African American adolescents. *Family Relations Interdisciplinary Journal of Family Studies, 64,* 233–248.

Seaton, E.K., E.W. Neblett, R.D. Upton, W.P. Hammond, and R.M. Sellers. (2011). The Moderating capacity of racial identity between perceived discrimination and psychological well-being over time among African American youth. *Child Development, 82*(6), 1850–1867.

Sellers, R.M., N.C. Linder, P.M. Martin, and R.L. Lewis. (2006). Racial identity matters: The relationship between racial discrimination and psychological functioning in African American adolescents. *Journal of Research on Adolescence, 16,* 187–216.

Simon, D. (2002). *The wire.* HBO Productions.

Sleeter, C.E. (2001). Preparing teachers for culturally diverse schools research and the overwhelming presence of whiteness. *Journal of Teacher Education, 52*(2), 94–106.

Sleeter, C.E. (2008). Preparing white teachers for diverse students. In J.A. Banks and C.M. Banks (Eds.), *Handbook of research on multicultural education* (pp. 560–582). San Francisco: Jossey-Bass.

Solórzano, D.G. (1998). Critical Race Theory, race and gender microaggressions, and the experience of Chicana and Chicano scholars. *Qualitative Studies in Education, 11*(1), 121–136.

Solórzano, D.G., and T.J. Yosso. (2002). Critical race methodology: Counter-storytelling as an analytical framework for educational research. *Qualitative Inquiry, 8*(1), 23–44.

Spencer, M.B. (2006). Phenomenology and ecological systems theory: Development of diverse groups (Chapter 15). In W. Damon and R. Lerner (Eds.) *Handbook of child psychology, vol. 1* (R. Lerner, Ed.): *Theoretical models of human development* (6th edition), (pp. 829–893). New York: Wiley.

Spencer, M.B., D. Dupree, and T. Hartmann. (1997). A phenomenological variant of ecological systems theory (PVEST): a self-organization perspective in context. *Development and Psychopathology, 9*(4), pp. 817–833.

Tatum, B.D. (1997). *"Why are all the black kids sitting together in the cafeteria?" And other conversations about race.* New York: Basic Books.

Taylor, E., D. Gillborn, and G. Ladson-Billings (Eds.). (2009). *Foundations of Critical Race Theory in Education.* New York: Routledge.

Taylor, R.D., R. Casten, and S. Flickinger. (1993). The influence of kinship social support on the parenting experiences and psychosocial adjustment of African American adolescents. *Developmental Psychology, 29,* 382–388.

Tyack, D.B. (2003). *Seeking common ground: Public schools in a diverse society.* Cambridge, MA: Harvard University Press.

Werner, E.E. (1993). Protective factors and individual resilience. In S.J. Meisels and J. Shonkoff (Eds.), *Handbook of early childhood intervention* (pp. 78–96). New York: Cambridge University Press.

Wong, C.A., J.S. Eccles, and A. Sameroff. (2003). The influence of ethnic discrimination and ethnic identification on African American adolescents' school and socioemotional adjustment. *Journal of Personality, 71*(6), 1197–1232.

Yosso, T.J. (2002). Toward a critical race curriculum. *Equity and Excellence, 35*(2), 93–107.

Zumwalt, K., and E. Craig. (2005). Who is teaching? Does it matter? In J.A. Banks and C.A. Banks (Eds.), *Handbook of Research on Multicultural Education* (pp. 931–975). San Francisco: Jossey-Bass.

Schooling You on the Domains of Power in *The Wire*

Tia Sherèe Gaynor *and* Brandi Blessett

Introduction

Liberal arts disciplines like psychology, sociology, political science, education, social work, American studies, criminal justice, history and urban affairs, among others, often incorporate discussions relating to power, inequity, democracy and fairness into course content. In these instances, students may be exposed to historical events or discipline specific theories/theorists that present discourse regarding inequities and power differentials. Some faculty may present examples of discrimination or discuss issues related to diversity. Yet, fewer faculty critically uncover and explore issues of oppression, inequity, and injustice, particularly as they require in-depth explorations of the embedded structural, institutional, social, and cultural factors that create and perpetuate the marginalization of those deemed undesirable and hopeless (Winkle-Wagner & Locks, 2014). Arguably, the lack of a multicultural faculty correlates with the lack of critical engagement with these issues in the classroom. For example, the National Center for Education Statistics (NCES) (2015) reports that as of fall of 2013, 79 percent of full-time faculty in degree-granting postsecondary institutions were White, 6 percent were Black, 5 percent were Hispanic, and 10 percent were Asian/Pacific Islander. It is not to suggest that faculty who are not of color are not capable of critically engaging with lessons that explore the institutional and structural systems that perpetuate the marginalization of communities of color. Indeed many do. However, more do not. These individuals may not feel comfortable or not consider themselves an expert in such areas and therefore, choose not to incorporate these discussions into classroom lectures, assignments and readings. Consequently, students are left with an incomplete understanding of the complexities involved in social mobility, racial injustice, and economic inequities.

The Wire, the HBO television series first airing in June 2002, presents the viewer with unflinching storylines that demonstrate how U.S. society, public servants, the public school system, politicians and politics, as well as private industry create and sustain practices that limit equity and democracy. Although fiction, episodes of *The Wire* provide the audience with numerous examples to fuel a critique of these systems and examine how they operate to limit the characters' access to opportunity. Educators specifically can use the show to demonstrate to students practices in place that limit access to equity, equality, and democracy.

Within this essay, we use the Critical Race Theory (CRT) and the domains-of-power (DOP) frameworks to evaluate the injustices presented in the public school system depicted in *The Wire*. Critical Race Theory allows the authors to explore the issues present in the show through a lens that considers the importance of history, race, voice, interpretation, and praxis (DeCuir & Dixon, 2004; Dixon & Rousseau, 2006; Zamuido, Russell, Rios, & Bridgeman, 2011). Therefore, an appropriate examination of power domains requires a discussion that is reframed to illustrate the perspective of those groups directly impacted by the injustices exhibited. We use Collins' (2009) domains-of-power to deconstruct Season Four of *The Wire* and identify the four domains—structural, cultural, disciplinary, and interpersonal—of societal power within the show.

CRT and DOP are especially useful to the examination of *The Wire* because both are unsympathetic in critically analyzing how the current societal arrangement has been created to justify and propagate systems of difference by race, gender, class, ability, sexuality, and other personal characteristics. CRT and DOP offer an evaluative analysis of institutions and their respective organizational practices, the ideas and ideologies that inform public and political discourse, and the types of interactions that reinforce or resist systems of power and oppression.

Ultimately, we suggest that using *The Wire* in college classrooms can aid educators in helping students discover answers to questions like: what role does structural, cultural, or interpersonal factors have in contributing to systems that result in disproportionate outcomes? How do structures, institutions, and processes perpetuate the widespread marginalization of historically disenfranchised groups? Why does it take a critical praxis, or tipping point, before society is concerned with the lived realities of people of color? These questions initiate a critical analysis of hegemony, whereby students no longer blindly accept the discourse that is perpetuated, but begin to reassess the world around them.

Critical Race Theory and Domains of Power: A Framework for Studying The Wire

Critical Race Theory

CRT is a unique framework because it is rooted in the assumption that history, race, voice, interpretation, and praxis are valuable counternarratives to hegemonic discourse (Dixon & Rousseau 2006; Zamuido et al., 2011). History recognizes the social, economic, political, and cultural backgrounds of individuals and the power structures that promote difference within a given society. In the examination of *The Wire*, historical injustice is used to frame the context of contemporary problems, particularly through an acknowledgement that race, both implicitly and explicitly, is thoroughly embedded in how society functions.

Race continues to influence the social constructions of people and place. These constructions consequently, contribute to disparate treatment and outcomes experienced by those who are constructed negatively and powerlessly (Schneider & Ingram, 1993, 1997). The negative constructions of the young black male middle school students of Season Four are of particular importance as the narratives about who they are and what they represent serve to limit the students' opportunities to transcend the deprivation of their neighborhood.

Voice and interpretation use counter-narratives and/or storytelling to authenticate the experiences of the marginalized "Other" (Zamudio et al., 2011). Counter-narrative is the term CRT scholars use to describe a method of storytelling from those people whose experiences are rarely told (Solórzano & Yosso, 2009). In other words, it legitimizes the voice of marginalized people to share their stories. *The Wire* gives voice to those struggling with drug addiction, children, gangsters, individuals in a lower socio-economic status, and street level bureaucrats, populations who in U.S. society rarely witness the elevation of their collective voice or an acknowledgement of their lived experience.

Finally, praxis requires that educators and scholars are active, not passive in the fight for social justice for the purposes of transforming education to better serve the needs of all students (Zamudio et al., 2011). Unlike traditional theories that ignore context, CRT recognizes the importance of challenging the dominant discourse about societal phenomena and its related interactions (Dixon and Rousseau, 2006; Zamuido et al., 2011).

CRT evolved from "...a tradition of interrogating or questioning the ideologies, narratives, institutions, and structures in society through a critical conceptual lens" (Zamudio et al., 2011, p. 11) and is used to examine the role of race and racism within systems and structures. In summary, CRT reflects six common themes, it:

    (1) recognizes that racism is a pervasive and permanent part of American society;

    (2) challenges dominant claims of objectivity, neutrality, colorblindness, and merit;

    (3) challenges ahistoricism and insist on a contextual/historical analysis of the law;

    (4) insists on recognition of the experiential knowledge of people of color in analyzing law and society;

    (5) is interdisciplinary; and

    (6) works toward eliminating racial oppression as part of the broader goal of ending all forms of oppression (as cited in Dixon & Rousseau 2006, p. 4).

We will later use a CRT lens to deconstruct the power systems found in Season Four of *The Wire*. First an examination of domains-of-power is warranted.

The Domains-of-Power Framework

    The domains-of-power framework is a model that recognizes the impact that structure, discipline, culture, and interpersonal relationships have in either creating or restricting access to equality and democracy, thus serving as power domains. These four domains are controlled and manipulated to reinforce dominant preferences on non-dominant groups. The structural domain of power refers to inequitable practices that are organized through U.S. social institutions. These institutions may be "banks, insurance companies, police departments, the real estate industry, schools, stores, restaurant, hospitals, and government agencies" (Collins, 2009, p. 53). The establishment of rules and regulations is responsible for creating an arrangement that supports the existing social organization of people and institutions to maintain the status quo (Collins, 2009). For example, lending bias, insurance practices, and restrictive covenants operate legally to produce racially segregated neighborhoods. With the example of housing, the policies, protocols, and regulations embedded within the housing industry have created neighborhoods—with vastly different amenities and property values—for people of color versus their white counterparts. Between 1934 and 1968, financial institutions systematically engaged in redlining to deny mortgages based on neighborhood. This practice disproportionately impacted potential homeowners of color and "created systemic disinvestment in economically distressed communities" (Gaynor, 2013, p. 95). The federal urban renewal policy, while touted as a program to rehabilitate lower-income urban communities, ultimately benefited central business districts, leaving communities far worse than they were before revitalization efforts (Gaynor, 2013). While homeownership is associated with the 'American dream,' it has been purposefully denied to lower income individuals and people of color. Ultimately, affecting the quality of life, educational opportunities, and ability to accumulate intergenerational wealth for marginalized populations (Collins, 2009).

The disciplinary domain-of-power denotes how people and organizations exercise power and use the rules and regulations of everyday life to uphold racial, economic and other power hierarchies (Collins, 2009). Embedded within this power domain are "two sets of behaviors—how the rules of organizations regulate who can say and do what, and how people actually carry about these rules in their day-to-day behavior" (Collins, 2009, p. 64). In thinking about discipline within an educational environment, the assignment of police officers as security in schools has significant implications for students of color. Despite being in schools, police officers often operate with the intent to punish criminal offenses, not discipline school-aged children. In these instances, the officer's behavior may be overly aggressive and beyond the scope of traditional punishment sanctions in schools. In this regard, police function within the organizational protocols of law enforcement, not within the dictates of a school environment, thus exacerbating disparities experienced by students of color. For example, "a 5-year-old boy in Queens, NY was arrested, handcuffed and taken to a psychiatric hospital for having a tantrum and knocking papers off the principal's desk" (Heitzeg, 2009, p. 10). More recently, a cell phone recording showed "a white school police officer in a Columbia [South Carolina] classroom grabbing an African-American student by the neck, flipping her backward as she sat at her desk, then dragging and throwing her across the floor" (Fausset & Southall, 2015, para 1). Since students of color are oftentimes constructed as deviants, they experience differential and frequently harsher punishment than their white counterparts.

A cultural domain-of-power refers to the creation and proliferation of the ideas that justify social inequity. Within this domain are societal and personal institutions including the family, religious institutions, and schools. Institutions within the cultural domain of power develop "a system of beliefs (ideology)" that is grounded in assumptions that inequity and injustice no longer exists in U.S. society (Collins, 2009, p. 69). This set of beliefs or ideology then shapes behaviors that justify and uphold social inequality. Colorblind racial attitudes are problematic as they argue that race should not and does not matter, however ignoring the importance of race ignores the continuance of racism within the U.S. context (Neville, Lilly, Duran, Lee, & Browne, 2000). Davis (1998) argued, "By relying on the alleged "race-blindness" of the law, black people are scrumptiously constructed as racial subjects, thus manipulated, exploited, and abused, while the structural persistence of racism—albeit in changed forms—is ignored (p. 62). The ideology of color blindness suggests fairness and deservedness because race based discrimination is no longer allowed in public spaces (Collins, 2009). This is illustrated in thinking about how many individuals verbalize how everyone, regardless of race, gender, and sexuality, should not receive discriminate treatment, however, few are willing to "concern themselves" (p. 76) with the struggles of "Others" in order to fight against such treatment.

Interpersonal is the last domain of power. This domain shapes race relations among individuals in everyday life. In describing the interpersonal power domain Collins (2009) argued:

> The interpersonal domain of power reveals that the true measure of our docility and/or our rebellion lies in recognizing what I call "social scripts" that are handed to each of us. Based on how we are defined within structural power relations, by how belief systems construct us for others, and by the types of experiences we have had with institutions that strive to discipline us into our proscribed place, we each have some sense of who we should be and how we should understand and treat others. Despite its manipulation by other spheres, the interpersonal domain is the one place where we can think for ourselves and can be responsible for the consequences of our speech and actions [p. 78].

In essence, the interpersonal domain is characterized by the thoughts, ideologies, behaviors, values, and attitudes of individual people and how these attitudes shape interactions with others.

The domain-of-power framework is used to expose the authoritative configurations that inform macro-and micro-level, internal and external decisions within social structures, including public institutions. Although discussed separately, the four domains-of-power are not mutually exclusive, as inequity is not an either/or phenomenon. Oftentimes, inequities occur because of institutional and individual variables where each domain-of-power enlightens and influences the other (Collins, 2009). Therefore, it is important to examine the totality of these concepts in relation to one another to comprehend the ramifications structure, culture, discipline, and interpersonal relationships have on individuals specifically and society at-large.

Each domain-of-power is evident in *The Wire*. In this regard, we highlight Season Four as it focuses primarily on one of the most vulnerable populations, children. Through a CRT lens, the authors evaluate the stories of the children depicted in Season Four, and demonstrate the presence and impact of each of the four power domains.

Public Education in the United States

In the United States, education has been deemed the greatest equalizer (Nagpal, 1995). The landmark 1954 Supreme Court *Brown v. Board of Edu-*

cation ruling outlawed the practice of 'separate but equal,' however government policies have since created funding structures that undermine investment in educational resources (e.g., books, teachers, and infrastructure) for low-income students, therefore continuing segregation within the public school system (Bell, 2009). These policies disproportionately impact Black, Latino, and Native American students who are purposefully denied access to a quality education and confined to inferior facilities (Taylor, Gillborn, & Ladson-Billings, 2009). Receiving a quality education, in the United States, is directly related to the environment in which a person is born (e.g., poverty, abuse, or unstable family structure, among others). Although there is an expectation that all children in the U.S. will receive a free and decent primary education, there are distinct differences in resource allocations by race (e.g., White, Black and Latino), location (e.g., urban, rural, and suburban), and school type (e.g., public, private, or charter). For students of color, like those in *The Wire*, the intersection of race, class, location, and school type are important factors that can dictate quality of life outcomes.

Gaynor (2014) argues that "media, particularly, television, is regularly used to teach concepts ranging from basic definitions to complex issues" (p. 370) and recommends *The Wire* as a pedagogical tool to train culturally competent public administrators. Furthermore, we extend that discussion to suggest that *The Wire* can be used to help students explore U.S. systems through the DOP (structural, disciplinary, cultural and interpersonal) framework. In this regard, students are able to see examples of the interplay of the four domains and how they perpetuate inequity, limit opportunity, and maintain the status quo. University and college instructors, on the other hand, are able to help students critically examine power structures; discuss the implications for students, teachers, and the broader community; and apply techniques to overcome real-world structural, disciplinary, cultural, and interpersonal domains-of-power. The next section of the paper examines the DOP through *The Wire*.

Evidence from The Wire

Structural Domain: Depictions of Public Schools as Social Institutions

The social institutions presented in *The Wire* exist not just as a background to the human characters of the show, but as non-human characters themselves. Structures of government and politics, the criminal legal system,[1] public schools, institutions of higher education, and the "game" are illustrated as power bearing and depicted as regular producers of inequities.

The public school system serves as the focus of Season Four and begins with the close of summer vacation and the start of the new school year. The school depicted in *The Wire*, in general, is shoddy. A security guard had difficulty opening the building's doors. When new and returning teachers (and administrators) of Edward Tilghman Middle School gather for professional development before students return, the training offered little professional development for instructors and was incongruous and inapplicable to the experiences that teachers will have in the classroom once school begins. Many faculty are ill-prepared to teach the school's student population, all do not have adequate supplies or resources, nor do they have properly operating equipment. For example, Roland Pryzbylewski (Prez), Baltimore police officer turned middle school math teacher, is shown cleaning and organizing the gum covered, slovenly thrown desks in his classroom. The disarray of the classroom desks can be seen as a representation of the disorder within the school structure. While faculty and administrators are well-meaning, the school structure is organized in such a way that it serves more as an oppressive institution than one of learning. Therefore, the facetiously wished "good luck" to teachers at the start of the new academic year is foretelling.

The totality of the issues within the school system—as depicted on the show—represents what Collins (2009) deems a rigged system. In this case, rigged systems produce "consistent winners and losers—some groups benefit from one generation to the next, whereas others perpetually lose" (p. 57). *The Wire* does not show who the perpetual winners are as it relates to public education, however, the losers are clear. The students of Tilghman Middle School are, through the educational system, put in a position where the likelihood of success (outside the drug organizations of their communities) is limited.

The depictions of educational inequities in *The Wire* serve as a representation of the marginalization created by social structures, generally. In the United States, people of color have historically and continue to be on the losing side of the structural domain-of-power. Persons of color, as a social group, receive inequitable access, particularly as it relates to economic and educational opportunities. The consequences of these inequitable opportunities (poor public education, limited economic mobility, poor health, etc.) are associated with negative social constructions and a public and political discourse that ultimately justifies the creation of a second-class (Blessett, 2015). Therefore, to be uneducated is often equated with being part of a perpetual class of laborers that are exploited by the powerful for financial gain.

Federal, state, and local government policies support the unequal educational experience of students relegated to social groups characterized and treated as a deprived class. For instance, it was once illegal in the United States to teach enslaved persons to read and write. Native American students, in the 1850s, were sent to boarding schools designed to strip them of their cultural identities, and in the 1960s Chicano children in the Southwest were offered limited education in order to keep them working in the fields (Zamudio et al., 2011). More recently, the passage of Propositions 63 (1986) and 227 (1998) in California and Title III of the No Child Left Behind Act devalues the inclusion of bilingual education and endures inaccurate "at-risk" labels for children who are not monolingual (Zamudio et al., 2011). Such practices reveal the complicity of all levels of government to support the systematic marginalization of students of color in the United States. This lens offers a context and explanation as to why racial disparity persists, why persons of color are confined to the most distressed communities, and why quality of life outcomes are devastating for low-income populations of color. Young (1990) argues these are all representative examples of how dominant, powerful groups oppress targeted, social groups.

Pedagogically, faculty can use the example of the public school system as a way to impart upon students the vital role social institutions play in enduring marginalization and discrimination. The depictions of the school system in *The Wire* parallel the real-life experiences of many young children "whose race, class, ethnicity, or immigrant status leaves them assigned to inferior schools" (Collins, 2009, p. 84). Public schools, are then, a social institution that serves as "a gatekeeper for privilege" (Collins, 2009, p. 88), limiting opportunity and perpetuating inequity.

The structural domain-of-power can also serve as a framework for resistance. Faculty can guide students in using the classroom as a political space, where students are able to develop, explore, debate and adjust their beliefs and ideologies. If instructed to exist outside the constraints of traditional social institutions, students can learn how to challenge normative conceptions and structures, therefore, breathing "life into the structures that they inherit" (Collins, 2009, p. 97). Incidentally, the restrictions and disparities set forth by traditional social structures are challenged as are the symbols, rules, and regulations that marginalized individuals are forced to navigate. As university faculty engage in shifting the traditional operations of their respective schools, classroom instruction can explore the ways in which *The Wire* illustrates the transcendence of the confines imposed by the public school structure. Prez using dice and Monopoly money to teach students probabilities may best exemplify this transcendence. By going outside the prescribed methodology, Prez was able to communicate with his students in a way other teachers were not, and thus, able to have students grasp a relatively complex math operation. Prez and his students present a contradiction to the ideology that low-income, inner-city, children of color are intellectually inferior and do not want to learn. In this example, going beyond the structural confines of the institution challenges the rules and regulations of the classroom.

Disciplinary Domain: Exploring
the School-to-Prison Pipeline

In Season Four of *The Wire* an innovative program is proposed to Tilghman Middle School administrators by a professor at the University of Maryland. The professor is interested in starting a pilot program in the school to address social, educational, and disciplinary needs of at-risk youth. These at-risk youth or "corner kids" are described as being unable to sit in a classroom and are often removed from traditional classrooms based on reduced expectations of their academic abilities. The term at-risk has significant implications for any student given such a label. At-risk youth are essentially the manifestations of the structural, disciplinary, cultural, and interpersonal dysfunctions of the broader society. "Scholars have found that pejorative stereotypes of African Americans pervade the classroom. Research indicates that teachers perceive African American students as more defiant, disrespectful, and rule-breaking than other groups" (as cited in Unnever & Gabbidon, 2011, p. 82). Applying such language, reinforced by limited expectations, places the responsibility for dysfunction on the students and their respective families without criticizing the power structures that perpetuate inequity in all aspects of life and society. In this regard, *The Wire* and existing research demonstrates the importance of recognizing the role language and perception have in interactions with students and vice versa.

Gregory and Weinstein (2008) suggest that African American students are likely to be defiant when they perceive that teachers underestimate their academic ability or are uncaring because of their race. In contrast, the teachers who treat African American students with care and high expectations were more willing to comply with authority of teachers who had earned their trust (Gregory & Weinstein, 2008). For students like those depicted in Season Four of *The Wire*, schools too often function as a pipeline to prison through the use of colorblind disciplinary policies that produce racially disproportionate outcomes. The American Civil Liberties Union (ACLU) (n.d.) defines the school-to-prison pipeline as

> the policies and practices that push our nation's school children, especially our most at-risk children, out of classrooms and into the juvenile and criminal justice systems. This pipeline reflects the prioritization of incarceration over education [para 1].

Furthermore, numerous "stops" were identified that reinforce the path to incarceration, which includes: failing public schools, zero tolerance and other school discipline policies, policing school hallways, disciplinary alternative schools, and court involvement and juvenile detention (ACLU, n.d.).

The school-to-prison pipeline has recently become the topic of significant discussion in the public discourse. The statistics are alarming, the Office of Civil Rights Data Collection Statistics (2014) reports

- Black children represent 18 percent of preschool enrollment, but 48 percent of preschool children receiving out-of-school suspension.
- Black students are suspended and expelled at a rate three times greater than white students.
- Black girls are suspended at higher rates (12 percent) than girls of any other race/ethnic group and most boys.
- Students with disabilities represent 25 percent of students arrested and referred to law enforcement, even though they are 12 percent of the overall student population. More than one out of four boys of color with a disability (served by the Individuals with Disabilities Education Act) and nearly one in five girls of color with disabilities receive out-of-school suspensions.

Such awareness has resulted in media outlets, scholars, advocacy groups, and activists from around the country giving public visibility to a problem that has been festering for decades in communities of color. The extent that disciplinary policies have become increasingly harsh, applied disparately, and introduce students into the juvenile or criminal legal system is problematic. An acknowledgement of even the best intentioned policies, those designed to keep students, faculty and administrators safe in school, have been implemented in ways that produce more harm than good is the first step toward examining the role of discipline within public schools. The second step requires an analysis of existing policies and the development of alternative approaches to improve academic success. Third, recognizes the role of reflection as an opportunity to enhance interactions with students and therefore, cultivates safe and brave learning spaces. Pedagogy, in this regard, is a wide-ranging concept that considers institutional and professional practices as well.

Over the course of Season Four, Prez's relationship with the students evolves from being confrontational to respectful. He demonstrated his care and concern for students when he explained the rationale for his rules, set high expectations for their behavior, encouraged and rewarded them for their efforts, and created a space where unconventional learning could happen— i.e., using Monopoly money and dice to teach probability. Overall, Prez's fortitude to be innovative and committed to his job and his students was evidenced by the respect the students displayed as the season progressed. Taken collectively, the policies, practices, perceptions, and school infrastructure reveals the overlapping forms of power that influence student behavior, teacher perceptions, and ultimately the way these groups interact with each other—for better or worse.

Cultural Domain: Codes of "the Game"

Like social institutions in *The Wire*, "the game" serves as a primary non-human character in the show. "The game" is the informal (in some cases illegal) structures that exists in West Baltimore whereby engagement with or participation in requires the adherence to a certain set of rules and regulations. Within the context of *The Wire*, "the game" appears in various ways and with various characters. Elected officials working to maintain their political power, stevedores working the docks and helping to smuggle contraband, the media focusing on stories that will sell papers, and the drug organizations all operate within "the game." While "the game" is often associated with the distribution of illegal drugs, *The Wire* broadens this conception to include varying informal and/or illegal systems that allow individuals to advance their social mobility. Those in "the game" (or those who move in, out, and alongside of it) operate with certain codes. These rules, regulations, and codes are necessary for networking within and across groups and territories, operating informal economic organizations, and as survival techniques. The ideologies and ideals that govern the behavior of those that operate within "the game" are key to its continuation. Perhaps the most important ideology or code to abide by is that of not talking to the police. Snitching is uniformly frowned upon by anyone with tangential connections to "the game." Those who snitch are often shunned, badly harmed, or killed, therefore, community members rarely violate this tenet.

As Moore discussed in an earlier chapter, Randy, a Tilghman Middle School student, is a rare entity in this sense as he snitches, both to police and school administrators. When a young female classmate finds herself engaged in sexual activity with several male students in the boy's bathroom, school administrators look to Randy for information on what occurred. Subsequently, a Baltimore police Sergeant, Herc, questioned Randy on the "disappearance" of a young man affiliated with a rising drug cartel. Randy's willingness to snitch stems from not wanting to create instability in his home life. As a young man, who has previously been in trouble, Randy wants to ensure that his foster mother, Ms. Anna, does not learn of his involvement in either of these incidents. Randy is quite fearful that Ms. Anna will choose to no longer serve as his foster mother once she finds out about him getting in trouble. For Randy, ensuring a safe home environment with his foster mother is worth jeopardizing his safety outside the home (via breaking the code of "the game"). In this regard, Randy's snitching serves as a challenge to the ideologies and codes of "the game," thus challenging the inequities embedded within this informal system. While Randy's insubordination of the ideals of the streets is not intentional (he is merely trying to survive), his actions suggest that residents do not need to submit to the codes. Paradoxically, the fact that, as a middle school student, Randy is forced to navigate "the game" and its ideals and ideologies is, in itself, a representation of inequity. Randy's suburban counterparts, even those who may be in the foster care system, rarely have to traverse an environment that routinely threatens their personal safety and limits their opportunities for upward mobility.

The codes of "the game" have instituted behaviors, actions, and a culture in which anyone who is remotely connected must engage. Thus, creating a reality that justifies the culture of "the game." For students using *The Wire* as a text, seeing Randy's actions as contesting the norms and beliefs of "the game" challenges the hegemonic structures that exist even within the informal arrangements of the street. Randy's reality contextualizes why snitching may be deemed necessary, particularly if it is linked to survival and stability. Students learn, through the lived experiences of the characters, the importance and validity of voice. On one hand, students find truth in another's experiences. Through their exposure to lived experiences, students expand upon traditional notions of intellect and knowledge. Is Randy, as Heather Moore suggested, intelligent because he is able to navigate snitching in "the game"? How does Randy challenging the codes of the street make him an anomaly? On the other hand, students' increased understanding of the importance of voice and experiences helps students develop their own voice and recognize the validity in their stories and experiences. Through Randy, students can be led to ask themselves how their own truth may serve as nontraditional yet equally valid, knowledge.

Interpersonal Domain:
Law Enforcement Behavior

The interactions between the children of Season Four and representatives of the Baltimore Police Department best exemplify the marginalization and inequity that occurs through the interpersonal domain-of-power. Collins (2009) argues that individuals' understanding of their social standing is largely "based on how we are defined within structural power relations, by how belief systems construct us for others, and by the types of experiences we have had with institutions that strive to discipline us into our proscribed place" (p. 78). The middle school students of Season Four are bombarded with interpersonal exchanges that invade their personal space/environment and devalue their bodies. In particular, the interactions initiated by the Baltimore police are grounded within constructions that prescribe criminal behavior and activity prior to initial contact. The messages as communicated suggest that these young people are powerless delinquents whose opportunities are limited solely to being players or pawns in "the game."

Baltimore Police Officer Eddie Walker, routinely, uses aggression and violence during his interactions with the residents of West Baltimore. When he catches Randy in an alleyway, he illegally seizes the $200 Randy is carrying, despite being told that the money came from his foster mother for school clothes. This example exemplifies how ideologies and constructions influence the behaviors of individuals within social structures. Officer Walker's interactions are symptomatic of the Baltimore Police Department (BPD), in general, particularly as the "Western District Way" of conducting police business is defined by the mantra, "banging heads and taking names." Officer Walker and the various other representatives of the BPD who interact with Randy and his friends work to strip away any agency the young middle school students may have over their personhood. These young boys are treated as criminals, despite any notion that a crime has been committed. The actions of the BPD are a constant reminder that their behaviors are routinely surveilled and at any given time may be subjected to a (undeserved) consequence for conduct deemed undesirable.

As the interpersonal domain is "a domain of individual choice, of deciding to follow the rules, to break them, or to write new ones altogether" (Collins, 2009, p. 78), it is important for students to understand the role individual choice plays in perpetuating or resisting inequity. The example provided via Officer Walker demonstrates, for students, the choice to use the power afforded by his profession as a means of oppression and discrimination. Students can be challenged to consider an alternative role for Walker, where he chooses to use his power to provide opportunity and practice resistance.

Conclusion

This essay explored the domains-of-power through the lens of critical race theory using *The Wire*. Critical race theory contextualizes the realities of students in *The Wire* in critical ways that link their oppression and marginalization to the existing societal structure. Within the structural domain, the historical legacy of policy decisions (e.g., education, employment, housing) offer a contemporary explanation for the divergent experiences some students of color face on a daily basis. Navigating communities of disrepair to attend schools with crumbling infrastructure and inadequate resources, these students are saddled with the reality that their opportunities are limited. This is profoundly reinforced by the colorblind disciplinary policies that oftentimes target students of color. Whether based on perceptions by teachers and administrators that students of color are perceived to be defiant or deviant, punishment is not allocated fairly. The result increases the chances for students of color to interact with the juvenile and criminal legal systems at earlier ages. For example, "racial disparities in out-of-school suspensions also start early; black children represent 18 percent of preschool enrollment, but 42 percent of preschool children suspended once, and 48 percent of preschool children suspended more than once" (Office of Civil Rights, 2014, p. 7).

The cultural domain of power recognizes that while all major stakeholders in *The Wire* are playing "the game," dominant narratives of dysfunction and illegality are concentrated primarily on the drug dealer, while the dishonesty of politicians and law enforcement, those actually responsible for ensuring the safety and well-being of the citizens of Baltimore, is glossed over as politics as usual. This reality serves to place the blame on residents and criminals for the downfall of the city without ever considering the role of institutional racism, unethical and corrupt behavior by city leaders as relevant issues that need to equally be addressed. Furthermore, the behavior of law enforcement officials throughout the series demonstrates a need for a more accurate discourse about the role of police as those that "protect and serve" their communities. The interpersonal connections people of color have with law enforcement officials are oftentimes drastically different than their white counterparts. As witnessed by Randy and Officer Walker's interaction in *The Wire* or the numerous testimonials of police brutality by residents in Ferguson, MO (DOJ, 2015) and Baltimore, MD (DOJ, 2016), these lived experiences are valid and need to be recognized as such. Society's inability (or unwillingness) to acknowledge the structure, discipline, culture, and interpersonal apparatus that adversely affects marginalized individuals and groups seeks to sustains domains-of-power as Collins has articulated.

The authors highlight the DOP as deeply embedded structures that require critical examination if they are ever to be dismantled. Therefore, using *The Wire* to illustrate how these multifaceted issues impact individuals in society (particularly marginalized groups) allows for a meaningful assessment of power, oppression, race, class, status, privilege, worth, deservingness, deviance, etc., in a non-threatening way. Paired with critical race theory, students are given a historical context and appropriate language to understand how these structures are reinforced and legitimized through public discourse, institutions, and everyday practices. *The Wire* mimics the social, political, and economic realities of the real world, thus the fictional imitation of life presents students with opportunities to develop and strengthen the skills of cultural competency and critical thinking (Gaynor, 2014). In this regard, students are not required to disclose their proximity to any given situation or scenario, but can freely discuss the issues and related implications. The use of media, particularly *The Wire*, may serve as an effective way to help students develop ways to challenge the structural, cultural, disciplinary, and institutional forces create "Other" experiences.

NOTE

1. Mogul, Ritchie, and Whitlock (2011) note the term criminal legal system reflects an acknowledgment that the "criminal justice system" has not resulted in anything approximating justice for the vast majority of people in the United States—particularly for people of color, poor people, immigrants, and queers—but rather bears major responsibility for continuing the institutionalization of severe, persistent, and seemingly intractable forms of violence and inequality.

REFERENCES

American Civil Liberties Union (ACLU). (n.d.). What is the school-to-prison pipeline? Retrieved from https://www.aclu.org/fact-sheet/what-school-prison-pipeline.
Bell, D.A. (2009). *Brown v. Board of Education* and the interest convergence dilemma. In E. Taylor, D. Gillborn, and G. Ladson-Billings (Eds.). *Foundations of critical race theory in education* (pp. 73–84). New York: Routledge.
Blessett, B. (2015). Disenfranchisement: Historical underpinnings and contemporary manifestations. *Public Administration Quarterly, 39*(1), 3–50.
Collins, P.H. (2009). *Another kind of public education: Race, schools, the media, and democratic possibilities.* Boston: Beacon Press.
Davis, A. (1998). Racialized punishment and prison abolition. In J. James (Ed.), *The Angela Y. Davis reader* (pp. 96–110). New York: Blackwell.
Decuir, J., & Dixson, A. (2004). "So when it comes out, they aren't that surprised that it is there": Using critical race theory as a tool of analysis of race and racism in education. *Educational Researcher, 33*(5), 26–31.
Department of Justice (DOJ). (2015). Investigation of the Ferguson police department. Retrieved from http://www.justice.gov/sites/default/files/opa/press-releases/attachments/2015/03/04/ferguson_police_department_report.pdf.
Dixson, A.D., and C.K. Rousseau. (2006). *Critical race theory in education: All god's children got a song.* New York: Routledge.
Faussett, R., and A. Southall. (2015, October 26). Video shows officer flipping student in South Carolina, prompting inquiry. *New York Times.* Retrieved from http://www.nytimes.com/2015/10/27/us/officers-classroom-fight-with-student-is-caught-on-video.html?_r=0.
Gaynor, T.S. (2013). Building democracy: Community development corporations' influence on democratic participation in Newark, New Jersey. *Operant Subjectivity: The International Journal of Q Methodology, 36*(2): 93–113.
Gaynor, T.S. (2014). Through "The Wire": Training Culturally Competent Leaders for a New Era." *Journal of Public Affairs Education*, July, 20(3).
Gregory, A., and R.S. Weinstein. (2008). The discipline gap and African Americans: Defiance or cooperation in the high school classroom. *Journal of School Psychology, 46*(4), 455–475.
Heitzeg, N.A. (2009). Education or incarceration: Zero Tolerance policies and the school to prison pipeline. Retrieved from http://files.eric.ed.gov/fulltext/EJ870076.pdf
Mogul, J.L., A.J. Ritchie, and K. Whitlock. (2011). *Queer (In)Justice.* Boston: Beacon Press.
Nagpal, T. (1995). Voices from the developing world: Progress toward sustainable. *Environment: Science and Policy for Sustainable Development, 37*(8), 10–35.

National Center for Education Statistics (NCES). (2015). *The condition of education 2015* (NCES 2015–144). Retrieved from http://nces.ed.gov/pubs2015/2015144.pdf

Neville, H.A., R.L. Lilly, G. Duran, R.M. Lee, and L. Browne. (2000). Construction and Initial Validation of the Color-Blind Racial Attitudes Scale (CoBRAS). *Journal of Counseling Psychology,* 47(1), 59–70.

Office of Civil Rights. (2014, March). Data snapshot: School discipline (Issue Brief No. 1). Washington, D.C.

Schneider, A., and H. Ingram. (1993). Social construction of target populations: Implications for politics and policy. *The American Political Science Review, 87*(2), 334–347.

Schneider, A.L., and H. Ingram. (1997). *Policy design for democracy.* Lawrence: University Press of Kansas.

Solózano, D.G., and T.J. YossoJ. (2009). Critical race methodology: Counter-storytelling as an analytical framework for educational research. In E. Taylor, D. Gillborn, and G. Ladson-Billings (Eds.), *Foundations of critical race theory in education* (pp. 131–147). New York: Routledge.

Taylor, E., D. Gillborn, and G. Ladson-Billings. (2009). *Foundations of critical race theory in education.* New York: Routledge.

Unnever, J.D., and S.L. Gabbidon. (2011). *A theory of African American offending: Race, racism, and crime.* New York: Routledge.

Winkle-Wagner, R., and A.M. Locks. (2014). *Diversity and inclusion on campus: Supporting racially and ethnically underrepresented students.* New York: Routledge.

Young, I.M. (1990). *The politics of difference.* Princeton: Princeton University Press.

Zamudio, M.M., C. Russell, F.A. Rios, and J.L. Bridgeman. (2011). *Critical race theory matters: Education and ideology.* New York: Routledge.

From Sentimentalism to Grief

Pedagogies of Humanization
in Waiting for "Superman" and The Wire

MARK STERN

You gonna help, huh? You gonna look out for me? ... You mean it? You gonna look out for me? You promise? You got my back, huh?—Simon & Chapelle, 2006

Finals

"It humanized the readings," is a common refrain I hear from my mostly very White and mostly very wealthy students after they watch season four of *The Wire* for their final exam in my Politics and Education class. With names like Caitlin and Laura and Ted, my students fumble a bit in the early parts of their oral final as they look for affirmation or reassurance when they start talking about Omar, Namond, or Bodie. They look to me, their very White professor, to see if they are pronouncing the names correctly or if they have the right to be saying the names at all—they are clearly nervous to be talking about Black people, not wanting to say something egregiously wrong or offensive. Their hesitations are only amplified as I stage these conversations at the local coffee shop in my own little attempt to facilitate a kind of public sphere. We attend a small liberal arts school in a small town and being overheard talking about "racialized capitalism" or "neoliberalism," never mind nail guns and boarded up row homes, brings about more than a few askance glares. I try to use the affective registers my students feel in speaking publicly about the show—self-aware, awkward, and uncomfortable—to draw attention to their own social locations: Why, compared to how easy it is for you talk about *social welfare* and *democracy* and *racism* and *education* in class, is this television show so hard to talk about? What does this say about you and your world? Where are *you* in *The Wire?* Might there be something about what *The Wire* does so well—the refusal to account for individual actions outside of a social context—that might help us to think through how you have experienced the show and now try to speak about it? Why are you whispering?

Watching season four of *The Wire* is the last thing we do in class—one side of a bookend. The other bookend, what we do first in this class, is watch *Waiting for "Superman"* (*WFS*)—a media artifact that weds stories about poor Black and brown children (and one White, upper-middle class youth) to a triumphant narrative about the current corporate "reform" agenda dominating contemporary education policy.[1] Between the bookends, the students are introduced to critical literature that contextualizes the discourses and institutions that make up the corporate reform agenda within larger conversations of political economy. This course is structured as something like Neoliberalism and Education Policy 101. Students are introduced to a framework for thinking about contemporary education policy through lenses such as deregulation and accumulation by dispossession in terms of testing regimes and charter schools (Saltman, 2007; Lipman, 2011). They are asked to consider the colonial ideology that underscores programs like Teach For America (TFA) (Anderson, 2013). And they are pushed to grapple with the differences between market-based choice and democracy (Beane & Apple, 2007). Much of what this class speaks back to are the kinds of theoretical and empirical claims that are present in *WFS* about the effectiveness of charter schools, standardized testing, and non-unionized teachers—claims many of my students walk into class already having and claims that currently dominate public discourse.

This essay is not concerned about theory or empirical evidence about the efficacy of contemporary neoliberal education policy. There has already been much written about the neoliberal assault on public education in the United States that manifests throughout season four of *The Wire* (Fabricant and Fine, 2012; Kumashiro, 2012; Lipman, 2011; Watkins, 2011). This theoretical literature has shown, with astute insight and rigor, that the current iteration of education reform follows a logic symptomatic of time marked by rampant social stratification, racial/class-based austerity measures (decreased services for some, tax breaks for others), and the privatization of social and public life. The money backing these reforms has direct ties to Wall Street and multinationals looking for new markets from which to extract surplus capital (Burch, 2009). And, as the scholars who contribute to places like The National Education Policy Center (NEPC, n.d.) have been suggesting for quite a while, quantitative research supporting these "reforms" are inconclusive at best and duplicitous at worst. Moreover, qualitative research, found in relatively accessible places like the pages of the grassroots and educator-driven *Rethinking Schools*, documents the misogynistic levels of control, surveillance, and accountability over mostly female teachers, the plight of students with disabilities who are "counseled out" of charter schools, and parents who, because their neighborhood schools have been closed, now have to worry about their child traveling great distances to get to school—ones that are most likely just as under-resourced and overburdened as the ones closed down (Lipman, 2011).

Though *The Wire* supports many of the critiques that scholars and community-based activists have waged against neoliberal reforms—such as the adverse pedagogical effects of high stakes standardized testing and the degree to which these reforms disproportionately affect communities of color—it is not my interest to rehearse them here. Pedagogically, season four of *The Wire*, which traces the relationship between deindustrialization, gentrification, street-based entrepreneurialism, crime rates, public schools/test scores, and a mayoral "race," most certainly provides a narrative rejoinder—what Walter Been Michaels calls the "most serious and ambitious fictitious narrative of the twenty-first century so far" (cited in Williams, 2011, p. 209)—to the scholarly work of the likes of Pauline Lipman (2004, 2011) and Alexander Means (2013). These scholars have done critical ethnographic work mapping out the constellation of factors that destabilize already disenfranchised urban communities, putting youth in an especially precarious relationship with real and material safety and citizenship. As David Simon and Ed Burns, creators of *The Wire*, show with great care, season four offers its viewers a didactic representation of how schools, under the regimes of accountability and testing, form a pivotal node in the topography of accountability culture and the militarization of some urban spaces—mostly those inhabited by poor Black and Brown bodies.

Thinking pedagogically, this essay instead focuses on the way *The Wire* (specifically season four) resonates with students in relationship to their affective registers—in conversation with, but different than, the theory and empiricism of critiques of neoliberal education policy. There is much to be mined from *The Wire* in terms of how it portrays teachers (Blum, 2011), tracking, and culturally relevant pedagogy (Trier, 2010). And though students gain a good deal from watching season four looking for the echoes of neoliberalism lurking on and around the *corners*, this essay is more interested in that common refrain noted above: "It humanized the readings." What might students mean by humanized? Who is the *human* that gets humanized? How might this process of humanization lend itself to thinking about ethics and politics?

In what follows below, and in conversation with how my students tend to respond affectively to *WFS*, the essay addresses these questions in an attempt to explore why *The Wire* might be used to teach about urban issues—educational and otherwise—to mostly non-urban, mostly White, and wealthy, students. Using my own classroom and teaching experiences as a site of study, this essay offers a critical reflection on how media artifacts about education structure and scaffold different kinds of pedagogical and political responses from students who have pedagogical and political questions about the future of public education in the United States.

From Crying

In order to talk about how my students understand and experience *The Wire,* it is first necessary to situate the show within the discursive media environment in which it gets viewed/heard. Education policy, as many scholars have recently pointed out, has come front and center within the mediasphere (Henig, 2008). As No Child Left Behind produced a discourse of failure in the public imaginary, media outlets found that drama of high stakes testing and the apocalyptic undertones of the United States falling behind in the global economy had a captive audience. Quick to frame the discourses of failure were think tanks, policy institutes, and (in)vested stakeholders who constructed narratives that provided a specific kind of structure for understanding the issues and, therefore, the answers to those issues (discussed below in more detail). Rather than providing a structural analysis of the intersections of racism, imperialism, and education in the United States, many of these stakeholders instead aimed to, as Herman and Chomsky (2002) call it, manufacture neoliberal consent through a double critique of public bureaucracies limiting choice and bad teachers (Kumashiro, 2012). Many of these narratives, as I discuss below, traded on White sentimentalist representations of race and class in America: poor Black and brown children who are stuck in "failing" schools who just need to be saved from their culture of poverty through introducing choice and accountability into educational markets. *WFS* is, perhaps, the most forceful and most widely viewed artifact in this realm. As such, and in thinking about student and public reception of *The Wire,* it is first necessary to provide an analysis of the discursive topography set forth by *WFS,* most especially in regard to the way affect was used in accruing consent/hegemony.

Appropriations

A few years ago, I wrote an article about *WFS* and crying (Stern, 2012). More specifically, I was interested in why, after a semester of learning about neoliberalism and the current education reform regime—testing, accountability, charter schools, TFA, and so on—my students and I cried after watching *WFS.*[2] We had spent an entire term poking holes in every claim the film made, and yet, with two weeks left, we all found ourselves in a movie theater red-eyed and blue. Some of us were embarrassed about having these feelings, some angry, others ready to get away from the class and the critiques and join TFA and start "helping" to "close" the "achievement gap." The film had validated all kinds of racialized and class-based tropes that spoke to hegemonic common sense ideologies, what the problems were, and the best ways to go about solving them (Gramsci, 1971; Kumashiro, 2008).

The narrative the film provides is quite compelling: *Public schools in urban areas serving poor Black and Brown students are failing those communities. Populating these schools are bad teachers who are protected by their evil unions, who are made up of adults who do not care about students, only themselves. Charter schools, which do not tend to have unionized teachers, which means they have good teachers, do care about students. Charter schools offer parents a choice about where to send their kids to school. Charter schools and the good non-unionized (mostly White) teachers send kids to college. And everyone wants to send their kid to a charter school, as evidenced by the lotteries to get in. Moral: It is not poverty or the historical legacies and contemporary manifestations of life in a White supremacist state that perpetuates educational and social injustice in the United States. Instead, it is bad teachers, schools, and a public monopoly over the educational marketplace. And you* (audience member) *can help by supporting charter schools, Geoffrey Canada* (CEO of the Harlem Children's Zone), *Michelle Rhee* (then–Chancellor of the Washington, D.C., public schools), *and their friends at TFA and KIPP* (the Knowledge is Power Program charter school chain).

Using Nancy Frazier's theories on the *politics of needs and needs discourses*, Swalwell and Apple (2011) suggested that the film "creatively appropriate[d] the language and issues [that come from below (i.e., the disenfranchised)] in such a way that very real problems expressed by multiple movements are reinterpreted through the use of powerful groups' understandings of the social world and of how we are to solve 'our' problems" (p. 369). In other words, the film had to speak to the real needs of the urban poor who want the best for their children and have been fighting for education since being captured and brought to this country (Jones, 2010). At the same time, WFS had to speak to middle-class sensibilities about civil rights and meritocracy in a "post-racial" America in order to gain political clout and legitimacy. Swalwell and Apple (2011) suggested that the narrative of WFS preyed on these needs and desires, repackaging them in a way that supported a particular kind of ideological (neoliberal) policy regime. This is something of an instance of what Critical Race scholars (like others in this volume) might call interest convergence: policy transformation occurring when the interests of the dominant/ruling/corporate/White class converge with the needs and demands put forth by the underclass (Bell, 1980; Spade, 2011). In this example, the dominant class usurps the demands for better educational opportunities and repackages them with their own interests of control and capital layered under a veneer of social justice rhetoric.

Sentimental Hope

WFS follows five families in their attempt to get the best education for their children, which in the film gets cast as charter schools. These are real people, with real impediments to getting their children the education they need and deserve. No one doubts that; however, the sentimentalist American Dream plotline of the film preys and pulls on heartstrings. Jensen, Janak, and Slater (2012), in their study on the impact of *WFS* on future teachers, argued that "documentaries have the potential to be equally, if not more, powerful [than fiction films]" (p. 26). Cinema, with its magical abilities to manipulate time and space, is a captivating and seductive medium. And so it is not to say that *WFS* manipulates whereas other screen-based media, like *The Wire*, do not manipulate. The question is about the slant of the manipulation: how, why, and to what end—not to mention the wealthy venture philanthropists supporting production costs (Miner, 2010). Cameos by trusted male-figures such as Stanford's Eric Hanushek, venture-philanthropist Bill Gates, and journalist Jonathan Alter are weaved seamlessly into the emotional fabric of the plight of families, the helpless children, and a bunch of statistics offered through visually compelling cartoons. It is close to impossible not to be affected by this film. It is a story about underdogs, about people who have gotten the short end of the stick, and about good people who just want the best for their kids. Even with various kinds of critical faculties doing acts of demystification, the film most certainly contains all the elements necessary to be affecting.

After over an hour and a half of messaging with plot lines that sentimentally resonate within the contemporary public imaginary—a young Black male student whose father died from drugs and was being raised by his grandmother who wants to live a better life, a young Latina student who wants to be a veterinarian or a doctor in order to help people—the audience is pulled into the climax: a gut-wrenching fifteen-minute drama of the lottery. The odds are stacked against the families and, as an audience, we are positioned as observers to the cruel vicissitudes of a certain-strand of market-based school choice. Given everything we have been told, it is difficult to not be rooting for the families. Thinking reflectively and affectively, I cry when students' numbers are called in the lottery and when they are not; but I think I cry more for those who do not get in. These kids and their families are *so* close, *so* close to being "saved." So close to being able to achieve the American Dream. So close to getting *out* of their *ghetto schools*—those things the film portrays as ahistorical and magically reoccurring in poor areas that just so happen to serve communities of color. Rather than leading students to think critically about what lotteries say about rights and citizenship, *WFS* gives the audience real-life melodrama. Desires for creating fairer opportunities for young people are externalized into an affective policy platform that, behind the scenes, also works to push a neoliberal ideological approach toward social, political, and economic life.

Feeling Helpful

WFS teaches students, particularly those at Predominantly White Institutions, little about urban issues that fall outside of their already White and upper/middle-class sensibilities. Students learn that the issues faced by the poor, people of color, and those deemed Other can be addressed by tweaking the system in such a way that fails to call into question any of the underlying systemic and structural injustices that involve the privilege and violence associated with Whiteness, global capital, or notions of merit. The film does not ask students to consider how the system that continues to fail communities of color is the same system that has benefitted them. Privileged students who have profited from cultures of whiteness are not asked to consider how their successes and social locations are connected to the historical disinvestment in poor urban communities. They are not asked about the cultural production of knowledge in the classroom or on tests. Most students at small liberal arts schools like I teach at have done well in school and on tests. They have always been told they are smart; tests and grades merely affirm/ed that. *WFS* does not question the social and cultural capital that allows them to succeed with a good deal of consistency. The unwritten tautology of testing masks their capital as well as legitimates their social location at a highly selective liberal arts school. There is no gesture toward thinking relationally—the matrices and interconnections of political economy, race, class, globalization, and politics. Nothing calls the audience into question; the gaze never ends up on the viewer. Instead, the students/viewers from the dominant culture are called upon to act on behalf of those on the screen—to help save them. In *WFS*, teaching is depicted as a teacher opening a student's head and filling it with stuff. That stuff, we are to believe, makes that student smarter. Critical scholars refer to this as the banking model of education, a model that has long been critiqued in regard to power relations, passivity, and rigid automation (Freire, 2000). *WFS* serves as an example of this banking model by assuming a passive audience and uses sentimentalism and tropes of whiteness in order to facilitate an ideological processes of policy and political legitimation.

In *Ugly Feelings*, Sianne Ngai (2007) differentiated between affects that are less useful for politics (paranoia, anxiety) and affects that are more useful (anger, fear). The kinds of affects generated in *WFS* are useful for (a certain kind of) politics. Crying to the film, or at the film, or with the film, sutures a kind of solidarity. Because students, at least in the beginning of class, have not been primed with questions that might engender an active conversation about contemporary educational issues, solidarity is coerced through sentimental manipulation, rather than achieved dialogically. The cry of frustration, sadness, or anger is met with a supplementary positive affect that invites the student into a political order—an order premised on colonial mentalities of White saviors and capitalist fantasies about reforming education through market-driven politics. The film literally asks the viewer/student to join their mission to help the students depicted in the movie. Students like those in my classes are actually interpellated into a possible savior-subject. With a kind of imperial hope, students are called to help lead the "reform movement"— a calling where they can both do good and be good (Labaree, 2010). With billions of dollars backing the reform movement, this kind of hope is relatively easy to believe in especially with the ways *WFS* accrues legitimacy through discursive uses of sentimentalism and the sensibilities of cultures of Whiteness.

To Grieving

Hope is not something that students talk about getting from *The Wire*— at least not a kind of sentimentalized hope as produced from *WFS*. Sentimentalized hope carries with it a certain kind of relationship to the future. Malabou and Derrida (2004), suggested that sentimentalized hope's relationship to the future is relatively predictable. There is a future and in that future one can imagine what the world might look like, especially in relation to education policy. *WFS* wants an audience to think that the world can pretty much look like the same place it does today—just with a few more charter schools making middle-class life seemingly more accessible to students of color (predicated on an idea that middle-class life is desirable). *WFS* offers easy answers to unsophisticated questions.

The Wire, on the other hand, refuses to ask easy questions. In turn, it refuses to offer easy answers. In interviews, Simon and Burns have stated that they want viewers to feel "morally outraged" at how "raw, unencumbered capitalism" has diminished human life and the relationships we form between each other (Talbot, 2007, para 6). The overarching feel of the show—the city, the particular spaces within the city the show depicts, and the situations that characters find themselves in—is something like trapped. Happy endings like getting out of "'da hood" or beating the odds, themes that characterize many popular representations of urban life geared toward White audiences that romanticize political notions of meritocracy and the protestant work ethic, do not get played out in this series. Students do not walk away from *The Wire* with feelings of traditional hope—that there will be a future and it will be bright and sunny. Instead, in the conversations with my students, I continually hear about how "fucked" the system is—fucked being a technical term I use throughout the semester to try to connote, in conversation with authors like June Jordan, Chester Himes, and Donald Goines, the very much non-consensual penetration of violence, racism, colonialism and capitalism within urban communities of color.

Hopeless Hopefulness

And yet, in this affective space of seeing the thing as "fucked," a different kind of hope emerges—a hope that characterizes what Robin D.G. Kelley (2002) called freedom dreams and what Derrida (Malabou & Derrida, 2004) in his work called l'avenir: the radical and revolutionary future to come. Whereas the future as imagined through WFS is portrayed in a relatively knowable way and remains afflicted with classed and racialized ideologies, freedom dreams or l'avenir call into being a revolutionary relationship with the future characterized by a kind of faith in the unknowability of what might be in a world of radical justice. L'avenir emerges from what Malabou and Derrida (2004) referred to as aporetic spaces: "the difficult or the impracticable, here the impossible passage, the refused, denied, or prohibited passage, indeed the non-passage, which can in fact be something else, the event of a coming or of a future advent ... the point where the very project of the problematic task becomes impossible..." (p. 250). Aporetic hope, then, is precisely a kind of hope that emerges when one has no hope, or when hope seems impossible, or when things seem "fucked"—when the logics of hope predicated on a present moment are unavailable for they are insufficient for the task at hand or will always and already be insufficient in dealing with structural issues. It is a hope grounded in critique, having a sophisticated analysis of a problematique, and an ethical engagement with a future that is not contingent on what already is.

Resonating with this, and in a letter to fans about the hopelessness of the show, Simon writes that the neoliberal imaginary wants the kinds of "simple solutions," which WFS offers. He goes on to say, "We enjoy being provoked and titillated, but we resist the rigorous, painstaking examination of issues that might, in the end, bring us to the point of solving any of them" (cited in Vint, 2013, p. 86). Anderson wrote that *The Wire* is not in the business of presenting solutions, "but rather that, 'The resolution is elsewhere, in the residue of affect that lingers long after the television is turned off, and the viewers' relationship to the characters, which is an empathetic relationship exactly because the characters are flawed, ambiguous and contradictory figures'" (cited in Vint, 2013, p. 88). Clear distinctions between good and evil, fiction and documentary, and right and wrong are stripped from their traditional function in moralized storytelling and instead the audience bares witness to complexity, compromise, and, at times, compunction. The hope students get from *The Wire* stems from their inability to arrive anywhere at the end of the series. "There is no complete picture," wrote Fuggle (2009) of the series, "no ultimate truth, no tidy conclusion..." (para 1). Denied sentimentalized answers and heroic identities, students end up in a different kind of affective space—a space characterized by a certain kind of political mourning and grief.

Mourning, Grief, Humanization

From students' early hesitations about names and talking about the show, they usually end up finding their feet. There is a difference between being hard to talk about and not having anything to say. The first part of the semi-structured conversation of the final is open-ended. Students are prompted with nothing more than: "What did you think?" After the initial fumbling, they almost always start rehearsing the litany of issues that emerge in the post-industrial city—no jobs, no social support, gentrification, political corruption, blackmail, few venues for meaningful education, and so on. These issues, of course, are not particular to Baltimore or the post-industrial, but they nonetheless provide scaffolding for thinking symptomatically about neoliberalism. For students, the portrayal of systemic violence on the screen, rather than unfolding on the pages being read during the term, does something. The use of local actors and local residents, the way the show unfolds in realist fashion, the character development, and the general blending between fact and fiction, what Simon calls, "non-fiction truth-telling," somehow crystallizes the issues we have been discussing in class into a reality: this really happens and, the corollary, this really happens to real people (cited in Vint 2013, p. 86).

Real people like Bodie, who students think represents some sort of ethical center of the season/show, which cements my personal belief that he is the protagonist and hero of a show that resists, at all costs, protagonists and heroes. Talk of Bodie easily moves into conversations about Michael. "And Michael...." usually say with an exasperated and saddened inflection and then stop and look up at me as if I know what they are talking about. And I think I do. Some of them say things like, "I get it." They have had thought experiments in philosophy classes about if they had to steal or do something against the law to protect one of their family members, would they do it? I like to believe that, with Michael, the students get an affective rejoinder to their more logical understanding of what it means to be young and Black and poor growing up in the United States in an age of racialized austerity. When they say, "It humanized the readings," I see this as evidence that the show has created a kind of pedagogical ecology whereby, when a student might hear a statistic or a story in the news ("One dead on the corner in drug turf war"), they might see Bodie, they might see Michael, and they might see Bug.

But the show demands more than just that, too. *The Wire*, with the relationality called out in the title itself (wires connect things), forces the students to see themselves in West Baltimore—how their lives of affluence, of relative decadence, and of safety are not just predicated on, but are radically contingent upon the lives on the screen. Michael and Bug and drug addiction and accidental deaths like Sharrod's and Duquan's life of continual dispossession all exist within a field of relation, wired as it were, to the students who are watching from a historical, social, and geographical distance.

This wiring contains the possibility for students to feel a sense of complicity, a sense of also feeling trapped in a very different way in Baltimore. Though just about all of the students have not grown up in places like they see on the screen, they gain an understanding that their skin color, their class, their educational opportunities both shape life in Baltimore and have been shaped by it. The show presents an aporetic space of impasse where easy plans of escape—from accountability structures to raising test scores—are utterly disqualified. The focus on schools in *The Wire* is antithetical here to *WFS*, rejecting the central tenants suggesting that a tweak of policy or charter schools equal messianic change. Simon has written that schools were once "the way out for us and our parents" but that today schools "cannot save us" (cited in Williams, 2011, p. 223). This is not to say that schools cannot play a huge role in the formation of a better world, but that, as scholars have long argued and as Season Four attempts to portray, schools are used as a dumping ground for all social issues and are also impossibly asked to make them all go away (Wells, 2009). Pedagogically, *The Wire*, in articulating circuits of relation, denies students this fantasy and denies them savior-like temptations.

Pedagogical Grief

Precluded from answers, and having formed a certain kind of relationship with some of the characters, students are engaged with a kind of pedagogical grief for the "fictitious" characters. For *The Wire*, as Butler (2004) in *Precarious Life* might say, has made the lives it depicts grievable. Though the families and children in *WFS* are grievable, the way their struggle is depicted suggests that the grief can be outsourced through externalized reforms—not much is demanded of an audience except a certain kind of charity. *The Wire*, however, in resisting the tropes of externalization and savior creates the conditions for different kinds of humanization and, therefore, different kinds of grief.

What Butler argues in relation to humanization and grief stems from three inter-related questions: "Who counts as human? Whose lives count as lives? And, finally, what *makes for a grievable life?*" (p. 20; emphasis original). In conversation with Freud and Benjamin on mourning and melancholia, Butler sees grieving as an affective manifestation of relationality—a recognition of the ways in which individuals are contingent on others and the social fields that provide an ecology for the emergence of such subjects. In grieving, Butler wrote, "something about who we are is revealed, something that delineates the ties we have to others, that shows us that these ties constitute what we are, ties or bonds that compose us" (p. 22). Through the loss of someone else, she argued, we lose a sense of who we are. In this loss of self, it is revealed that we are not independent and autonomous beings in the world, but radically contingent on others for meaning and material life. Far from being a private process one goes through, Butler argues that grieving is an ontologically public process for it reveals the vulnerability and publicness of bodies and selves—it is, to be sure, a certain kind of political and public revelation. Grief discloses this interdependence and exposure and Butler argues that this can be a disclosure that holds hope for politics and ethics. If one can understand the ways in which materiality and language provide for *wires* of interconnectedness, about how my life is wrapped up in yours, about how Carcetti's life is wrapped up in the life of Randy, about how a viewer's life is wrapped up in the viewed, then one might enter into a different kind of relationality in thinking how to comport oneself politically and ethically in the world. One might rethink with for whom action is necessary in order to have hope.

Humanization

The prospect for thinking ethics relationally, though, is stipulated on an economy of humanness. When one loses a lover or a friend, that person is fully human to the other and their loss is felt intimately and closely. Not all subjects, though, have the same degree of humanness as a close acquaintance. Within the political sphere, a sphere marked by race, class, ability, gender, sexuality, nation, and so on, there are differing degrees of humanness. For most Americans, those who died in the Towers on 9/11 were completely human. Even though they were not known to most of the country, they were portrayed as human through things like public obituaries. These people had names, had children, had pasts, and futures that were all lost. These were human beings who died, and they were therefore grievable. Through the use of public obituary and covert jingoism as represented in such places like *The New York Times*' "Portraits of Grief," this humanness and likeness "put mourning to work" in shoring up consent for a political program around war and terrorism (Engle, 2007).

Contrast this to dead Palestinians. Dead Afghanis. Dead Iraqis. It is not hard to see how most of if not all of these victims, with brown skin and strange names, are never rendered human, and therefore, remain ungrievable. "Do they have names and faces, personal histories, family, favorite hobbies, slogans by which they live?" asked Butler (p. 32). For many, these are not real people—histories of coloniality, racism, and geopolitics rendering them inhuman, disposable, or worse, deserving. In a world where those who receive violence are not fully human, there is no chance to see relation, for there is no relation to see. If grief reveals our relations, and if one must be human to be grieved over, then without being rendered human there will be no revelation. And without revelation, there will be no action.

The Wire provides names, stories, families, and hobbies about people in Baltimore to audiences like my students. Unlike most television shows about urban America that operationalize stereotypes about the lives the racialized poor, *The Wire*, as Lorrie Moore put it, "transform[s] a social type into a human being, demography into dramaturgy" (cited in Williams, 2001, p. 221). Its ethnographic patience and generosity, combined with the way it shows interconnection and interdependence, provides for a process of humanization that opens up the possibility for pedagogical grief. Students are not left with a game plan about how to reform education policy or urban issues with quick fixes and grand schemes for cursory development, like *WFS*. Instead, they are left with, as Anderson is quoted above suggesting, "residue of affect that lingers long after the television is turned off."

This residue is the kind of sticky environment Derrida had in mind when thinking about aporetic spaces. There is a certain kind of resin that *The Wire* secretes. This stickiness represents the web of relations that emerge from watching the show—that the parts are connected, that everyone plays the game, that finding an alibi is all but impossible. The issues facing the urban poor cannot be externalized into simple institutions or programs that the privileged can join or support in order to save *them*. Instead, *The Wire*'s stickiness indicts its audience by exposing connection: you in the suburbs, you with White skin, you not living like this—you are a big part of this problem.[3] The metaphor of the wire calls out this relationship between viewers and viewed. *The Wire*, at the same time that it humanizes the urban poor through the kinds of manipulative devices available to media, it also humanizes the relations between people by making an audience see itself more honestly and, therefore, humanely. The trauma of *The Wire* is the trauma of neoliberal, militarized, urban life. It is the trauma of witnessing what is happening to humanized people. But it is also the trauma of alterity. It is the trauma of understanding the way dehumanization has failed to account for the instrumental ties that bind human beings together. For it is the trauma of interconnection, of being *wired* together, that students confront most formally in watching.

In this sense, grief is predicated on finding oneself in an aporetic space. *The Wire* can provide a kind of sticky impasse for students who are too easily swayed by the kind of marketing tricks employed in *WFS* or adverts for TFA. By not providing answers, *The Wire* rejects alibis. By refusing normative valuations of morality, *The Wire* rejects vindication. By providing names and nuance, *The Wire* provides the possibility for humanization. *The Wire* provides a space for students to get stuck, and in that getting stuck, to see things a bit differently. I do not want to overstate the process or the pedagogy and suggest that my students come out of the class engaged in the radical fight for justice. They do not. But I do know that they come out with a humility that is the result of being confronted with the complicated facts that pedagogical grief engenders—that we live in a world of interconnection, that these interconnections map material and ideological topographies that play out in their lives as well as in Bubbles,' and that these interconnections, though somewhat easily repressed in the comforts of upper/middle-class life, are always there, a spectral presence haunting social life (Regenspan, 2014).

(In)conclusion

Toward the end of the final, I ask my mostly very White and mostly very wealthy students—whom I actually believe do have a certain kind of fidelity toward social justice—how these two representations (*WFS* & *The Wire*) might be in conversation with each other. There are lots of answers to this question—cooking the books in schools and police precincts, the exploitation of Black and brown bodies for political clout, the symbolism at the end of season four of *The Wire*, with dead bodies literally packed into a middle school gymnasium and the deadening of education going on in the militaristic test-prep classrooms, and about the relationship between the market-logic privatization of education (represented best by Michelle Rhee in *WFS*) and the bottom-line drug business as run by Marlo. There is something about Rhee and Marlo that both my students and I find more terrifying than Geoffrey Canada and Avon Barksdale. Both Marlo and Rhee present themselves as ruthless, with nothing, no union, no larger community, no sentiment that will get in the way of doing business. Everything has profit-motive. Whereas, Canada and Barksdale represent some semblance of what Mike Davis called "crypto-Keynesianism" with their acknowledgment of family and community, Marlo and Rhee represent the more malicious version of profit over people (cited in Vint, 2013, p. 46). The insight here is that, even within neoliberal entrepreneurialism, there are differing degrees of dogmatism.

I end the oral final by asking the students what type of education policy might "help" people in Baltimore. More testing? More charter schools? More young and energetic and smart post-grads like themselves in classrooms with Black and Brown bodies? They are leading questions, coming from me, but I ask anyway. And, in stride, I get something of a negative theology answer— no, not more testing; no, not more charters; no, not more of us, even though we want to "help." They also say that the students represented in the show know more about neoliberalism than they do—that though Randy might not have "their" academic language or books, the continuing metaphors about chess and *the game* and their understanding of living under constant surveillance has provided an education about the world we live in that my students never got, or at least were never trained to see due to the blinders of whiteness and class. And so, and in turn, and instead of answering the question about what Baltimore needs, many of my students instead start asking questions about why this has been hidden from them for so long. Why did their enrichment programs or extracurricular activities or "volunteer work" not help them see the world in its enmeshed opacity? Why did no one explain to them that the upkeep of their lives were killing other people? Why did no one tell them that Whiteness is very much property?

And it is with this type of questioning that I start to find a bit of hope that when students say that, "It humanized the readings," they are not making overdetermined commentary about the people who experience the world radically differently. Rather, I understand "It humanized the readings" as being a self-reflexive gesture—that students are talking about themselves, and their human experiences, rather than what was on the screen. In ways both complementary and contradictory, watching *The Wire* gets students to reflect on their own education and their own personal/political lives.

Perhaps with a bit of naïve optimism, I want to think of my students' experiences watching *The Wire* as a pedagogical experience where they become more human to themselves. By human here I mean something akin to how Butler conceptualizes the human as noted above—relational, contingent, dependent, vulnerable, historical, and emergent. I want to think that the process of humanization, if we think about it relationally, if we think about it in regard to the *wires* that connect, bind, and subdue us, has a double function. It has the possibility to not only humanize those who were once statistics, but also create a more robust and complicated idea of the self. And in this sense, it is possible that grieving is both over the loss of life—of Omar, Bodie, Duquan—but also grieving over the loss of the kinds of easy answers and easy questions that once characterized a less precarious relationship to life and how they once understood their individuated personhoods.

The opening quote of this essay comes from Randy Wagstaff, one of the young students we meet in season four. After a series of events, Randy finds himself taken away from his foster mother (Ms. Anna) and transferred to a group home. Sergeant Carver, who Randy is talking to, had promised to take care of Randy, to protect him and his foster mother. Despite trying, Carver was not able to and the scene, which comes toward the end of Season Four, is one of a few storylines that are not ending well among the youth who the season follows.

Though directed at Carver, I believe a better way to read Randy's words are as if they were directed at the audience—and not just any audience, but an audience filled with people like my students and I. *You gonna protect me? You gonna help? You got my back?* It seems to me that we might be able to read these words against a backdrop of the current reform movement in education. There are lots of well-intentioned people out there in education claiming that *they* are going to help; that *they* are trying to protect young people; and that *they* have their backs. Though I do not doubt the earnestness with which people are working to help students in urban communities, the current fad of neoliberal policies do and will continue to fail the most vulnerable students and democratic ideals. For what does it mean to really have someone's back? What does it mean to try to help? Who gets to answer these questions, or frame the questions?

This essay and the introduction of pedagogical grief suggests that we need to start thinking about these questions from a place where privilege meets impasse rather than charitable habituation. Through getting stuck, in Baltimore or elsewhere, we might be forced to think about political and ethical questions differently. And, perhaps most importantly and pedagogically, we might think about political and ethical questions in relation to ourselves, in contingency, and through a kind of ethic of what it is to be *wired*.

Notes

1. To reform something usually has a positive connotation. Something is broken and one reforms it to work better. I use "reform" here in scare quotes to call attention to the critique of the self-proclaimed "reformers" working in education policy today that, for many of us, are eviscerating the *public* of education and draining education of its critical and civic potentialities. Like others, I would use deform rather than reform to describe the work of this policy regime (Watkins, 2011); however, I will use reform throughout the paper without scare quotes, but use it with critical distance.

2. When I first taught Politics and Education, I used *WFS* as the final and had

the students write a response. I then started using *The Wire* as a response text the next time I taught the course.

3. One might consider this kind of ethical imposition in relation to the poetic invocation to Primo Levi's (1996) *Survival in Auschwitz*, which begins: "You who live safe/In your warm houses,/You who find, returning in the evening,/Hot food and friendly faces:/" (n.p.).

REFERENCES

Anderson, A. (2013). Teach for America and the dangers of deficit thinking. *Critical Education, 4*(11), 28–47. Retrieved from http://ojs.library.ubc.ca/index.php/crit icaled/article/view/183936.

Beane, J.A., and M.W. Apple. (2007). The case for democratic schools. In M.W. Apple and J.A. Beane, *Democratic schools: Lessons in powerful education* (2nd ed., pp. 1–29). Portsmouth, NH: Heinemann.

Bell, D.A. (1980). *Brown v. board of education* and the interest-convergence dilemma. *Harvard Law Review 93*(3), 518–533.

Blum, L. (2011). "B5—its got all the dinks": School and education on *the wire. Dark Matter—The Wire Files.* Retrieved from http://www.darkmatter101.org/site/2011/04/29/b5-it-got-all-the-dinks-schools-and-education-on-the-wire/.

Burch, P. (2009). *Hidden markets: The new education privatization.* New York: Routledge.

Butler, J. (2004). *Precarious life.* New York: Verso.

Davis, M. (2006). *City of quartz.* New York: Verso.

Engle, K. (2007). Putting mourning to work: Making sense of 9/11. *Theory, Culture & Society, 24*(1), 61–88.

Fabricant, M., and M. Fine. (2012). *Charter schools and the corporate makeover of public education: What's at stake?* New York: Teachers College Press.

Friere, P. (2000/1970). *Pedagogy of the oppressed.* New York: Continuum.

Fuggle, S. (2009). Short circuiting the power grid: *The wire* as critique of institutional power. *Dark Matter: The Wire Files.* Retrieved from: http://www.darkmatter101.org/site/2009/05/29/short-circuiting-the-power-grid-the-wire-as-critique-of-institutional-power/.

Gramsci, A. (1971). *Selections from the prison notebooks.* New York: International Publishers.

Henig, J. (2008). *Spin cycle.* New York: Russell Sage Foundation.

Herman, E., and N. Chomsky. (2002). *Manufacturing consent: The political economy of the mass media.* New York: Pantheon.

Jensen, A., E. Janak, and T.F. Slater. (2012). Changing course: Exploring impacts of *Waiting For Superman* on future teachers' perspectives on the state of education. *Contemporary Issues in Education Research, 5*(1), 23–31.

Jones, B. (2010). The struggle for black education. In J. Bale and S. Knopp, *Education and capitalism: Struggles for learning and liberation* (pp. 41–69). Chicago: Haymarket Books.

Kelley, R.D.G. (2002). *Freedom dreams: The black radical imagination.* Boston: Beacon.

Kumashiro, K.K. (2008). *The seduction of common sense: How the right has framed the debate on America's schools.* New York: Teachers College Press.

Kumashiro, K.K. (2012). *Bad teacher!: How blaming teachers distorts the bigger picture.* New York: Teachers College Press.

Labaree, D. (2010). Teach for America and teacher ed: Heads they win, tails we lose. *Journal of Teacher Education, 61*(1–2), 48–55.

Levi, P. (1996). *Survival in Auschwitz*. New York: Touchtone.

Lipman, P. (2004). *High stakes education: Inequality, globalization, and urban school reform*. New York: Routledge.

Lipman, P. (2011). *The new political economy of urban education: Neoliberalism, race and the right to the city*. New York: Routledge.

Malabou, C., and J. Derrida. (2004). *Counterpath: Traveling with Jacques Derrida*. Stanford: Stanford University Press.

Means, A. (2013). *Schooling in the age of austerity: Urban education and the struggle for democratic life*. New York: Palgrave Macmillan.

Miner, B. (2010, October 20). Ultimate $uperpower: Supersized dollars drive "Waiting for Superman" agenda. *Not Waiting for Superman*. Retrieved from http://www.notwaitingforsuperman.org/Articles/20101020-MinerUltimateSuperpower.

National Education Policy Center. (n.d.). *Homepage*. Retrieved from http://www.nepc.colorado.edu.

Ngai, S. (2007). *Ugly feelings*. Cambridge, MA: Harvard University Press.

Regenspan, B. (2014). *Haunting and the educational imagination*. Boston: Sense Publishers.

Saltman, K.J. (2007). *Capitalizing on disaster: Taking and breaking public schools*. Boulder: Paradigm Publishers.

Simon, D. (Writer), and J. Chappelle. (Director). (2006). That's got his own. [television series episode]. In D. Simon (Executive Producer). *The Wire*. New York: Home Box Office.

Spade, D. (2011). *Normal life: Administrative violence, critical trans politics and the limits of law*. Cambridge, MA: South End Press.

Stern, M. (2012). "We can't build our dreams on suspicious minds": Neoliberalism, education policy, and the *feelings* left over. *Cultural Studies ↔ Critical Methodologies, 12*(5), 387–400.

Swalwell, K., and M.W. Apple. (2011). Reviewing policy: Start the wrong conversation: The public school crisis and "Waiting for Superman." *Educational Policy, 25*(2), 368–382.

Talbot, M. (2007, October 22). Stealing life. *The New Yorker*. Retrieved from http://www.newyorker.com/reporting/2007/10/22/071022fa_fact_talbot.

Trier, J. (2010). Representations of education in HBO's *The wire*, season 4. *Teacher Education Quarterly, 37*(2), pp. 179–200.

Vint, S. (2013). *The wire*. Detroit: Wayne State University Press.

Watkins, W. (2011) *The assault on public education: Confronting the politics of corporate school reform*. New York: Teachers College Press.

Wells, A.S. (2009). Our children's burden: A history of federal education policies that ask (now require) our public schools to solve societal inequality. In M.A. Rebell & J. Wolff (Eds.), NCLB at the crossroads: Re-examining America's commitment to closing our nation's achievement gaps (pp. 1–42). New York: Teachers College Press.

Williams, L. (2011). Ethnographic imaginary: The genesis and genius of *the wire*. *Critical Inquiry, 38*(Autumn), 208–226.

"Omar listening"
Queer Theory, Gender Play and The Wire

Jason P. Vest

Openings

The Wire (2002–2008), created by David Simon and first broadcast on the premium-cable network Home Box Office (HBO), transcends shallow representations of its gay and lesbian characters' inner lives, emotional complications, and flawed personalities. This program's two most notable queer characters, Omar Little (Michael K. Williams) and Shakima "Kima" Greggs (Sonja Sohn), are neither perfect nor perfectly drawn, making The Wire an exemplary text for illustrating important queer-theory concepts to university students. The Wire, indeed, enables more sophisticated understandings of queer theory's concerns about heteronormativity; its emphasis on the fluid, socially determined construction of gender roles; and its exploration of how artistic productions across disparate media represent queer lives. This final concern also interrogates how David Simon's—and, by implication, U.S. television's—casting choices influence the onscreen portrayal of gay and lesbian people, for Simon selected two straight actors to play The Wire's most notable queer characters. His program's investment in these issues not only assists interested educators in launching provocative discussions about queer theory but also offers college students fruitful opportunities for intellectual and scholarly growth.

These outcomes gain luster when considering how The Wire, in a clever bit of cultural allusiveness, reconfigures the narrative, thematic, and visual codes of the Western to position Omar and Kima as two classic Western figures: the daring outlaw and the brash peace officer. By unapologetically allowing Omar and Kima to fulfill these generic roles as capably as their heterosexual counterparts, The Wire exposes these stock characters' allure as the product of widespread, reactionary formulations of masculinity and femininity in the United States. As such, *The Wire*'s fascination with transforming Western settings, themes, and plots into urban crime drama allows Simon's series to contest careless assumptions about queer lives. By doing so, *The Wire* becomes a useful tool for teaching queer theory's foundational concepts to students who, more often than not, know little (or nothing) about them.

Western Promises

The opening of *The Wire*'s third-season episode "Middle Ground" (Pelecanos, 2004) exemplifies these pedagogical possibilities. This scene, even for viewers unfamiliar with Westerns, includes so many generic trappings that audiences may think the characters have stumbled into *High Noon* (1952), *The Man Who Shot Liberty Valance* (1962), *The Rifleman* (1958–1963), or *Deadwood* (2004–2006). Two men confront one another by pointing guns, exchanging words, and pursuing a primary rite of male passage, at least as far as twentieth-century U.S. film and television are concerned: the street shootout. The threat of violence raises expectations as *The Wire*'s viewers anticipate the moment when the sound of guns blazing heralds the bloody battle long promised by a narrative that forces the good guy to oppose, to fight, and, in the end, to kill the bad guy.

Yet the standoff's details distinguish this quarrel from the moment the screen first fades from black. The scene takes place at night, in a deserted alleyway in Baltimore, Maryland, not in broad daylight on a busy street in Hadleyville, New Mexico; Laredo, Texas; or Deadwood, South Dakota. The two men are not sheriff and rustler, or marshal and prisoner, but stickup artist Omar Little and hired assassin Brother Mouzone (Michael Potts), two inhabitants of Baltimore's criminal underworld who have crossed paths in the past. They are not White men replaying tensions fundamental to the United States' mythical conception of itself as a land whose inhabitants unfailingly fight evil in the name of liberty and justice, but rather Black men navigating the unequal political and moral terrain inherited by African Americans after centuries of racial oppression, cultural exclusion, and economic disenfranchisement. Omar and Mouzone, moreover, do not shoot one another, but instead catalog the weapons they brandish in a clever refashioning of the sparse, sterile dialogue that characterizes classic Western showdowns. The camerawork, in color rather than black and white, is not stark, but instead moody in the way that good urban thrillers are, with streetlights casting shadows in chiaroscuro patterns that manage to catch glints of color from the rain-slicked pavement. The costumes include no white hats, black hats, or tin badges, but instead Brother Mouzone's dark suit and bow tie, so preferred by the Nation of Islam that it has become—at least in the popular imagination—a virtual uniform, while Omar Little's duster, no matter how practical it may be for damp weather, recalls the regalia seen in hundreds of Western movies and television episodes.

Yet the most important aspect of this scene remains invisible. Omar, as anyone who has watched *The Wire*'s previous episodes knows, is a gay man who robs the drug dealers controlling and patrolling the downtrodden Baltimore neighborhoods he haunts. This fact provokes derision from Omar's foes, who call him a "dick sucker" and a "cocksucker" on numerous occasions, but Omar's intelligence, audacity, and bravery make him the most feared man on West Baltimore's streets. Despite the disgust about Omar's sexual orientation expressed by Avon Barksdale (Wood Harris), Russell "Stringer" Bell (Idris Elba), and Marlo Stanfield (Jamie Hector), they nonetheless admire his ability to organize and undertake the daring robberies that he regularly (and thrillingly) executes.

Omar's character, indeed, makes a strong case for employing *The Wire* to teach university students about queer theory's fundamental principles, arguments, and controversies. Simon's series, in a subtle narrative maneuver, positions Omar as an outlaw who resembles the traditional Western antihero, thereby calling forth orthodox conceptualizations of American masculinity that the series then unsettles by showing Omar to be a man who cares deeply for his male lovers. Despite this laudably complex characterization, Omar remains a minor (if memorable) presence in *The Wire*'s large pantheon of characters, which itself might indicate the program's hesitance to tread too far afield of the sexual conventions that typify the cops-and-robbers series so beloved by U.S. television. David Simon might protest this observation by claiming that he designed *The Wire* to subvert almost every expectation of standard network cop shows, but Simon did not resist the temptation, taken from so many previous entries in this genre, to make his lead character, Detective Jimmy McNulty (Dominic West), a heterosexual White man who pursues women with reckless abandon.

The Wire, thankfully, does not offer Omar as its only queer character. Simon chooses to include as a principal protagonist the redoubtable "Kima" Greggs, a narcotics detective so good at her job that, like McNulty, she frequently cannot believe the Baltimore Police Department's bureaucratic ineptitude, regressiveness, and incompetence. Although Kima's lesbianism fascinates her more unreconstructed male colleagues, particularly fellow narc Thomas "Herc" Hauk (Domenick Lombardozzi), Kima's long-term relationship with her live-in partner, a broadcast journalist named Cheryl (played by Melanie Nicholls-King and never given a surname), demonstrates *The Wire*'s value as a forum for discussing queer theory in both graduate and undergraduate classrooms. Kima, indeed, so capably manages her personal and professional lives in Season One's inaugural episodes that Laura Lippman (former reporter for the *Baltimore Sun*, author of the Tess Monaghan mystery novels, and wife of David Simon), comments upon this fact in her fine 2004 essay "The Women of *The Wire* (No, Seriously)" by writing, "Smart, tough, and hard-working, Greggs seemed almost *too* admirable in the early going— it's a bird, it's a plane, it's Super-Lesbian!" (p. 55). This remark acknowledges the tendency by enlightened heterosexual writers to create gay and lesbian personalities of unimpeachable virtue who resist the demeaning stereotypes that have long plagued Hollywood productions. Despite the increasingly complex gay and lesbian characters on U.S. commercial television (whether broadcast, basic cable, or premium channel) since Vincent Schiavelli played Peter Panama—network television's first openly gay recurring character—in Norman Barash and John Boni's situation comedy *The Corner Bar* (1972–1973) and Billy Crystal played Jodie Dallas—the medium's first regular gay character—in Susan Harris's *Soap* (1977–1981), Kima Greggs seems, at least to Lippman, almost too good to be true, as if Simon and *The Wire* wished to establish their dramatic legitimacy and artistic integrity by portraying Kima not simply as equal to, but as better than, her hetero colleagues.

The Wire quickly complicates this straitened depiction by dramatizing how Kima's many professional and personal responsibilities cause her work and home lives to suffer. Along with her job as a full-time narcotics detective, Kima attends night-school law classes, largely at Cheryl's insistence, because Cheryl, who worries about Kima's safety while working drug investigations, feels that being an attorney offers physical and fiscal protections that a career in law enforcement cannot. Cheryl's fears prove well-founded late in Season One when, in "The Cost" (1.10), Kima is shot while performing an undercover drug buy, leading to months of physical recovery that culminate in Kima accepting a desk job four episodes later, in the Season Two premiere, "Ebb Tide" (2.1), to placate Cheryl's anxieties. Yet Kima soon returns to investigative duty, preferring the active pursuit of wrongdoers to the sedentary life of an office bureaucrat in a decision that sees Kima develop the swaggering style associated with McNulty, Omar, and *The Wire*'s other Western-inspired characters. Kima not only begins to stray outside her previously monogamous relationship with Cheryl but also begins to buck the police department's rules.

These thumbnail sketches of Omar and Kima cannot capture their many nuances, drawn out over the program's sixty episodes, but they prove that *The Wire* is no simplistic Western doubling as a contemporary urban-crime drama. These queer characters' ongoing presence and narrative significance underscore how well *The Wire* aids classroom educators in the daunting task of explaining queer theory's fundamental precepts.

New Normals

Contextualizing the history of queer theory is crucial to appraising its influence, as anyone who teaches this body of critical work soon realizes. Such a venture becomes more urgent when introducing queer theory to undergraduate students who are acquainted with this subject's effects, inside and outside the academy, even if they do not realize it. The dramatic shift in U.S. attitudes regarding the civil rights of lesbian, gay, bisexual, transgender, and queer (LGBTQ) citizens since the 1990s, after all, could not have happened without activism by people familiar with queer theory's analytical techniques and evaluative strategies for questioning, exploring, and dislodging traditional assumptions about the primacy of heterosexual relationships in family arrangements, legal practices, business ventures, and cultural life. This ongoing process lays claim to diverse influences, but queer theory's significance lies in its ability to recognize the social, economic, medical, and historical forces that, for much of the United States' existence, enshrined heterosexual relationships as both proper and natural, thereby relegating gay and lesbian relationships to marginal positions frequently identified as deviant (see Foucault 1984, Jagose 1996, Sedgwick 1990, and Sullivan 2003 for incisive discussions of queer theory's political implications).

The term *theory*, however, carries so much baggage that launching students into queer theory's foundational works, including Judith Butler's *Gender Trouble: Feminism and the Subversion of Identity* (1990), Eve Kosofsky Sedgwick's *Epistemology of the Closet* (1990), and editor Michael Warner's scholarly anthology *Fear of a Queer Planet: Queer Politics and Social Theory* (1993)— or even Sedgwick's earlier, slightly more accessible book *Between Men: English Literature and Male Homosocial Desire* (1985)—risks alienating novices before they get going. As Terry Eagleton (1983), Fredric Jameson (1979), and Slavoj Žižek (1989, 1992) have long understood, student resistance to—and even outright hatred of—theory becomes easier to manage when demonstrating theory's relevance to pop-cultural texts that students sometimes understand better than their professors. This pedagogical strategy fails if it degenerates into empty exercises that deplore popular culture's influence on U.S. society, deride popular culture as a force that waters down theory, or presume pop-cultural texts to be bastardized commercial objects unable to compete in complexity or effect with the traditional Western canon's works of supposedly unassailable genius. This attitude's historical blindness about cultural production and canon formation, indeed, quickly deteriorates into a caricature of rigid, unsparing pedantry that scholars like Eagleton, Jameson, Sedgwick, and Žižek take pains to avoid. This viewpoint also ignores how popular culture simultaneously reflects, extends, and creates U.S. beliefs about LGBTQ people, a fact not lost on David Simon. *The Wire*, during its broadcast run and its afterlife as an object of mainstream and scholarly attention (thanks to the program's availability in various digital formats), participates in the United States' ongoing cultural conversation about LGBTQ representation in a development that, happily enough, illustrates queer theory's basic principles.

Omar Little and Kima Greggs, indeed, can assist students grappling with queer theory's most foundational idea: heteronormativity. Michael Warner (1993) identifies this concept's salient features in his introduction to *Fear of a Queer Planet*, saying that the essays he selects for his collection must advocate more than tolerance for LGBTQ people in public life

> because so much privilege lies in heterosexual culture's exclusive ability to interpret itself as society. Het culture thinks of itself as the elemental form of human association, as the very model of intergender relations, as the indivisible basis of all community, and as the means of reproduction without which society wouldn't exist [p. xxi].

Warner does not stop here, writing, "Materialist thinking about society has in many cases reinforced these tendencies, inherent in heterosexual ideology, toward a totalized view of the social" and that "it is certainly true that Western political thought has taken the heterosexual couple to represent the principle of social union itself" (p. xxi). Omar Little forcefully rejects this totalized formulation throughout *The Wire*, but nowhere better than in Season One's concluding episodes, when he begins a long campaign of vengeance against the Barksdale drug organization for torturing, mutilating, and murdering his boyfriend, Brandon Wright (Michael Kevin Darnall). The Barksdales leave Brandon's corpse lying atop a car in the mid-season episode "The Wire" (Simon, 2002a) not only to warn all neighborhood residents against opposing Avon Barksdale's power but also to repudiate Omar's successful raid on a Barksdale stash house three episodes earlier, in "The Buys" (Simon, 2002e).

Avon Barksdale and Stringer Bell keep an additional goal in mind. They order that Brandon be sexually tortured to spotlight Omar's gayness in the hope that doing so will publicly unman him. Their attitude demonstrates homophobia's irrationality, for Avon and Stringer know better than anyone how Omar's reputation as Baltimore's foremost stickup artist makes him a fearless street criminal who carries a sawed-off shotgun and announces his presence by whistling "The Farmer in the Dell" to evacuate bystanders before committing a robbery. Avon in particular cannot accept that Omar enjoys a committed relationship to Brandon, thinking that he (Omar) will see Brandon's death as little more than payback for robbing his (Avon's) operation. Avon, indeed, repeatedly defames Omar as a "dick sucker" during the scene in "Old Cases" (Simon, 2002f) where he (Avon) authorizes killing Brandon as vengeance for the stash-house raid. Avon's behavior, moreover, starkly illustrates the "chronic, now endemic crisis of homo/heterosexual definition, indicatively male, dating from the end of the nineteenth century" (p. 1) that Sedgwick (1990) identifies in *Epistemology of the Closet* as structuring "many of the major nodes of thought and knowledge in twentieth-century Western culture as a whole" (p. 1). Avon plays out the contradictions that Sedgwick's groundbreaking book analyzes, especially

> the contradiction between seeing homo/heterosexual definition on the one hand as an issue of active importance primarily for a small, distinct, relatively fixed homosexual minority (what I refer to as a minoritizing view), and seeing it on the other hand as an issue of continuing, determinative importance in the lives of people across the spectrum of sexualities (what I refer to as a universalizing view) [p. 1].

Avon expresses surprise about Omar's gayness when told of it in "Old Cases," having never considered that gay men (whom Avon stereotypes as flamboyantly effeminate) might execute drug robberies because, for Avon, such bold action is quintessential man's work. Despite banning LGBTQ people from his organization, Avon fixates on Omar's gayness to the exclusion of almost all other information about him. Avon, in fact, dismisses Omar's relationship with Brandon as little more than the deviant sex he presumes gay men single-mindedly pursue, only later realizing how sorely he has misjudged Omar's commitment to Brandon, particularly the rage that publicly displaying Brandon's cadaver provokes.

Avon may denigrate Omar's relationship with Brandon, but *The Wire*'s viewers become privy to its depth and tenderness as Season One unfolds. Omar, for instance, lightly criticizes Brandon's profane language in "The Buys" (Simon, 2002e) and "Old Cases" (Simon, 2002f), prompting Brandon to joke about Omar's puritanism and his small, irritating daily habits. These scenes illustrate their union's affectionate exasperation in a manner that also typifies *The Wire*'s straight couples, especially Jimmy McNulty's combustible relationship with Assistant State Attorney Rhonda Pearlman (Deirdre Lovejoy). *The Wire*, moreover, acknowledges Omar and Brandon's physical passion for one another. Both men hug, cuddle, and kiss in "Old Cases," discomfiting John Bailey (Lance Williams), their partner in the stash-house raid, whom Barksdale soldiers murder in the following episode, "The Pager" (Burns, 2002). They then capture and (unsuccessfully) torture Brandon for information about Omar's location, with Stringer Bell insisting that they publicly dump Brandon's body after he dies.

Avon and Stringer become living representatives of heteronormativity in *The Wire*'s first two seasons (a role taken up by Marlo Stanfield in the third, fourth, and fifth seasons). As Warner argues, they think that straight couples are the basis of all community. The many parties, barbecues, and gatherings that Avon and Stringer organize for their employees are object lessons in this regard, with only straight couples shown attending them. Avon also references his sexual prowess with multiple female partners in both "The Detail" (Simon, 2002d) and "The Pager" (Burns, 2002) as a sign not only of his potency but also his reputation as West Baltimore's most powerful man. Omar's many raids—along with his status as a gay man who openly, defiantly, and success-fully challenges Avon's primacy—so undermine this position that Avon feels himself financially, strategically, and symbolically emasculated by his gay nemesis. Avon's homophobia, indeed, reflects Eve Sedgwick's appraisal, influ-enced by Michel Foucault's (1976, 1984) pioneering work in his three-volume *The History of Sexuality*, that because

> modern Western culture has placed what it calls sexuality in a more and more distinctively privileged relation to our most prized constructs of individual identity, truth, and knowl-edge, it becomes truer and truer that the language of sexuality not only intersects with but transforms the other languages and relations by which we know [p. 3].

Avon comes to formulate his dispute with Omar almost exclusively in sexual terms, with Omar's gayness defying Avon's notions of proper manliness. This development, particularly acute in *The Wire*'s first season, assists students in understanding how queer theory identifies heteronormativity as a discursive construction with nearly pervasive influence on U.S. conceptualizations of sexual propriety, normalcy, and convention. Discussing how Michael K. Williams plays Omar as a man equally capable of expressing tenderness toward Brandon and hatred towards Avon also becomes key to understanding Omar's effectiveness as a character. Williams never indulges the mincing, falsetto-voiced mannerisms of Hollywood's worst gay stereotypes, but instead makes Omar brave in the face of danger, confident in asserting his authority, and compassionate toward his neighbors. Omar, for instance, gives a free fix to a young female drug addict suffering withdrawal in "Old Cases" (1.4), donates money from his raids to poor people in his West Baltimore neigh-borhood, and, in one of *The Wire*'s best character sketches, treats his grand-mother with unerring respect throughout the program's early seasons. Omar, therefore, resembles the classic Western hero more closely than the show's ostensible protagonist, Jimmy McNulty. Such traits, along with Omar's unflinching observance of his personal code—Omar only targets people who work in the drug trade, forswears profanity, and refuses to threaten his rivals' family members—explains why he became so popular with *Wire* viewers that then-Senator Barack Obama, during his 2008 presidential campaign, named Omar *The Wire*'s best character and reaffirmed this judgment during a 2012 interview conducted in the White House.[1]

Kima Greggs, by contrast, illustrates heteronormative thinking in dif-ferent ways. Her sexual relationship with Cheryl never provokes the derisive comments that attend Omar's interest in men, but instead becomes the object of lascivious attention by Herc Hauk and other male colleagues. Their behav-ior reflects, sometimes baldly, the double standard regarding lesbian sex, which retains its capacity to titillate, arouse, and hold straight men spell-bound. Herc and his partner, Detective Ellis Carver (Seth Gilliam), specu-late about how "hot" Kima and Cheryl's coupling must be in the series pilot

"The Target" (Simon, 2002c), while Carver interrogates Kima's lesbianism in "The Detail" (Simon, 2002d) by saying, "Kima, if you don't mind me asking, when was it that you first figured you liked women better than men?" Kima replies, "I mind you asking" not merely because Carver's question distracts her from the task at hand (snapping surveillance photos of Barksdale soldiers selling drugs), but because, despite Carver's polite demeanor, his question constructs her sexual orientation as something that she had to deduce, to calculate, or, in his words, to figure. Heterosexuality, Carver implies, is such a default position that neither he, Herc, McNulty, nor any straight woman in *The Wire* underwent a similar process of recognition about their orientation, thereby casting Kima's lesbianism as a foreign territory to be explored or, in the words of *The Wire Blog*'s Peter Honig (2012), "a math problem" to be solved. This short scene encapsulates heteronormativity so well that it can initiate provocative discussions about heterosexual privilege; the historical, cultural, and religious exclusion of gayness and lesbianism to marginal, unnatural, and deviant forms of sexuality; and male heterosexuality's primacy as the model by which all people are judged.

Kima's relationship with Cheryl begins deteriorating in Season Two to the point that, by the third-season episode "Dead Soldiers" (Lehane, 2004), while drinking bottled beer near the railroad tracks that McNulty uses as a personal, late-night getaway, the two colleagues begin discussing their career's effect on intimate relationships. Kima even says, "Don't tell my I'm the same kind of asshole…. Jesus, I'm turning into McNulty," in a scene that acknowledges *The Wire*'s heteronormative assumptions. This development is especially fruitful for demonstrating queer theory's approaches to heteronormativity. *The Wire*, in this and related sequences, discredits heteronormative assumptions as little more than the restrictive, binary formulations of human sexuality that privilege straight couples as culturally, legally, and morally superior to gay and lesbian relationships. *The Wire*, by foregrounding Kima and Omar, depicts a broader range of sexual orientations, interactions, and behaviors than standard commercial television normally permits, suggesting that gay and lesbian characters are as normal as their straight counterparts.

Building Gender

The multiple attitudes toward gayness and lesbianism that *The Wire*'s characters express also enable students to understand two significant principles that queer theory shares with feminism, critical-race studies, postcolonialism, and poststructuralism: (1) the cultural construction of identity, in this case one's sexual identity (or, more accurately, identities), and (2) essentialism. When students accept without question heterosexuality as the primary, fundamental, and natural way of being in the world, they engage in essentialist thinking without even realizing it. Annamarie Jagose (1996), for instance, famously defines the term *queer* as "mark[ing] a suspension of identity as something fixed, coherent and natural" (p. 98) in *Queer Theory* (known in subsequent editions as *Queer Theory: An Introduction*). Jagose explains how the term *queer*

> describes those gestures or analytical models which dramatise incoherencies in the allegedly stable relations between chromosomal sex, gender and sexual desire. Resisting that model of stability—which claims heterosexuality as its origin, when it is more properly its effect—queer focuses on mismatches between sex, gender and desire [p. 3].

Essentialism—or the belief that human identity comprises innate, universal traits (or essences) that fully describe a person's existence—cannot long survive Jagose's formulation, which decenters heterosexuality's dominance (as a method of describing "natural" human relations) by demolishing the primacy of any single sexual identity or orientation. For Jagose (1996), the term *queer* makes fixed, coherent, natural sexual identities impossible. Jagose does not deny that people identify themselves by specific sexual orientations in their personal lives, but rather emphasizes how these identifications remain provisional; how they develop against specific historical and cultural pressures that change over time; and how, as a result, we can never accept terms like *homosexual, heterosexual, gay, lesbian,* and *straight* (among many others) as stable indicators of human sexuality. These labels, in a move typical of poststructuralist theory, develop within a massively complex field of historical, economic, religious, and cultural signifiers to become fluid markers of sexual identity.

Nikki Sullivan (2003), indeed, opens the inaugural chapter of *A Critical Introduction to Queer Theory* by writing

> I want to begin with the suggestion that sexuality is not natural, but rather, is discursively constructed. Moreover, sexuality, as we shall see, is constructed, experienced, and understood in culturally and historically specific ways. Thus we could say that there can be no true or correct account of heterosexuality, of homosexuality, of bisexuality, and so on. Indeed, these very categories for defining particular kinds of relationships and practices are culturally and historically specific and have not operated in all cultures at all times [p. 1].

This paragraph so concisely summarizes the work of poststructuralist theory that it doubles as a good launching pad for students mystified by the frequently arcane discussions they encounter in essays and monographs devoted to queer theory. *The Wire* serves a similar function, particularly when students consider how Kima Greggs and Omar Little fulfill different (and occasionally conflicted) roles in the program's narrative that cannot be restricted to their status as lesbian or gay characters. By traversing this ever-changing, symbolic territory, both characters demonstrate their sexual orientation to be fluid, unfixed, and discursively formed.

Kima, for instance, receives no judgment from McNulty when she tells him that she dates women in "The Buys" (Simon, 2002e), to which McNulty responds, "that's another thing we have in common. I date women, too." McNulty's comfort with her revelation prompts Kima to tell him about her decision to "come out of the closet" early in her career, when she realized that lesbianism confers personal and professional benefits: her straight male co-workers, whom Kima refers to as "dogs," do not try to seduce her, while, more importantly, they perceive her as tough enough to do the hard job of policing Baltimore's streets. McNulty agrees with this final notion, saying that the only other female police officer he ever knew who was "worth a damn" was also a lesbian. Kima and McNulty's conversation demonstrates how lesbianism, at least for them, becomes what anthropologist Claude Lévi-Strauss (1987) calls a floating signifier, a term without fixed referents that, because it has no agreed-upon single definition, can mean whatever users wish (or need) it to mean. Associating lesbianism with toughness, for instance, invokes the well-known stereotype that all lesbians are rough, masculine characters who dominate the people around them rather than meekly making their way through the world. They are, in popular parlance, butch, and certainly not femme. Kima, however, is neither stereotypically butch nor femme, even saying, "I look like I could go either way" to illustrate how lesbianism is not a single, secure, or static identity for her (or, by implication, for anyone else). Kima, however, knows that projecting the image of a more masculine woman gains respect from colleagues in her straight, male-dominated workplace while also curtailing their sexual advances. Kima, in other words, plays the different roles set by American society for lesbians when she deems it necessary, navigating them so skillfully that McNulty, who asks, "So everybody figured this out but me?," remains mystified by Kima's sexual orientation until she reveals it.

McNulty's responses in this scene are fascinating precisely because they acknowledge how Kima's gender identity is a cultural construction, yet troubling because they depend upon essentialized ideas that reify rigid boundaries between male and female behavior (lesbian cops, for McNulty, are more manly/masculine than their straight female peers and more valuable as colleagues because they resemble straight men). McNulty's ignorance of Kima's lesbianism demonstrates that she does not behave in ways that he (the representative of straight, White American society) defines as stereotypically queer. McNulty also reveals his deeply seated, unthinking sexism by immediately associating Kima's professional competence (her logical mind, her willingness to challenge authority, and her physical aggressiveness) with masculine traits. Kima, by appearing neither butch nor femme, strengthens McNulty's respect for her because he judges their similarities to be greater than their differences. Kima, indeed, plays the various roles demanded by conventional U.S. social expectations (what Michael Warner calls "het culture") that she has traversed her entire career.

Kima, in this scene and throughout *The Wire*, embodies the gender role-playing that Judith Butler (1990) analyzes in *Gender Trouble*:

> The appearance of an abiding substance or gendered self, what the psychiatrist Robert Stoller refers to as a "gender core," is thus produced by a regulation of attributes along culturally established lines of coherence.... In this sense, *gender* is not a noun, but neither is it a set of free-floating attributes, for we have seen the substantive effect of gender is performatively produced and compelled by the regulatory practices of gender coherence.... There is no gender identity behind the expressions of gender; that identity is performatively constituted by the very "expressions" that are said to be its results [p. 25].

The expressions of Kima's lesbianism, in other words, help construct her sexual identity rather than emanating from an essential core that imposes lesbian traits, behaviors, and appearances upon her. The discursive nature of Kima's sexual identity exposes her ability to recognize which aspects of lesbianism suit her at particular moments, to play up or play down those traits as required, and to move among these various roles so fluidly that she not merely escapes, but indeed repudiates rigid labels (including the label *lesbian*, a word that Kima rarely utters in *The Wire*'s sixty episodes). Having inherited cultural, political, and social ideas about what a lesbian is (and may be), Kima not only creates her own spectrum of sexual identities but also navigates this continuum by choosing to embrace or discard different roles depending upon circumstances. Kima does not always do so consciously, but her conversation with McNulty in "The Buys" (Simon, 2002e) dramatizes her awareness of her sexual orientation's manufactured nature.

Kima, therefore, helps students understand how essentialist definitions of sexual identity are themselves fabrications that both restrict and liberate LGBTQ characters. Omar serves a similar purpose, with his gayness becoming secondary to his effectiveness in disrupting the Barksdale and Stanfield drug organizations' movements to acquire, consolidate, and perpetuate their own power on West Baltimore's streets. Omar never discusses his sexuality with anyone in the same fashion that Kima does with McNulty, but his ability to resist the hateful stereotypes with which Avon Barksdale, Stringer Bell, and Marlo Stanfield impugn him dramatizes how Omar's role as fearless stickup artist remains as powerful as his gayness. In his private life, Omar enjoys male companions and lovers. In his professional activities, Omar refuses to apologize for these preferences, but also does not allow them to define him so narrowly that they constrain his effectiveness or force him to develop a "gender core" in Stoller's sense of this term. Essentialist notions of gayness, of masculinity, and of femininity have little purchase with Omar or Kima, making them ideal test cases for graduate and undergraduate seminars in which students struggle to better understand queer theory's foundational concepts, especially the permeable, unstable, and porous boundaries among gender labels and identities that Butler, Jagose, and Sedgwick anatomize.

Another factor about Omar's and Kima's personalities bears upon this discussion. Both are terrific observers of the people and places around them whose patient concentration allows them to judge human motives and behaviors more accurately than many other *Wire* characters. Omar, for instance, willingly surveils Barksdale and Stanfield drug crews longer than the police, helping explain his successful stash-house raids. Kima becomes similarly astute in her detective work, developing what McNulty's longtime partner, Detective William "Bunk" Moreland (Wendell Pierce), calls "soft eyes": the ability to perceive every aspect of a crime scene, taking in details that other cops miss because they are not open to unexpected possibilities. Kima is a keen observer of human behavior, making her interrogations more successful than even McNulty's and Moreland's, while Omar adeptly ferrets information from Barksdale and Stanfield employees by using his fearsome reputation to intimidate them.

Both characters listen to others as much as they talk, best illustrated by Omar's willingness to hear out Brother Mouzone in the opening scene of "Middle Ground" (Pelecanos, 2004) despite Mouzone pointing a loaded weapon at him. Omar, betraying no fear when he recognizes that Mouzone seeks information for his own revenge campaign against Stringer Bell, simply says—in an iconic *Wire* moment—"Omar listenin.'" Omar, in this scene, resolutely refuses to degenerate into the crazed, fearful gay man that conventional Hollywood productions would endorse. He, like Kima, moves from one persona to another throughout *The Wire* to dramatize how the labels *gay*, *lesbian*, and *queer* are moving targets, floating signifiers, and cultural constructions.

Cast(ing) Away

Even so, Omar and Kima cannot choose to play whatever roles they wish at any time because, like all people, they exist within cultural, historical, and social limitations that intersect, overlap, and interpenetrate one another. This ceaseless play of influences constructs gender identities as complex constellations of habits, ideas, and behaviors that no one can fully articulate. Jonathan Culler (2011) highlights gender identity's performative aspects in *Literary Theory: A Very Short Introduction* by writing, "You become a man or a woman by repeated acts, which ... depend on social conventions, habitual ways of doing something in a culture" (p. 104). These socially established ways of being a man or a woman do not mean, according to Culler, that gender is a choice, a role you put on, as you choose clothes to put on in the morning. That would suggest that there is an ungendered subject prior to gender who chooses, whereas in fact to be a subject at all is to be gendered: you can't, in this regime of gender, be a person without being male or female [p. 104].

Culler's analysis of Judith Butler's vital contribution to queer theory underscores the complex interplay of ideas, traits, and behaviors that stage gender identity as what Butler calls, at different points in *Gender Trouble*, both a cultural construction and a social production. Omar and Kima, by this reckoning, play different roles (or adopt various personae) to fashion their gender identities, which, in the end, forces them to remake themselves depending upon the circumstances they face, the needs of the moment, and the sociocultural forces in play. Omar and Kima, in other words, do not simply cast themselves in whatever role seems most convenient, even if their intermittent control of this process accounts for a good deal of their character development throughout *The Wire*'s sixty episodes, but instead respond, often unconsciously, to the social conventions that form, influence, and limit how they perceive themselves. Omar's and Kima's behavioral norms, or, in Butler's terms, the expressions that simultaneously reflect and constitute these norms, help manufacture their sexual identities, becoming part of the unending cultural cycle of identity construction, production, and performance that Butler examines in *Gender Trouble*.

This more nuanced appraisal of Omar and Kima's roleplaying in *The Wire* resonates with their status as characters in a commercial television series. Issues of casting become crucial because choosing the wrong actor for a role can condemn the character, the performer, the audience, and the program to years of misery. David Simon, thankfully, selects two accomplished actors whose talent and hard work make Omar and Kima fascinating to watch. Michael K. Williams and Sonja Sohn are so good in their roles that Omar and Kima become remarkable small-screen characters that Williams and Sohn, along with *The Wire*'s writing staff, sustain across five seasons. This notable achievement causes Francine Prose (2010), in "Ten Things Art Can Do," her speech accepting Washington University in St. Louis's 2010 International Humanities Medal, to identify "every moment of Michael K. Williams's portrait of Omar Little in David Simon's *The Wire*" (p. 6) as an example of her first dictum, "Art can be beautiful" (p. 5).

That Simon chose two straight actors to play these queer roles can trigger productive student discussions about the history of cinematic casting practices. For decades, Hollywood's unwritten rules forbade gay, lesbian, and bisexual actors from revealing their orientations for fear of offending mass audiences, whose homophobia was presumed by studio and network executives to run so deep that learning about their favorite stars' LGBTQ identities would cost their parent corporations significant profits. The best-known example, at least from Hollywood's so-called Golden Age of the 1940s through the 1960s, was Rock Hudson (stage name for Roy Scherer, Jr.), an actor who so completely embodied American masculinity that he married his agent Henry Wilson's secretary, Phyllis Gates, in 1955 to hide his homosexuality. Hudson so carefully guarded his private life that his 1985 death (due to AIDS complications) shocked many fans by exposing his gayness to public scrutiny. LGBTQ actors, as a result, have long played straight roles, with Jodie Foster, Ian McKellen, Cynthia Nixon, and George Takei being notable examples. Hollywood, in an unsurprising development, has an equally long tradition of straight actors playing gay roles, with Billy Crystal in *Soap*; Hilary Swank in *Boys Don't Cry* (1999); Philip Seymour Hoffman in *Capote* (2005); and Annette Bening and Julianne Moore in *The Kids Are All Right* (2010) being relevant examples.

These factors raise questions about Simon's decision to cast Williams and Sohn as *The Wire*'s most notable queer characters. Were good gay and lesbian actors unavailable for these roles? Did Simon specifically search for gay and lesbian actors to play these parts or did he encourage an open casting call? Were other straight actors considered to play Omar and Kima who perhaps refused to perform queer sex scenes? How did Simon prepare Williams and Sohn to play their characters, if at all? Such queries demonstrate the fraught territory that casting represents in American cinema and television, particularly when issues of accurate representation become part of the discussion. The dearth of queer characters on American television, once almost total, may have changed since the 1980s and the complexity of queer characterizations may have improved since the 1990s, but debating whether or not queer performers should play queer roles gets to the heart of how we define gender identity: as an essence, as a social production, or as a mediation of these possibilities. That Williams and Sohn so capably play Omar and Kima suggests that sexual identity is, indeed, multivalent and flexible, just as Rock Hudson's firm command of heterosexual roles (particularly in 1959's *Pillow Talk*, 1961's *Lover Come Back*, and 1964's *Send Me No Flowers*, the trilogy of romantic comedies he made with Doris Day) demonstrates that gay actors can convincingly play straight roles.

Producers frequently resort to clichés about wanting the best actor for the role, but the longtime exclusion of LGBTQ actors from American film and television (or the demand that such performers hide their sexuality) means that they endured decades of unfair treatment that only began reversing itself in the late 1980s and early 1990s. Queer theory permits students to think more deeply about how such representations affect viewers and performers. In terms of *The Wire*, discussing the credibility of Michael K. Williams' and Sonja Sohn's acting helps students interrogate concepts such as heteronormativity (does Simon endorse heteronormative assumptions by casting straight actors in queer roles?), essentialism (what does it mean to play a role as "straight" or "gay"?), and the cultural construction of gender identity (how do Williams and Sohn succumb to, resist, or modify queer stereotypes when playing Omar and Kima?). These questions may not have definitive answers, but they indicate just how rich a text *The Wire* can be, especially in courses devoted to queer theory.

David Simon's *The Wire*, therefore, is a boon to educators struggling to find ways to make queer theory pertinent to university students. The program's complex representations of Omar Little and Shakima Greggs, along with its other LGBTQ characters, can provoke passionate discussions among students who may never have encountered queer theory before stepping foot on a university campus. Assigning *The Wire* in courses (or units) devoted to queer theory should produce intelligent conversations and lively seminar essays that avoid the somber pedantry that besmirches literary theory's reputation after decades of academic institutionalization. Students and instructors, indeed, will have tremendous fun watching, analyzing, and evaluating *The Wire* in light of queer theory's insights. This development, in perhaps the best testament to *The Wire*'s effectiveness as a pedagogical tool, demonstrates just how alive, relevant, and significant queer theory has been (and remains) to understanding the shifts in America's civic regard for its LGBTQ citizens.

NOTE

1. See Coolican (2008) and Simmons (2012) for more information. Obama, after naming Omar his favorite character, tells the *Las Vegas Sun*'s J. Patrick Coolican, "That's not an endorsement. He's not my favorite person, but he's a fascinating character." Obama tells *Grantland*'s Bill Simmons, in a March 2012 interview conducted in the White House, "It's got to be Omar, right? That guy is unbelievable, right?" when Simmons asks Obama who the best *Wire* character of all time is.

REFERENCES

Barash, N., and J. Boni. (Creators). (1972–1973). *The corner bar* [Television series]. Hollywood: American Broadcasting Company.

Burns, E. (Writer), D. Simon and E. Burns. (Story), and P. Medak. (Director). (2002, June 30). The pager [Television series episode]. In Simon, D. (Producer), *The wire*. Baltimore, MD: Blown Deadline Productions & Home Box Office.

Butler, J. (1990). *Gender trouble: Feminism and the subversion of identity*. New York: Routledge.

Cholodenko, L. (Director). (2010). *The kids are all right* [Motion picture]. United States: Focus Features and Gilbert Films.

Coolican, J.P. (2008, January 14). Obama goes gloves off, head-on. *The Las Vegas Sun*. Retrieved from http://www.lasvegassun.com/news/2008/jan/14/obama-gloves-off/.

Culler, J. (2011). *Literary theory: A very short introduction*. Oxford: Oxford University Press.

Eagleton. T. (1983). *Literary theory: An introduction*. Minneapolis: University of Minnesota Press.

Ford, J. (Director). (1962). *The man who shot liberty valance* [Motion picture]. United States: Paramount Pictures and John Ford Productions.

Foucault, M. (1976 & 1984). *The history of sexuality* (Vols. 1–3). Paris, France: Éditions Gallimard.

Gordon, M. (Director). (1959). *Pillow talk* [Motion picture]. United States: United Artists.

Harris, S. (Creator). (1977–1981). *Soap* [Television series]. Hollywood: American Broadcasting Company.

Honig, P. (2012, July 6). 1.3: Kima's one true love. [Web log comment]. Retrieved from http://www.thewireblog.net/season-1/episode3_thebuys/kima-one-true-love/.

Jagose, A. (1996). *Queer theory*. New York: New York University Press.

Jameson. F. (1979). Reification and utopia in mass culture. *Social Text, 1*, 130–148.

Jewison, N. (Director). *Send me no flowers* [Motion picture]. United States: United Artists.

Laven, A. (Creator). (1958–1963). *The rifleman* [Television series]. Hollywood: American Broadcasting Company.

Lehane, D. (Writer), D. Simon and D. Lehane (Story), and R. Bailey (Director). (2004, October 3). Dead soldiers [Television series episode]. In Simon, D. (Producer), *The wire*. Baltimore, MD: Blown Deadline Productions & Home Box Office.

Lèvi-Strauss, C. (1987). *Introduction to the work of marcel mauss*. (F. Baker, trans.) London: Routledge & Kegan Paul. (Original work published in 1950).

Lippman, L. (2004). The women of the wire (no, seriously). In Alvarez, R., *The wire: Truth be told* (pp. 55–58). New York: Pocket Books.

Mann, D. (Director). (1961). *Lover come back* [Motion picture]. United States: United Artists.

Milch, D. (Creator). (2004–2006). *Deadwood* [Television series]. Hollywood: Home Box Office.

Miller, B. (Director). (2005). *Capote* [Motion picture]. United States: Sony Pictures Classics.

Peirce, K. (Director). (1999). *Boys don't cry* [Motion picture]. United States: Fox Searchlight Pictures.

Pelecanos, G. (Writer), and J. Chappelle (Director). (2004, December 12). Middle ground [Television series episode]. In Simon, D. (Producer), *The wire*. Baltimore, MD: Blown Deadline Productions & Home Box Office.

Prose, F. (2011 January/May). Ten things art can do. *Belles Lettres, 9*(2), 5–9.

Sedgwick, E. (1985). *Between men: English literature and male homosocial desire*. New York: Columbia University Press.

Sedgwick, E. (1990). *Epistemology of the closet*. Berkeley: University of California Press.

Simmons, B. (2012, March 1). B.s. report transcript: Barack Obama. *Grantland*. Retrieved from http://grantland.com/the-triangle/b-s-report-transcript-barack-obama/.

Simon, D. (Writer), D. Simon, and E. Burns (Story), and B. Anderson (Director). (2002a, August 11). The cost [Television series episode]. In D. Simon (Producer), *The wire*. Baltimore, MD: Blown Deadline Productions & Home Box Office.

Simon, D. (Writer), D. Simon, and E. Burns (Story), and E. Bianchi (Director). (2002b, July 7). The wire [Television series episode]. In D. Simon (Producer), *The wire*. Baltimore, MD: Blown Deadline Productions & Home Box Office.

Simon, D. (Writer), D. Simon, and E. Burns (Story), and C. Johnson (Director). (2002c, June 2). The target [Television series episode]. In Simon, D. (Producer), *The wire*. Baltimore, MD: Blown Deadline Productions & Home Box Office.

Simon, D. (Writer), D. Simon, and E. Burns (Story), and C. Johnson (Director). (2002d, June 9). The detail [Television series episode]. In Simon, D. (Producer), *The wire*. Baltimore, MD: Blown Deadline Productions & Home Box Office.

Simon, D. (Writer), D. Simon, and E. Burns (Story), and P. Medak (Director). (2002e, June 16). The buys [Television series episode]. In Simon, D. (Producer), *The wire*. Baltimore, MD: Blown Deadline Productions & Home Box Office.

Simon, D. (Writer), D. Simon, and E. Burns (Story), and C. Virgo (Director). (2002f, June 23). Old cases [Television series episode]. In Simon, D. (Producer), *The wire*. Baltimore, MD: Blown Deadline Productions & Home Box Office.

Simon, D. (Writer), D. Simon, and E. Burns (Story), and E. Bianchi (Director). (2003, June 1). Ebb tide [Television series episode]. In Simon, D. (Producer), *The wire*. Baltimore, MD: Blown Deadline Productions & Home Box Office.

Sullivan, N. (2003). *A critical introduction to queer theory*. New York: New York University Press.

Warner, M. (1993). Introduction. In M. Warner (Ed.), *Fear of a queer planet: Queer politics and social theory* (pp. vii–xxxi). Minneapolis: University of Minnesota Press.

Zinneman, F. (Director). (1952). *High noon* [Motion picture]. United States: United Artists.

Žižek, S. (1989). *The sublime object of ideology*. London: Verso Books.

Žižek, S. (Ed.). (1992). *Everything you always wanted to know about Lacan (but were afraid to ask Hitchcock)*. London: Verso Books.

What Then?

The Cultural Forum of The Wire

JOE ALLEN *and* CHRISTOPHER S. TOENES

Television and Popular Culture

Film has long been accepted as a field worthy of study and instruction in academia while the mass medium of television less so. However, in the last two decades, television has undergone a radical transformation. In *Difficult Men*, Brett Martin (2013) argues the cultural importance of this recent development, "The open-ended, twelve-or thirteen-episode serialized drama was maturing into its own, distinct art form. What's more, it had become the signature American art form of the first decade of the twenty-first century" (p. 11). David Chase's *The Sopranos* (1999), as has been well documented by Martin and others, dramatically altered the landscape of television and subsequently the way television is used in academia. David Simon and Ed Burns took full advantage of the space *The Sopranos* created on HBO and developed *The Wire* (2002), a show that further pushed the literary, social, and political envelope of television with a drama so rich in characters, themes, and issues that it has proven to be well-suited to rigorous analysis and real-world applications in a wide variety of college classrooms.

Using a television show that dramatically examines income inequality in the confines of a college class raises a number of questions for students. What has been the impact of the endless war on drugs and mandatory minimums on urban communities? What has caused the loss of jobs, increasing poverty, crumbling infrastructure, and abandoned buildings in the rust belt? Why do politicians "juke-the-stats" rather than speak the truth? Asking students to consider *The Wire*'s impact on American culture is still a formidable task. Did *The Wire* have any direct or tangible impact on American culture, power structures, and institutions? Is it simply enough to be drawn into the debate over the significance of the show, the cultural forum of *The Wire*? This essay hopes to examine the pedagogical implications of the show, using the authors' experiences in two arenas, Allen's use of full seasons of *The Wire* in teaching undergraduates two different courses, Popular Culture and Introduction to Cultural Studies, at a community college in upstate New York, and Toenes' research supporting a course for undergraduates on social welfare solutions at a university in North Carolina.

The Wire's unflinching honesty and brutal realism help to make it so teachable, but prior to *The Wire* such realism was not accepted by major network television producers or audiences. In *The Revolution Was Televised* (2012), Allan Sepinwall writes in his intro about *Oz*, the HBO show that helped set the stage for *The Sopranos* and *The Wire*, "When Fontana pitched even mild versions of Oz to the broadcast networks, he says he was told, 'Oh, they're all too nasty. Where are the heroes? Where are the victories?' These questions simply didn't apply to HBO" (p. 25). When Tony Soprano brutally strangles the "rat" Febby Petrulio just after he drops off his daughter on a college visit in the infamous "College" episode (Manos Jr., Chase & Coulter, 1999), the scene is still hard to watch. Chris Albrecht, president of HBO Original Programming at the time, yelled at Chase after reading the script, "You've created one of the most compelling characters on television in the last twenty years and you're going to ruin him in the fifth episode! We're going to lose the audience" (Martin, 2013, p. 92). Chase would not relent. Tony had to kill Petrulio. Sepinwall accurately notes, "it left no possible confusion about what kind of man we were watching and what kind of show this was" (p. 41). Nonetheless, audiences really could not turn away. Other creators, writers, and show-runners took note, as did FX, AMC, Showtime, and Netflix.

Today, TV audiences, including college students, are quite comfortable consuming season or multi-season long story arcs, without clear-cut heroes or resolutions, either in real-time or in marathon binge-viewing sessions after-the-fact. Shows such as *The Walking Dead, Breaking Bad, Orange Is the New Black, Game of Thrones* and the like are now the media texts of choice for many college students. They would rather binge watch *House of Cards* than go see the latest Hollywood superhero predetermined blockbuster. Meaning is also made in real-time with live blogging and twitter posts, and then that meaning is endlessly refracted around our culture both online and in print.

For *The Wire*, a show so unpopular it was almost canceled after every season, it is enjoying a vibrant second life. What once seemed so revolutionary is now widely accepted both inside academia and out. Probably the best-known scholar to lead academia's praise of the show is esteemed sociologist William Julius Wilson of Harvard, who exclaimed in a 2008 seminar about *The Wire*,

The Wire's exploration of sociological themes is truly exceptional. Indeed I do not hesitate to say that it has done more to enhance our understandings of the challenges of urban life and urban inequality than any other media event or scholarly publication, including studies by social scientists [Wilson, 2010].

The Ongoing Cultural Forum of The Wire

David Simon, though, is skeptical of all the after-the-fact accolades and class debates. Yet, because of the ever increasing cultural relevance of *The Wire*, his willingness to publicly engage any latecomers keeps the dialogue ongoing. He honestly expressed his disdain in a *New York Times* J. Egner interview in 2012:

I do have a certain amused contempt for the number of people who walk sideways into the thing and act like they were there all along.... For people to be picking it apart now like it's a deck of cards or like they were there the whole time or they understood it the whole time—it's wearying. Because no one was there in the beginning, or the middle, or even at the end. Our numbers continued to decline from Season 2 on [para. 14].

Season Five's attack on the media already began questioning why his show and the issues examined had been ignored, by viewers, by the news, by politicians. No best-drama Emmy! Simon's long-simmering anger is palpable. He is unmistakably not comfortable in the clear change in status of his show and, in the broader sense, current television itself.

When students encounter *The Wire* in the classroom for the first time, they are engaging with a visual text that gained cultural relevancy from Simon's embattled sense of its cultish status to garner acknowledgements from policymakers who could actually affect change on the social issues it addresses. Former Attorney General Eric Holder in a speech asked David Simon to do another season of *The Wire*, in hopes of showing off his ability to drop hip popular cultural references. Simon later replied, "The attorney general's kind remarks are noted and appreciated. We are prepared to go to work on season 6 of The Wire if the Department of Justice is equally ready to reconsider and address its continuing prosecution of our misguided, destructive and dehumanizing drug prohibition" (Gustini, 2011, para 2). Did Holder watch Season Three and the critique of politicians and their empty rhetoric of reform, especially on the war on drugs and the war on poverty?

President Obama also watched *The Wire* and even noted that Omar was his favorite character. In "Obama's TV Picks: Anything Edgy with Hints of Reality, " according to Michael Shear (2013), David Simon "wonders whether Mr. Obama was drawn to the show because it dealt so directly with the issues of social and economic strife" (para. 11). Shear quotes Simon's response to Obama's praise, "'The Wire' was one of the few shows that was about the other America. It was set in the inner city. The characters were of a class that has been left behind economically and politically" (para. 12). Obama's second term has at times made fighting social and economic inequality the highest priority. Season Four's emphasis on the inner-city school vividly portrays the challenges and obstacles. "The idea that a child may never be able to escape that poverty because she lacks a decent education or health care, or a community that views her future as their own," Mr. Obama said, "that should offend all of us and it should compel us to action. We are a better country than this" (Shear, para. 14). Here, Simon probably agreed. He hoped his show would compel us to action.

However, Simon anticipated the possibility that *The Wire* would not spur meaningful economic and political change, even if presidents and attorney generals were keenly watching. One of *The Wire's* recurring characters in later seasons is Bunny Colvin, who is a nod to former Baltimore Mayor Kurt L. Schmoke but can also sound a bit like Simon at times. Colvin's commentary in Episode 13, "Final Grades," the finale of Season Four, when the "corner boy" school support program dies, it foreshadows Simon's frustration over the lack of meaningful impact of his show (Simon, Burns & Dickerson, 2006). Colvin and David Parenti, a Professor of Sociology at the University of Maryland, meet with Mayor Carcetti's advisors in hopes of saving and ideally expanding their corner boy program (Simon, Burns, & Dickerson, 2006). As soon as Colvin bluntly states "As it is, we're leaving them all behind anyway. We just don't want to admit it," the meeting is over. Bunny is furious as they exit, "It seems like every time I open my mouth in this town, I'm telling people something they don't want to know" (Simon, Burns & Dickerson, 2006). Parenti envisions all the great research that will come of the project. In this episode, (Simon, Burns, & Dickerson, 2006), rich with critique of the hollow role academic research can play in education reform, Parenti continues, "We get the grant. We study the problem. We propose solutions. If they listen, they listen. If they don't, it still makes for great research. What we publish on this is going to get a lot of attention." Bunny quickly replies, "From who? From other researchers. Academics." Bunny laughs and says, "Academics? What, they gonna study your study. When do this shit change?" (Simon, Burns, & Dickerson, 2006). In one swipe, Simon deconstructs the whole enterprise of teaching *The Wire* to undergraduates. Will *The Wire* compel us to action beyond the class discussions?

Interestingly, Simon has actively kept the conversation going about *The Wire* by continually discussing it in interviews and commenting on the responses of others. His post on his blog "The Audacity of Despair" (2013) regarding former Baltimore police commissioner Fred Bealefeld, "Mr. Bealefeld's Come-to-Jesus Moment" is a useful example of his debate strategy. After retiring, Bealefeld commented on the misguided war on drugs, "We wound up alienating a lot of folks in building this gigantic jail system in our country." Simon, though, is quick to criticize Bealefeld who made these comments from the safety of retirement. Bealefeld also never liked *The Wire*. Simon explains, "He argued that *The Wire* was instead a reflection of 20-year-old truth and therefore a dated narrative of Baltimore." Even though his show finished filming in 2007, Simon still clearly wants to be part of the debate of the war on drugs:

> We were, in fact, making arguments that had never been voiced or acted upon by anyone in Baltimore politics or law enforcement in any way, that these arguments had yet to find any favor in the department or at City Hall, and we were doing so because we believed and still believe in those arguments.

The more Simon engages Bealefeld, President Obama, Eric Holder, the late-comers to *The Wire*, and anyone else who appears in his crosshairs, *The Wire* attains more and more cultural currency and meaning. Plus, now on many college campuses, semester after semester, class after class discussions about the meaning of *The Wire* and about the crucial question of the show's impact on American culture and income inequality are held. *The Wire* is what television critic James Mittell (2010) calls a "cultural forum" (284) in his comprehensive *Television and American Culture* where "differing visions coexist within programs" and "diverse ideas can be seen and heard" (284). Such forums can challenge and negotiate dominant ideologies of American culture.

Cultural Studies, the Classroom and *The Wire*

Still, the question remains: What is accomplished, both inside and outside the classroom, by exposing college students to *The Wire*? Learning how to apply a theoretical framework to a media text starts to answer this question. The field of cultural studies is notoriously difficult to define. Introducing its defining, and often debatable, characteristics to undergraduate students presents unique challenges; nonetheless, cultural studies is an ideal framework to analyze *The Wire*. Cultural studies is a mix of intellectual theory and political practice—both the creator and the critic hope to produce radical social change and cultural transformation. David Simon is no exception. In PBS's documentary about television *American in Primetime* (Yellin & Kramer, 2011), Simon states that his goal was journalistic: "What I'm interested in is politics and sociology and economics.... We were left alone and given sixty hours of television and at that point it's kind of incumbent on you to have something to say." Simply, figuring out what *The Wire* has to say about any of a number of social issues is exactly what makes the show so teachable.

Simon goes on to identify one of his central themes, "It was a show about the rigged game of modern life." *The Wire* analyzes the systems of power and the institutions that govern inner-city life. In *Cultural Studies and the Study of Popular Culture*, John Storey (2003) explains, "the relations between culture and power ... is the core interest of cultural studies" (p. 4). In the world of *The Wire*, the gangsters, the police department, the politicians, the education system, and the media all operate within hierarchies with well-established codes of behavior. The show examines how such structures operate from the perspective of both the dominant ideology and that of those trying to negotiate, resist, or reform dominant ideologies. Cultural studies is concerned with contesting power structures and institutions. As Storey explains, "Popular culture is an arena of struggle and negotiation between the interests of dominant groups and the interests of subordinate groups" (p. 4). *The Wire* itself negotiates so many of the dominant tropes of popular television. The scenes where the "corner boys" go to the steakhouse alone exemplify a class divide rarely glimpsed in primetime.

When students write open-ended response papers where they can explore whatever catches their attention the most, their endlessly varied reactions show they are already actively engaged in the process of making meaning regarding *The Wire*. Here, cultural studies can be easier to do than explain. Many note the realism of the show while others see a side of American cities that is largely invisible on television and in popular culture. They often note that *The Wire* feels far more real than any reality show they have ever seen.

The Wire is simply so uniquely engrossing, especially tracking multiple, complex, and overlapping plotlines of narratives that are not usually covered in the popular culture students are drawn to on their own, students naturally begin placing the show in the context of other television shows (or media) or other aspects of American culture. Cultural practices and texts, such as *The Wire*, must be understood in terms of other traits of the culture and ideology in question. According to Cary Nelson in *Manifesto of a Tenured Radical* (1997), "Cultural studies conceives culture relationally." Analysis is in relation "with other objects and cultural forces" (p. 65).

For Simon, the primary context is the globalization of capitalism, which has abandoned both the people and the infrastructure of American inner cities, particularly in the Northeastern rust belt. In "Yesterday's Tomorrow Today: Baltimore and the Promise of Reform," David Alff (2009) cites data: "Following World War II, the city lost over 213,00 residents.... Between 1970 and 1995, Baltimore lost over 95,000 manufacturing jobs" (p. 30). As the jobs left and the production lines closed, the population loss rapidly increased. In 1950, Baltimore's population was 949,708 and in 1970 it was 905,759, but by 2009 it had fallen to 637,418. With such a loss of capital, the infrastructure is likewise abandoned. In 1998, Baltimore had 40,000 vacant houses out of about 300,000 according to David Harvey in *Spaces of Hope* (2000). In "We ain't got no yard," Peter Clandfield (2009) accurately identifies the vacant houses as a central image in Season Four. Note how many scenes linger on the boarded up row houses, for instance in the last scene in Episode 11 after Detective Lester Freamon realizes they are serving as a tomb for the current kingpin Marlo Stanfield's bodies, the wide angle shot of Bunk looking at a street of vacant homes and pondering the unthinkable. The vacants and what they represent are, for many, the main character of Season Four.

Simon (2013) continues to speak widely about the failures of late-stage capitalism and its representation on the show: "It was about people who were worth less and who were no longer necessary, as maybe 10 or 15 percent of my country is no longer necessary to the operation of the economy." As cities are emptied of jobs and people, a chain of events follows. In *Bomb the Suburbs*, William Upski Wimsatt (2001) described Chicago's spiral in 2001, well before the recent recession:

> White and middle-class fear, white and middle-class flight, flight of jobs and capital, shrinking tax base, degradation of public services, accelerated suburban sprawl, destruction of countryside, race and wealth polarization, regional polarization, higher cost of government, declining public institutions, less contact between rich and poor, top-down poverty programs rigged to fail, more hostility toward the poor; more industries that exploit fear ... [prison, law, media], less opportunities for poor people, more desperation, more crime, more public fear, tighter security, less community life, less public life, less political participation, worse politicians, and less support for the common good [pp. 98–99].

Upski and Simon would have much to talk about. After *Homicide: A Life on the Killing Streets* (1991), Simon, now with former cop and middle-school teacher Ed Burns, shifted to the people left behind in the non-fiction book *The Corner: A Year in the Life of an Inner-City Neighborhood* (1998). In addition to the powerful story of Gary and Fran McCullough, their son Andre, and a host of other Baltimoreans drawn to the corner, the book has sections on corner ideology, the war on drugs, education, and welfare that set the stage for the broader perspective presented in *The Wire*. The section on the values of the corner is especially useful in redefining the corner as an economic engine of the inner city. With assembly lines shut down, the plants gone, the port being run down (see *The Wire*'s Season Two), Simon and Burns write, "The corner has a place for them, every last soul. Touts runners, lookouts, mules, stickup boys, stash stealers, enforcers, fiends, burn artists, police snitches—all are necessary in the world of the corner .... The corner *is* the neighborhood" (pp. 58, 70). Simon's previous work adds context to the realities of inner city life, which helps students understand the devastating impact of the loss of jobs in the rust belt and the way the corner fills the economic void.

The police, though, view the corner as occupied territory in the war on drugs. Like any war, this one has been good for business. Simon and Burns note that it is a "growth industry" for the "DEA, Customs, ATF, the joint regional task forces, local narcotic squads" who are "vested in this debacle" (p. 164). In *The New Jim Crow*, Michelle Alexander (2012) presented a devastating account of the war on drugs and the prison-industrial complex. Her statistics are staggering. Between 1980 and 1984, FBI antidrug funding increased from $8 million to $95 million (p. 49). The Department of Defense antidrug funding jumped from $33 million in 1982 to $1,042 million in 1991; during the same years, DEA anti-drug expenditures had a similar increase, from $86 to $1,026 million (p. 49). In August 1989, President Bush characterized drug use as "the most pressing problem facing the nation" (p. 55). One poll at the time reported that 64 percent thought "drugs were the most significant problem facing the nation" (p. 55). The dramatic surge in funding and likewise the surge in public sentiment were, as Alexander described "the product of a carefully orchestrated political campaign" (p. 55). The prison population exploded as Alexander documents: in the last 25 years, 350,000 to 2.3 million in prison (p. 93) with 7.3 million "under correctional control" (p. 101) and "more than 31 million people have been arrested for drug offenses since the war began" (p. 60). Politicians, who are at the mercy of public perception, must always be tough on crime, and no one would dare speak the truth about an unwinnable war by tallying its true cost to our society. Alice Goffman's recent book *On the Run: Fugitive Life in an American City* (2014) further examines the far-reaching impact of mass incarceration on families and neighborhoods, specifically in Philadelphia. Her powerful text provides more context for Simon's Baltimore and this unwinnable war.

One casualty of the war on drugs is the alienation of the inner-city community from public institutions and values. The dominant ideology of the American dream, and for Simon and Burns, "the rest of America—its dreams, myths, standards—has walked away from West Baltimore (*The Corner*, 1998, p. 278). In one scene from Season Four of the *The Wire*, Marlo Stanfield, the latest kingpin, steals a piece of candy in plain sight of the security guard. The guard reluctantly must respond and uphold his values. After all, he is just doing his job, working hard for his family. Marlo responds, "You want it to be one way." The guard looks perplexed, so Marlo repeats, "You want it to be one way. But it's the other way." This vague exchange provides an apt metaphor for examining many of Season Three and Season Four's themes and the way those issues challenge the dominant American ideologies of race, class, and geography.

One of those themes is the emphasis on statistical platitudes that elevate image over reality for a vaguely defined "public" or as Mayor Royce says near the end of Season Three, "for the sake of public perception." This is known as "juking the stats," from crime rates to test scores. The students who have been tested and tested since grade school in the No Child Left Behind era have an affinity for this concept. Examining how "juking the stats" operates in a political context is a central argument of *The Wire*'s institutional critique. In "In the Life of *The Wire*," Lorrie Moore (2010) explains:

> The most intriguing phrase Simon has used regarding *The Wire* is to say it is about the "the death of work." By this he means not just the loss of jobs, though there certainly is that, but the loss of integrity within our systems of work, the "juking of stats," the speaking of truth to power having been replaced with speaking what is most self-serving and pleasing to the higher-ups.

Such loss of integrity is inherent in institutional imperatives and hierarchal structures of power. In order to maintain the structure and one's position in the hierarchy, one must follow the chain of command rather than attempt any true reform. In *Discipline & Punish*, Michel Foucault (1979) theorizes at length on what he terms the carceral network. For power to function automatically:

> one must have a station in life, a recognizable identity, an individuality fixed once and for all.... In short, one should have a master, be caught up and situated within a hierarchy; one exists only when fixed in definite relations of domination ... [for] order to be maintained [p. 291].

Over and over in *The Wire*, characters, both on the street and in the law, follow the chain of command. The relationship between the individual and an institution runs through Seasons Three and Four. Simon and Seth Woods discuss this in a *Rolling Stone* interview (2006):

> SIMON: Every character, except for Omar, is a prisoner of an institutional malaise that is distinctly American and very typically postmodern.
> WOODS: But isn't the individual overcoming the institution a classic American dream?
> SIMON: Yet these stories feel so much more real to me. How many individuals are bigger than the institution they serve? How many devour an institution? I've never seen anybody devour an institution. You know what matters in America? The share price, that's what fucking matters.

For Seasons Three and Four, analyzing the relationship between an individual and an institution, especially potential reformers, and then broadening that analysis to other aspects of American culture and ideology is a project that attracts many students.

Moore (2011) noted students would best understand a television show's powerfully critical view of social problems when they could dialogue using things like blog posts but, ultimately, need a fair bit of guidance regarding how to watch the show and how to analyze the narrative. It is important to realize the preconceptions students often have about social welfare programs and economic inequality. While academics and analysts view social inequality as a systemic phenomenon, "Americans remain strongly disposed to the idea that individuals are largely responsible for their own economic situations," and two-thirds of Americans think that Blacks in the U.S. who cannot get ahead "are mostly responsibly for their own condition" while 18 percent say it is a result of discrimination (Chadda and Wilson, 2011, 2). Near the end of *The Corner*, Simon and Burns talk about the same mythology, "the required lie that allows us to render our judgments," that allows the rest of America to distance itself and ignore those left behind in its cities. They write, "If it was us … we'd get out, wouldn't we. We'd endure. Succeed. Thrive. No matter what, no matter how, we'd find the fucking exit" (pp. 477–8).

Season Four smashes these myths when the stories of middle-school students Randy, Duquan, Michael, and Sherrod are concluded. Much earlier in *The Corner*, Simon and Burns ask, "How do we bridge the chasm? How do we reconnect with those now lost to the corner world?" and then immediately answers their question with perhaps the best reason and outcome for using *The Wire* in a college classroom: "As a beginning at least, we need to shed our fixed perceptions and see it fresh. From the inside" (p. 60). A reader is able to discard such preconceived notions by living with Gary, Fran, and DeAndre for a year of their lives on *The Corner*. For the vast majority of students who study *The Wire*, so does watching and discussing either Season Three and Four in their respective entirety.

While examining the pedagogical implications of using this show in the classroom, it is important to remember *The Wire* itself focused on public education throughout an entire season. In "That's Got His Own," (Pelecanos, Burns, & Chappelle, 2006), Mr. Pryzbylewski, "Prez," the former police-turned-teacher is trying to teach a lesson on math and percentages, but the students press him on his marriage, leading to a discussion of intimacy. The scene starts with Prez introducing a math problem involving two couples, then the discussion turns to marriage, Prez's own marriage, and a definition of intimacy (Simon, Dickerson, 2006). Dutro and Kantor (2011) found that this scene

> shows Prez moving toward a pedagogy of reciprocal testimony and witness in which his role as witness to the life experiences of his students is reciprocated as he allows his students to bear witness to his own life outside of the classroom.

"Bearing witness" is a perfect way to describe Simon's realism when it comes to showing the characters. It is left to the audience to decide from the characters' representation in the show, how to judge them or by witnessing their story, become engaged in the struggle of which they are a part. Likewise, an underlying tenet of cultural studies believes that the audience is actively involved in the creation of meaning, and the meaning is multiple, diverse, and often contested.

Meanwhile, in Baltimore...

Actors from the show often deeply entrenched themselves in Baltimore's real life story. The cameos from Baltimore residents have been well documented by Marshall and Potter (2009) and others. Former Baltimore Mayor's Kurt L. Schmoke uttering the line to Mayor Royce, as Royce debated the free zones near the end of Season Three, "Soon, they will be calling you the most dangerous man in America" was the line he heard as Mayor when he argued drugs should be decriminalized. Melvin Williams, who played The Deacon, was once a powerful drug kingpin in Baltimore, known as "Little Melvin," arrested in a wiretap case by Ed Burns when he was Baltimore police. Williams is said to be the inspiration for character Avon Barksdale (Smith, 2008). Baltimore native Felicia Pearson, who portrayed Snoop, spent several years in prison for killing someone in self-defense before going to work on the show, and in March 2012, was accused of being involved in a drug ring (Hermann, 2012). Again, casework involved a wiretap. The real homicide detective Jay Landsman from *Homicide* plays officer Dennis Mello. The real women and men from *The Corner*, Fran Boyd, DeAndre McCullough, and Tyreeka Freamon all had small roles in later seasons. For Marshall and Potter, blurring the lines of Baltimore reality and fiction provide an "understanding of the urban life of modern America and ... some sense of hope for the American Dream" (12).

Other actors from *The Wire* took the show back to reality. New Orleans resident Wendell Pierce, who played officer Bunk Moreland, returned to his hometown after Katrina and first began building low-cost homes in Pontchartrain Park and then opened convenience stores with nutritious offerings in low-income areas (Black, 2012). Sonia Sohn, who played Shakima "Kima" Greggs, co-founded a nonprofit called Rewired for Change, which works with young people who are out on parole, and Sohn uses "scenes straight from *The Wire* to help make her point through education, media and advocacy" ("Fresh Air," 2012). Like Simon and Burns, according to Zabriskie (2012), her "facilitators needed credibility, so she recruited 'Elder' Ted Sutton, who in the late 1980s had been a shotgun-toting lieutenant under legendary Baltimore drug kingpin Melvin Williams but now counseled gang members looking to get out of the game, and Greg 'Shamsuddin' Carpenter, a convert to Islam who spent two decades in prison but now helped former inmates adjust to life on the outside." In addition, cast members of *The Wire* served on the board and helped fund the project.

"You gonna look out for me?"

The show's creators set up a revelatory lens for their players that in turn fosters a critical view that students can use to examine the preconceptions they often have. That is, the characters are conscious of being restricted by circumstances they did not create, but they continue to analyze their situations, and produce inventive alternatives (Zborowski, 2010). Character Duquan "Dukie" Weems has the most tenuous home life with family members struggling with drug addiction. He lives in abject poverty and is teased about it in school. Dukie lives largely outside of the social services world, and early in the season rejects actively participating in the drug commerce of the neighborhood, a readily available shortcut to escaping poverty. Yet, he is presented as knowledgeable about his situation, a scenario that clearly shows the failure of the "social contract." Dukie is teased for his body odor after not being able to shower regularly, and his only reprieve comes from his teacher, Prez, who is working outside of his official role. Ultimately, though, Prez cannot rescue Dukie who turns away from his promotion to high school and ends up on the corner.

Randy Wagstaff, another student focused on in Season Four and friend of Dukie's, is involved in the social services system and has a foster mother who is supportive until their home is firebombed. Randy ends up "getting chewed up by the system" (Pelecanos, Burns, & Chappelle, 2006) as Prez had feared, after this incident. He is sent to a group home, where he succumbs to more retribution for being suspected of being an informant. Sergeant Carver, who had been trying to protect Randy from the system, is in the end unable to prevent the firebombing nor the return to the group home. "That's Got His Own" (Pelecanos, Burns & Chappelle, 2006), the penultimate episode in Season Four, ends with the indelible image of Randy, who is like Dukie keenly aware of his scenario, yelling at Carver, "You gonna look out for me? You gonna look out for me!" (Pelecanos, Burns, & Chappelle, 2006) as Carver slowly and painfully walks down the hospital hallway. In these two examples, college students studying social issues like child welfare and social services policy are presented with a first-person view of just how these systems work and do not work. The show displays a safety net so tattered and torn, it barely catches anyone in its reach.

If reform mostly fails in *The Wire*, students should be challenged to examine the hard-to-quantify possibility of the show reforming an aspect of our culture. When Simon writes in "Finale Letter" (2008) before Season Five begins, he is essentially posing an essay topic:

> Why, if there is any truth to anything presented in *The Wire* over the last four seasons, does the truth go unaddressed by our political culture, by most of our mass media, and by our society in general…. *The Wire* is about the America we pay for and tolerate. Perhaps it is possible to pay for, and demand, something more.

However, the interplay between popular culture texts and the cultural forces is difficult to pinpoint. Did MTV's 16 and Pregnant lower the teen birthrate, as Kristof (2014) argues, "seriously?" However, at the very least, by watching and discussing *The Wire* in undergraduate classes, students, like Simon, are engaged in the cultural forum of a host of interconnected social, political, and economic issues. There exists a keen interconnectedness between Burns' and Simon's *Wire*-world and real life, and ultimately the opportunities the show provides for students to bridge the gap between writing assignments and social change.

The effectiveness, pedagogically, of teaching *The Wire*, might be in the teacher's ability to present topics using the lens of the show, but to also bear witness to students' own realization that they may see themselves in those students in Prez's classroom, and think the state of education was wrong-headed when they were in school, too. Or that students' take away not only be learning about the given topic but that there is an engagement piece, a call to action, that does not exist in other television shows. This is another reason *The Wire* feels so revolutionary in the classroom; it is the television novel that calls people to action, not on one social issue, but against an all-encompassing system and institutionalized power structure that affects students, right down to the desk in which they are seated. Dutro and Kantor (2011) continue that the students and Prez start to share what could be called a desire for "a space in which life experiences can converge" (p. 158) and perhaps intersect with learning in meaningful ways. Ultimately, Prez starts to turn away from the rigid, institutional model of education, i.e., standardized tests and minimal one-to-one engagement, and embraces honest responses to his students' needs, experiences, and embracing a mutual need for connection (Dutro and Kantor, 2011). When the show displayed this level of reconciliation between teacher and students, it proposed a desired alternative to the conventional methods in public education. First, the show clearly demonstrates the inherent flaws and failures in the depicted education system, then Prez and the students in that classroom discover a Frierian pedagogy (2000), described in *Pedagogy of the Oppressed* as a process of education that "must begin with the solution of the teacher-student contradiction, by reconciling the poles of the contradiction so that both are simultaneously teachers *and* students" (p. 86). Using *The Wire* in college classrooms exemplifies this process during the semester and allows for the very real possibility, or hope, for students to become actively engaged in social and economic issues in future endeavors. *The Wire* challenges educators to use its cultural forum to rethink the classroom itself in addition to applying critical analysis to the society at large. Peter Beilenson (2012), a public health officer in Maryland and instructor at Johns Hopkins University who was depicted on the show, used *The Wire* in his teaching, brought in guest speakers for "real life" perspectives, and asked students to write about social issues they encountered. Levine, an instructor who taught a course entitled, "The Crisis of the American City—Viewed through HBO's *The Wire*," in a conversation hosted by Lageson, Green and Erensu (2011) said, "The sustained argument of *The Wire*, and the powerful depictions of the key themes in multiple episodes, is what makes it so valuable as a pedagogic tool" (pp. 12–15). As others in this volume have highlighted and as bell hooks (1994) said in her book *Teaching to Transgress: Education as the Practice of Freedom*, "It is crucial that critical thinkers who want to change our teaching practices talk to one another, collaborate in a discussion that crosses boundaries and creates a space for intervention" (p. 129).

Coda

Would Simon still echo Bunny's frustration—"When do this shit change?"—at the end of our classes that use *The Wire*, or the end of this essay? Would we appear in his blog skewered for missing the point? Honestly, we hope so. Just as next semester, another group of students will be exposed to *The Wire*, any project or forum that continues debating the meaning and cultural significance of the show is a worthy endeavor. In the spring of 2015, President Obama felt strongly enough about Simon's voice to amplify *The Wire* himself, interviewing Simon for the White House YouTube channel. During the end of the interview, Obama states, "If we can start down this path, to thinking about a more productive way of dealing with drugs and its intersection with law enforcement, twenty years from now, we can say to ourselves, 'We got a little smarter.' We didn't get here overnight, we're not gonna get out of it overnight. But the fact that we've got people thinking about it in a smarter way, gives me a little courage." (The White House, 2015). Simon simply responds, "From your mouth, to God's ears."

Simon did not intend for the seasons to be viewed and tossed away, but for there to be an inherent call to action. This is evidenced in his vehement efforts to keep a conversation going about policies skewered in the show, and the wide embrace academics continue to give it, both in their classrooms and in the literature. Covering *The Wire* in college classrooms, without question, leaves an indelible mark on students who actively engage in such conversations, either verbally or in writing. Whether the show has caused more students to be politically or socially engaged in society has not been measured (yet), but pedagogy should be asking viewers what they will do about the question "what then?" To ignore this, is to ignore the implications of the show itself. The class discussions, debates, essays, and projects are a crucial component of thinking about a productive way to become aware of and ultimately address the social, political, and economic forces at work in American cities. The odds are that some of the now thousands of students who have been exposed to *The Wire* in classrooms will, like Wendell Pierce and Sonja Sohn, work in a way that confronts social and economic inequality, which as Obama has asserted, is the "defining challenge of our times."

REFERENCES

Alexander, M. (2012). *The new Jim Crow: Mass incarceration in the age of colorblind-ness*. Revised Edition. New York: New Press.

Alff, D. (2009). "Yesterday's tomorrow today: Baltimore and the promise of reform." In T. Potter & C.W. Marshall (eds.), *The wire: Urban decay and American televi-sion*. (23–36). New York: Continuum.

Beilenson, P.L., and P.A. McGuire. (2012). Tapping into the wire: The real urban crisis. Baltimore: Johns Hopkins University Press.

Black, J. (2012, March 6). In New Orleans, an actor turns grocer. *New York Times*. Retrieved from http://www.nytimes.com.

Chadda, A., and W.J. Wilson. (2011). "Way down in the hole": Systemic urban inequal-ity and the wire. *Critical Inquiry, 38*(1), 164–188. doi:10.1086/661647.

Chase, D. (1999). *The sopranos: Season 1*. HBO.

Clandfield, P. (2009). 'We ain't got no yard': Crime, development, and urban envi-ronment. In T. Potter & C.W. Marshall (eds.), *The wire: Urban decay and Amer-ican television*. (37–49). New York: Continuum.

Dutro, E., and J. Kantor. (2011). "Can we talk about intimacy?": The Wire and a ped-agogy of testimony and witness in urban classrooms. *Review of Education, Ped-agogy, and Cultural Studies, 33*(2), 132–160. doi:10.1080/10714413.2011.569460.

Egner, J. (2012, May 12). The game never ends: David Simon on wearying "wire" love and the surprising usefulness of twitter. *New York Times*. Retrieved from http://artsbeat.blogs.nytimes.com/.

Foucault, M. (1979). *Discipline & punish: The birth of the prison*. New York: Vintage Books.

Fresh Air. (2012). WHYY. Sonja Sohn: Changing Baltimore long after "the wire." NPR.org. Retrieved June 1, 2014, from http://www.npr.org/2012/03/15/148294942/sonja-sohn-changing-baltimore-long-after-the-wire.

Goffman, A. (2014). *On the run: Fugitive life in an American city*. Chicago: University of Chicago Press.

Gustini, R. (2011, June 11). 'The wire' creator David Simon has a counteroffer for Eric Holder. Retrieved from http://www.thewire.com.

Harvey, D. (2000). *Spaces of hope*. Oakland: University of California Press.

Hermann, P. (2012). Case offers look into drug ring involving "Snoop" of "The Wire." *The Baltimore Sun*. Retrieved from http://articles.baltimoresun.com/2012-03-05/entertainment/bs-md-ci-drug-bust-pearson-20120305_1_operation-usual-suspects-drug-ring-felicia-snoop-pearson.

hooks, bell. *Teaching to transgress*. New York: Routledge, 1994. Print, 129.

Kristof, N. (2014, March 19). TV lowers birthrate (seriously). *New York Times*. Retrieved from http://www.nytimes.com.

Lageson, S., K. Green, and S. Erensu. (2011, Summer). The wire goes to college. *Con-texts, 10*(3), 12–15.

Manos, J., Jr., D. Chase (Writers), and A. Coulter (Director). (1999). College [Televi-sion series episode]. In D. Chase, B. Gray (Producers), *The sopranos*. New Jersey & New York: Home Box Office, Brillstein Entertainment Partners.

Marshall, C.W., and T. Potter. (2009). "I am the American dream": Modern urban tragedy and the borders of fiction. In T. Potter and C.W. Marshall (eds.), *The wire: Urban decay and American television* (pp. 1–14). New York: Continuum.

Martin, B. (2013). *Difficult men: Behind the scenes of a creative revolution: The Wire to mad men and breaking bad*. New York: Penguin.

Mittell, J. (2010). *Television and American culture*. New York: Oxford University Press.

Moore, A. (2011). Teaching HBO's the wire. *Transformative Dialogues: Teaching & Learning Journal, 5*(1). Retrieved from http://kwantlen.ca/TD/TD.5.1/TD.5.1.9_Moore_Teaching_The_Wire.pdf.

Moore, L. (2010, October 14). Life of *the wire*. *New York Review of Books*, Retrieved from http://www.nybooks.com.

Nelson, C. (1997). *Manifesto of a tenured radical*. New York: New York University Press.

Pelecanos, G., E. Burns (Writers), and J. Chappelle (Director). (2006). That's got his own [Television series episode], In D. Simon, N. Koble (Producers), *The wire*. Baltimore: Blown Deadline.

Sepinwall, A. (2012). *The revolution was televised: The cops, crooks, slingers, and slayers who changed TV drama forever*. New York: Simon & Schuster.

Shear, M. (2013, December 29). Obama's TV picks: Anything edgy with hints of reality. *New York Times*. Retrieved from http://www.nytimes.com.

Simon, D. (1991). *Homicide: A year on the killing streets*. New York: Henry Holt.

Simon, D. (2008, March 10). "Final letter: A final thank you to the wire fans." HBO. Retrieved from http://www.hbo.com.

Simon, D. (Creator). (2008). *The wire: The complete series*. HBO.

Simon, D. (2013, July 14). Mr. Bealefeld's come-to-Jesus moment. *The audacity of despair*. Retrieved from http://davidsimon.com.

Simon, D. (2013, December 7). David Simon: "There are now two Americas. My country is a horror show." *The Guardian*. Retrieved from http://www.theguardian.com/world/2013/dec/08/david-simon-capitalism-marx-two-americas-wire.

Simon, D., E. Burns (Writers), and E. Dickerson (Director). (2006). Final grades (Television series episode). In D. Simon, E. Overmyer (Producers), *The wire*. Baltimore: Blown Deadline.

Smith, V. (2008). Redemption song and dance: Little Melvin Williams is not the deacon he played on the wire. *Baltimore City Paper*. Retrieved from http://www2.citypaper.com/news/story.asp?id=15478.

Storey, J. (2003). *Cultural studies and the study of popular culture*. Second ed. Athens: University of Georgia Press.

The White House. A conversation with President Obama and the wire creator David Simon. 2015. Web. 30 Mar. 2015.

Wilson, W.J. (2010). Why both social structure and culture matter in a holistic analysis of inner-city poverty. *The ANNALS of the American Academy of Political and Social Science, 629*(1), 200–219. doi:10.1177/0002716209357403.

Wimsatt, W.U. (2001). *Bomb the suburbs*. Berkeley, CA: Soft Skull.

Woods, S. (2006, October 5). HighWire. *Rolling Stone,* 38 39.

Yellin, T., L. Kramer (Producers), and L. Kramer (Director). (2011). *America in prime-time: The crusader*. United States: PBS.

Zabriskie, P. (2012, January 27). After "the wire" ended, actress Sonja Sohn couldn't leave Baltimore's troubled streets behind. *The Washington Post Magazine*. Retrieved from http://www.washingtonpost.com.

Zborowski, J. (2010). The rhetoric of *the wire*. *Movie: A Journal of Film Criticism, 1*(6).

It's All in the Game

How NOT to Teach The Wire
in Predominantly White Institutions (PWI)

Peggy Jones

Myth: An unproved or false collective belief that is used to justify a social institution.

Epistemology: The philosophical study of knowledge and belief. Justified true beliefs.

Ignorance: Lack of knowledge, learning, information, etc.
                                            —Dictionary.com, 2015

Predominantly White educational institutions (PWIs) will often have rhetoric in their official documents claiming a desire for diversity. As faculty members at these institutions, we are encouraged to include diversity in our pedagogy. Given its mix of a classical tragedy told over five seasons in a contemporary, urban setting, the academy has been drawn to the narrative of *The Wire*. While I am concerned about the images and depictions of African American families in *The Wire*, I agree with the need for students at PWIs to be exposed to depictions of majority Black urban experiences. It is extremely important and relevant for those using this series that they help students understand and recognize the humanity of the characters. I wrote this essay with the goal of assisting those using *The Wire* in their teaching in a way that does not increase racial stereotyping, essentializing, or epistemologies of ignorance.

As a Black, multi-generationally middle-class, feminist university professor, I was both personally and professionally drawn to *The Wire* for the rather simple, yet revolutionary and (for me) unprecedented depictions of African descended characters on a television series. Via their acting, the cast displayed the widest array of humanity I had ever seen. As a viewer, I saw the Black actors demonstrating the range of human experience; like in real life, "good" characters did "bad" things and "bad" characters did "good" things. The program also displayed the humanity in urban life so often lacking in other programs situated in larger cities. It represented more of my intimate life experiences than had any other program with majority Black casts. *The Wire* was not just *The Cosby Show*, with its depiction of an upper-middle class Black Huxtable family, which owned a multi-storied home in New York City. It was not merely a family and their friends and neighbors living on public assistance in housing projects, like the Evanses in *Good Times*. The Evans family and the Huxtables are both represented in *The Wire*, with families and individuals all along the socio-economic ladder.

I teach at a PWI in the Midwest.[1] In addition to White students from varying life experiences, in the last eight years, I have also seen a diversity of non–White students, including native born Black students and those directly from the continent of Africa, along with Hispanic students from Spain and Latino students, locally born and bred. Many of the non–White students, especially those born in the U.S. and from the local metropolitan area, seem to have a strong connection to Eurocentric norms and values. Their paradigms seem to arise from a desire to "go along to get along. I believe their paradigms are also part of a (possibly) unconscious survival strategy and or a desire to be seen not as "other" but as the "same" as the majority students. While many of these students "have not and cannot be exposed to the complexity of urban social problems in an intimate way" (T. Gaynor & J. Taliaferro, personal communication, October 8, 2013), I have also had students, usually African descended, who have lived lives that could have come directly from *The Wire* storylines. I never ask those students; the revelations come as part of class discussions or more recently as a part of the program we do to explore our emotions and empathy for others.

Using a methodology of autoethnography, a key paradigm I wish to consider in this essay is the *epistemology of ignorance*, which must be, for some, the height of paradox. How does one perform a study of knowledge on a lack of knowledge? According to editors Shannon Sullivan and Nancy Tuana (2007), their text *Race and Epistemologies of Ignorance* contains essays which produce "an examination of the complex phenomena of ignorance, which has as its aim identifying different forms of ignorance, examining how they are produced and sustained, and what role they play in knowledge practices" (Sullivan, 2007, p. 1). Like the authors, I seek to examine how "race, racism, and White privilege…[are products of knowledge and how] especially in the case of racial oppression, a lack of knowledge or an unlearning of something previously known is actively produced for the purposes of domination and exploitation" (Sullivan, 2007, p. 1). I will also examine how when race is situated in urban settings, there are additional epistemologies of ignorance.

Finally, in this essay I will discuss how to teach *The Wire* in ways that will not add to the existing epistemologies of ignorance of race and urban environments in the United States that have existed since the founding of this country, especially those epistemologies that have been traditionally disseminated via educational institutions.

Reading, 'Riting, and Racism?

On the University of Kansas' catalog web page for their department of Women's, Gender and Sexuality Studies (2012), the question is asked why one should study this discipline. The answer is: "Because much of what people *think* about women, gender, and sex is a *myth*" (emphasis added). While I agree with this answer, I might change the wording slightly, substituting *think* to *believe*. I have rarely witnessed much deep, critical thought about these topics, but I have endured hearing in my classrooms many (false) beliefs. I would also personally include *race* as an area where many false beliefs prevail and are perpetuated by my very colleagues. To me and countless others, race sometimes feels like the third rail of the U.S. experience, where to discuss race can cause debilitating injury.

I currently teach in a PWI in the largest city of a Midwestern state. In 2010, according to the United States Census Bureau's QuickFacts webpage (2015), the state's Black population was 4.5 percent, while the city was 13.7 percent African American. Eighty-nine percent of the cities in the state have fewer than 3,000 people. The county in which the PWI is situated is very densely populated, relative to the majority of cities, with 1,574.4 people per square mile. Demographics show that race and urban areas are fairly synonymous in this city.

I struggle to find ways to teach, sometimes highly resistant, students of all racial backgrounds from areas outside of the largest city in the state about how race is seen and (attempted by some to be) unseen. To give them context, I have often assigned a book chapter which contains the following excerpt:

> Throughout its history in the US, (the concept of race) has been used to create a dividing line between those who were White and those who were non–White and to determine who would and would not have political rights (and by extension, political power.) In addition, cultural traditions created and adhered to by persons of European descent have come to be the "norm," while those from non–White races are deemed to be a less significant other. In the end, race (and, by extension, racism) has been constructed as a great divider and the avenue by which people of certain ethnic groups have come to be framed as inferior to Whites [Caliendo & McIlwain, 2011, p. 3].

It is one thing to present this information, but an entirely other thing to have students believe it, especially in the face of what they deem "evidence" to the contrary. A few years ago, a reporter from the local newspaper with the largest circulation in the state contacted me. He wanted to talk about White privilege. In my opinion, based on many experiences in the classroom, he did not believe White privilege existed, because he was mistakenly using the common micro-view of how one White person was (or in his case, wasn't) privileged, rather than the macro-view of realizing the systemic privilege of being White in America. Peggy McIntosh (2010) has come to see White privilege as "an invisible package of unearned assets which (she as a White person) can count on cashing in each day, but about which (she) was 'meant' to remain oblivious" (p. 14). The reporter clearly did not see his privilege, though in agreement with McIntosh, he is not meant to be aware of it.

My current pedagogy as a Black Studies professor consists of a multi-pronged approach to help students acquire the theoretical frameworks and vocabulary to form critical questions regarding race, gender, and sexuality in U.S. media. I give them a multidisciplinary-based lexicon of theory and relevant terms, initially gleaned from Patricia Hill Collins' (2000) *Black Feminist Thought*, with additions as necessary from a variety of disciplinary sources. I feel this text most accurately represents both my ideology as well as is the most effective for deconstructing the (heretofore unseen and *unknown* for many students) mainstream paradigms of racism, sexism, heterosexism, classism, and heteropatriarchy rampant in U.S. media. For me, this is the heart of the intersectional approach to teaching Black Studies that is most representative of reality. If *The Wire* is taught without these considerations, to White students with little to no exposure to those from different racial, economic, and geographic backgrounds, continued epistemologies of ignorance would be the inevitable result. Students have told me of their experiences in other, non–Black Studies courses, where the instructor, at the same PWI where I teach, has made comments demonstrating extraordinary ignorance, if not explicit racism. Statements have ranged from assumed gang membership to "what do those protestors in Ferguson, Missouri, have to complain about, anyway?"

Students in my Black Studies courses range from having an understanding of some of the terms, albeit not always from a critical race/gender perspective, to very little to no understanding or awareness of the conditions the terms explicates/defines. I have recently began requiring students to view a series of videos created to help students be more successful in college, in large part by aiding them in discovering their metacognition, or do they *know* what they *know*? These videos were presented and based on research by Professor Stephen Chew (2008) on students' misconceptions about learning. Chew states in the video that "weaker students are grossly over confident in how well they know the (course) material," or in other words, they have a high level of ignorance regarding what they do and do not know, and are stunned when they perform poorly in academic settings (Chew, 2008).

My eventual goal is that students have a deeper and meaningful understanding of the terms and can recognize the presence and continued nurturing of heteropatriarchy or structural domains of power, especially via cultural products they have most likely consumed without critical awareness. That consumption would be damaging enough; students are also learning from these entertaining media tropes in TV, film, and other contemporary media knowledge (or epistemologies of ignorance) regarding race, gender, sexuality, and other ways of identifying the self and/or connecting to groups.

I have also incorporated Stuart Hall's (1973) theories from his essay *Encoding and Decoding in the Television Discourse*. Students read a synopsis of this essay and we then analyze the dominant/hegemonic, negotiated, and oppositional subject positions to decode cultural products. Essentially, many students are generally unconsciously positioned (or consciously position themselves) in the dominant/hegemonic, where they accept with little question the coded messages in cultural products created by majority members because they themselves are majority members, or have adopted a similar position even if not visibly majority members. These messages are often stereotypical with regard to race, gender, sexuality, class, and other social positions. Other students utilize negotiated positions, which acknowledge the dominant messages, but do not accept them without critical inquiry. The final group, and most often in my experience students of color, reject the stereotypical messages and desire to create a truer message, often inspired by their own epistemologies.

As I have used cultural products in the past, I have typically excerpted scenes relevant to the topics/theory we are discussing and deconstructing in class. I work to separate students from (for many) their default, passive mental state when viewing entertainment, where it would rarely occur to them to question critically what they are consuming. For an example of this, one day in class we were analyzing a Super Bowl commercial for an insurance company that stereotypically continued epistemologies of ignorance using the Sapphire trope, where a Black woman is shown controlling "men through her emasculating insults and jibes" (Beaulieu, 2006, p. 475). A Black woman student who was usually very thoughtful and astute told me, "Aw, Ms. Jones, it's not that deep for me; I just watch (the commercials)." Perhaps she minimized the effect of the commercial on her because she knew a wider range of truths about Black women, but for many of the other students, especially the White ones, it was "that deep" in the student's vernacular. As a Black woman educator, those commercials are also "that deep" because I must work against and educate to groups which often have unconscious biases and stereotypes of who a college professor is and what that person looks like. These products mis-educate all who view them uncritically.

Educational institutions are all too often where myths are learned as "objective facts." In *Race and Epistemologies of Ignorance*, the contributor Lucius T. Outlaw, by focusing

> on practices of education ... explains how schools have been a primary site for the production and distribution of white ignorance of other races. From the nineteenth century onward, schools have been institutions of "Americanization," a process of teaching a hierarchical racial ontology in which white people dominate all others [Sullivan, 2007 p. 7].

This explanation would mightily offend many students who have enrolled in my classes. I once had an eighteen-year-old White male student in 2012 send me an email about how unfairly the policies of Ronald Reagan were viewed and experienced by people of color in a documentary. The people in the documentary had actually lived and been directly affected by those policies. The student was born in 1996, a full eight years after the last day Reagan was in office. Based on other items in the email, I have very little doubt this student would disagree with Outlaw's premise, especially in the framing of Americanization as an oppressive process.

In a class from the 2013 fall semester, another young White male upper class student, strongly affirmed that unlike in New York, no person in Nebraska would have ignored a younger Black mother asking for help for saving her two toddlers swept away during Hurricane Sandy (Rivas, 2012). Many Black (and some White) students openly guffawed at his naiveté, optimism or ignorance. When I assigned an excerpt from a book chapter asking students to look at their college or university and analyze any similarities between it and a plantation (White men in charge, White women helpmates, people of color doing the physical labor) one of the vociferous denials came from a young woman of African descent (a graduating senior), who seemed not to do the reading, but rather used her own definition of a plantation and then claimed she had never been whipped or made to pick cotton and everyone essentially got along, irrespective of their race. She went on to describe all of the marvelous opportunities the university had afforded her. I found myself wondering not entirely in jest, whether she was working in the school's public relations office.

While anecdotal, these three students are not so different from many students I have encountered in my approximately 26 year college-level teaching career. There has been, and currently is, a large amount of ignorance found in academic institutions—from uninformed faculty and students. Outlaw (2007), in his chapter *Social Ordering and the Systematic Production of Ignorance,* writes about the ignorance on all sides of racial areas where for centuries, White children are taught "both knowledge and ignorance to grow into confirmed, practicing racial supremacists... and ... successive generations of children—Black, brown, yellow, red, mixed—would be *mis-educated* to be racially inferior adults subordinate to White adults and children" (Outlaw, 2007, p. 197). Of course, the children of color could not help but also learn what the White children were taught, thereby doubling down on the amount of ignorance distributed in educational settings. Prior to Outlaw, Carter G. Woodson (1933) famously wrote *The Miseducation of the Negro*, with its telling quote about White supremacist practices via education, gendered word choice notwithstanding, "If you make a man feel that he is inferior, you do not have to compel him to accept an inferior status, for he will seek it himself" (Woodson, p. 60).

In an attempt to meld humor with education, I have often shown a clip from The Daily Show (Melkman, 2011) where the previous host, Jon Stewart, and the "Senior Black Correspondent" Larry Wilmore, discuss the coded language politicians use to discuss race, so the politicians will not be seen as overtly racist. In addition, I have shown a TedX talk by Jay Smooth (2011), titled, "How I Stopped Worrying and Learned to Love Discussing Race." In it, he states an aphorism that "race is dance designed to trip up the partners" (Smooth, 2011). The video is particularly effective because he uses the terms from the Black Studies lexicon I hand out at the beginning of every class I teach.

The lexicon began as a way to introduce students to theory terms mainly philosophical in origin, but also from other disciplines, including critical race studies, linguistics, social psychology and economics. Since using *The Wire* as a main component of my pedagogy in my Introduction to Black Studies class, I have put this course description in my syllabus:

> Given that societal processes and cultural products often educate unintentionally and, at times, with more lasting effect than what occurs in a formal academic setting, we will theoretically analyze how race, gender, and sexuality are presented in the media. This course will examine the foundation and development of the discipline of Black Studies via the theoretical deconstruction of the media depictions of African descended peoples in America. We will be paying particular attention to African Americans' efforts to shape and control their social, economic, and political institutions and to resist racial oppression. We will also be examining artistic and cultural contributions of African Americans to the larger American culture.

With the formation of my discipline, Black Studies, counter-narratives were created by academics and others to try and correct the ignorance aforementioned. In her book chapter, *Black Studies and Liberal Arts Education*, Johnetta Cole (2004) presents "a critical assessment of Black Studies," including how it came to be as a discipline and what its aims are in the context of educational institutions. One of the most relevant items is how the Black Studies critique "explicitly addresses shortcomings, omissions and distortions" in "curricula and institutions (as they affect African descended persons)" (Cole, 2004, p. 23). In her book, *The Black Revolution on Campus*, Martha Biondi (2012) describes how university students, desiring change from the racist and oppressive practices of educational institutions, created a revolution, usually in collaboration with community members, that enlarged the reach and breadth of Black Studies as an academic discipline at the college/university level.

You Don't Know What You Don't Know

As I mentioned, I have recently begun assigning a series of videos for my students to watch on the topic of succeeding in college. I assign these videos not only to help students learn how to learn, but also to introduce the meta-cognition to the concept of race and students' epistemologies of ignorance. As Sullivan (2007) describes it, "(While) ignorance ... (can) be a gap in knowledge, epistemic oversight... (s)ometimes what we don't know... (especially in the case of racial oppression) is actively produced for purposes of domination and exploitation" (p. 1).

A qualitative study showed that Millennials (aged 18–25 in 2011) who were White, often believed that racism was directly tied to *intent*; if they or others did not act intentionally or know that what they did would be considered a racist act, they could not be racist (Apollon, 2011). In other words, ignorance excused racist acts. Millennials of color were much more likely to take a macro-view of racism and look at systems of power and structures of oppression.[2] There were a few instances where White students described systems in conjunction with racism. Those students typically had taken sociological or ethnic studies classes. Also, there were students of color who tended to use the micro (or individual) view of racism rather describing structural domains of power or racial hierarchies. This is important for a few reasons. First, when racism is seen only as occurring by an individual, intentional actor (or at the micro-level), all systemic and institutional (or at the macro-level) can be dismissed or denied, leaving the great possibility of ignorance of that discriminatory reality persisting. By insisting that racism can only be intentional, one can completely dismiss the impact of racist acts. Second, the study showed how experiential systemic racism was for most of the students of color in ways it was not for other students. To honor the truths of the students of color, one must address this dialectical reality.

At times and especially in the case of racial domination and exploitation, "(a lack of knowledge or an unlearning of something previously known) can take the form of the center's own ignorance of injustice, cruelty, suffering, such as contemporary White people's obliviousness to racism and White domination" (Sullivan, 2007, p. 1). Evidence of this obliviousness could be found in a 2011 study by Tufts University's School of Arts and Sciences and Harvard Business School, where Whites now believe that they suffer more from racism than Blacks (Norton, 2011). A news release for the study stated, "It's a pretty surprising finding when you think of the wide range of disparities that still exist in society, most of which show black Americans with worse outcomes than whites in areas such as income, home ownership, health and employment," said Tufts Associate Professor of Psychology Samuel Sommers, Ph.D. (Thurler, 2011). This study would seem a prime example of an epistemology of ignorance of those who see Whites as suffering from more racial bias than Blacks.

If one showed the study respondents the wide range of disparities, my guess is that they would explain it away by using the fundamental attribution error, the tendency to *over-value* personality-based explanations for the observed behaviors of others while *under-valuing* situational explanations for those behaviors (Sherman, 2014). The case would be made that if Blacks really are suffering in those above listed areas, undoubtedly it is because they are inherently lazy, without character, and criminally minded, not because of systemic racist practices or any other external or situational factor. It is worth mentioning that gender has its own epistemologies of ignorance where the fundamental attribution error is strongly at play or in evidence. "Americans habitually over-emphasize biology (an internal trait) and underestimate the power of social facts (external situations) to explain sex and gender" (Spade & Valentine, 2008, p. 4). Additionally, it is totally valid to exchange sex and gender with race.

As I grapple with how to teach in ways that do not replicate or reinforce epistemologies of ignorance, I must consider the following: "Although racial oppression has been investigated as an unjust practice, few have fully examined the ways in which such practices of oppression are linked to our conceptions and productions of knowledge" (Sullivan, 2007, p. 2). One could easily say that since I am a college professor, knowledge production is my job. But I do not, for many of my students, look like I should have that power, given the dearth of Black women professors in the academy.

In 2013, Black women held 3.7 percent of tenure-track positions and 2.2 percent of tenured positions (Catalyst, 2015). I must also consider that "(t)racing what is not known and the politics of such ignorance should be a key element of epistemological and social and political analyses for it has the potential to reveal the role of power in the construction of what is known and provide a lens for political values at work in our knowledge practices" (Sullivan, 2007, p. 2). Johnetta Cole wrote about how "Black Studies during the '60s and '70s took a critical look at participants in American higher education" (Cole, 2004, p. 24). The examination revealed the reality of a great majority of White, male, middle-class professors who had been trained by a similar looking group and teaching a similar looking group of students. There was little to no statistical correlation to the U.S. population. Black Studies advocates questioned this anomaly and insisted on a more reasonable distribution of academic representation (Allen, Teranishi, Dinwiddie, González & Gonzalez, 2002). Not much has changed from then to now.[3] If students only *know* what a professor looks like from their experiences or others like them, how can they *know* what else exists? If they *know* from news coverage and other cultural products who holds power and who does not, how does one teach about other realities?

Since I teach at a Predominantly White Institution (PWI), I often ask myself, "What is known by students at a PWI?" In my class *Black Women in America*, a few years ago at the end of one semester, I had three young White women who cried because they did not *know* about race and gender intersections and the impact they had on Black women. In the same class period, I had three young Black women cry because their intersectional experiences, as young Black women, were so *unknown* by the young White women. Had we had more time or I had been more experienced, we would have analyzed how this came to be. Though the Black students did not say so explicitly, my guess is that they had much more accurate knowledge of these young White women than these White women had of them.

In that same semester of that class, when discussing Black directors whose work dealt with gender, I chose Spike Lee. I told my students that I had initially thought of Tyler Perry, but feared he would be *unknown* to many of the White students in the class. As some of the Black students expressed cynicism, a young White male student asked, "Who is Tyler Perry?" A young Black woman sitting in front of him spun around immediately and almost yelled, "Madea!" which did not clear things up for the White student at all.

Eugene Robinson (2010) wrote in his book, *Disintegration* on how experiences of Blacks and other non–Whites are rarely seen or *known* as universally as Whites see or *know* their own experiences (Robinson, 2011, p. 97). This especially seems to bear some truth with regard to *The Wire*'s second season, which has many more White characters and concomitantly higher ratings than the other four seasons with majority Black casts (Shelley, 2005). When I have shown excerpts of the films *Cadillac Records* (2008) and *Talk to Me* (2007) in my Introduction to Black Studies course, often the White students will show, by facial expressions, and will say during class discussions that they enjoyed the films. I will ask why they did not see the films in the theatre or by any other means (streaming digital, etc.), they said the movies did not seem to be "for them." To put it another way, the students perhaps assumed they would not *know* enough to enjoy or even understand the narrative.

Another challenge to using cultural products which feature many Black characters is how the media may frame the product. I often have my students read an article by Amy Binder (1993) in which she discusses how media depictions of harm (sexual and physical violence) by heavy metal groups with mostly

White members are seen as a threat to parental authority while rap performed by Black artists is a threat to all civilized society. I ask my students if they believe this is also true for television programs. We often have lively discussions, but have not come to any conclusions. In reality, I would be very surprised *not* to find the same type of framing of programming with a majority of African descended characters and how they are responded to by White viewers.[4]

How We Know What We Know to Be True

My family of origin is very different than that of the families depicted in *The Wire*. My family of origin included two parents and seven children, we have earned eleven college degrees from the undergraduate to doctoral level. My life differs greatly from some of the characters in *The Wire,* but not all of them. In my close extended family, I have a cousin who prostituted and she has a son who she encouraged to sling drugs, which might have led to the fact that he joined a gang and has committed multiple murders. But unlike others in my immediate family, I will acknowledge these family members in ways they will not. I have introduced my truths to my students as a counter-narrative to stereotypical depictions of Black life on U.S. television, as well as to elements of *The Wire*. Yet, or perhaps because of my family, I hesitate a little before showing my students excerpts of *The Wire* given the predominantly Black cast.

In the classroom, I have been made aware (via comments in class or assignments) students without any connection to the urban social situations in *The Wire* as well as students who have and are living those lives intimately. This is a perfect situation to understand (or begin to) how varying episte-mologies (or multiple *truths*) exist in the same place at the same time. When using *The Wire*, we see and experience multiple epistemologies or truths.

As such, in *The Wire*, unlike most other depictions of urban life, viewers see a much wider range than usual of African descended people's lives. For example, all levels of the Barksdale organization in Season One. To borrow, somewhat in reverse, the chess analogy skillfully used by a character to explain the roles of the pieces, we see a spectrum of representations, not just the pawns or kings and queens. This depiction of an African descended–run organization is so critically important because we see a coldly, rational universe. This portrayal, rather than the seemingly random, thoughtless, and nihilistic depictions of other programs or local news coverage of drug crime is logical, rational, and calculated. Black people are actors with a level of agency instead of mindless thugs, killing in sociopathic ways. They are making hard decisions and attempting to maximize their life chances within the context of their environment and reality.

In my teaching and personal experience, agency must be understood and approached as complex, dialectical, and nuanced. Hopefully, exerting one's agency in positive ways will aid oneself and brings little to no harm to others if possible. In *The Wire*, where viewers often see a "kill or be killed" environment, a character's agency has consequences and choices are rarely free ones. All life comes with nuance, but Black life is often depicted in the media with binaries of saintly good and egregious evil, with little of the complications and balancing of priorities. Cognitive dissonance rarely raises its head. Not that drama must be a product of verisimilitude, but when media is generally presented as a binary, there is an inadvertent byproduct when watching media where some beliefs are suspended while others are reinforced in the new reality being experienced. When using *The Wire* to teach, these beliefs can be challenged or at least exposed.

Notwithstanding the fact that the main creator of *The Wire* is White, the program could be arguably described as a "Black story." The question *Who gets to tell a Black story?* was the title of an article in the *New York Times* (June 2000). I have had students read it in preparation for viewing and deconstructing *The Wire* and systems that create cultural products, such as network television or commercial films. To summarize, the article is about the conflict between two men key to the planning and creation of HBO's *The Corner*. One is a genially drawn David Simon, a White writer who co-created *The Wire*. The other is Charles Dutton, who is depicted as a mostly furious, but esteemed Black actor and director. Dutton is originally from the very area of Baltimore depicted in both *The Corner* and *The Wire*.[5] In the writer's view, their conflict seems to originate and continue with Dutton's over-sensitivity to racially related issues.

Therein lies the complexity of teaching using *The Wire*. It can be very difficult to introduce *The Wire*'s depiction of "systematic urban inequality" without adding to epistemologies of ignorance regarding race in America. The question becomes, how does one make these truths *known* to those with little to no conception of a diversity of race in the United States without introducing other epistemologies of ignorance? I hope that information in this essay assists those who wish to do so.

NOTES

1. A telling feature of the university relative to this focus of the edited text can be found in the fact that when students do organized "Culture Walks," they only do them in local urban areas that are predominantly lower-income with majority Black or Brown populations. Areas in which Whites with higher incomes live seemingly don't have a "culture" since the walks have never taken place there.

2. The article included word clouds where when analyzing the White participants' language used to define "racism," the largest word after "RACE" and "RACISM" was "SOMEONE." When the language of people of color was analyzed, the only large word was "GROUP."

3. A Black male colleague at my university was told by his dean that as a Black professor, he was a good example to students of color. My colleague disagreed and said he was a better example to the White students, who make up the majority of the student population, to see a Black man in a position of authority.

4. George Yancy writes about "the gift of the Black Gaze and the Reinscription of Whiteness as Normative in *A Time to Kill* in *Race, Philosophy, and Film* which deals with some of these issues.

5. Dutton seems to feel as angry as I felt when hearing the line in the *The Help* spoken by a young, White woman reporter, that "they love us and we love them!" where the "they" are their Black servants, and "us" is the Whites that employ them.

REFERENCES

Allen, W., R. Teranishi, G. Dinwiddie, G. González, and G. Gonzalez. (2002). Knocking at freedom's door: Race, equity and Affirmative Action in U.S. Higher Education. *Journal of Public Health Policy, 23*(4), 440. http://dx.doi.org/10.2307/3343241.

Apollon, D. (2011, June 16) *What's racism? That's harder for youth to answer than you think.* Retrieved from http://colorlines.com/archives/2011/06/whats_racism_thats_harder_for_youth_to_answer_than_you_think.html.

Beaulieu, E. (2006) *Writing African American women: An encyclopedia of literature by and about women of color.* Santa Barbara, CA: Greenwood.

Binder, A. (1993). Constructing racial rhetoric: Media Depictions of harm in heavy metal and rap music. *American Sociological Review, 58*(6), 753. doi:10.2307/2095949.

Biondi, M. (2012). *The black revolution on campus.* Berkeley: University of California Press.

Caliendo, S., and C. McIlwain. (2011). *The Routledge companion to race and ethnicity.* London: Routledge.

Catalyst. (2015, July 9) *Quick take: Women in academia.* New York: Catalyst. Retrieved from http://www.catalyst.org/knowledge/women-academia#footnote36_pjqqt8j

Chew, S.L. (2008). Study more! Study harder! Students' and teachers' faulty beliefs about how people learn. In S.A. Meyers and J.R. Stowell (Eds.), *Essays from excellence in teaching* (Vol. 7, pp. 22–25). Retrieved from the Society for the Teaching of Psychology Web site: http://teachpsych.org/resources/e-books/eit2007/eit2007.php/.

Cole, J. (2004) Black studies in liberal arts education. In Bobo, J., C. Hudley, and C. Michel. *The black studies reader.* (pp. 21–34) New York: Routledge.

Dictionary.com. (2015). *Definitions of myth, epistemology and ignorance.* Retrieved 30 November 2015, from http://dictionary.reference.com/browse/myth?s=t.

Gordon, M. (Producer), and K. Lemmons (Director). (2007) *Talk to me* [Motion Picture]. United States: Universal Pictures.

Hall, Stuart. (1973). Encoding and decoding in the television discourse. Centre for Cultural Studies, University of Birmingham.

Hill Collins, P. (2000). *Black feminist thought.* New York: Routledge.

McIntosh, P. (2010) White privilege and male privilege. In M. Kimmel and A. Ferber (Eds.), *Privilege: A reader* (pp. 13–26). Boulder, CO: Westview Press.

Melkman, J. (Producer). (2011, December 13). *The daily show* [Television broadcast]. New York: Viacom. Retrieved from http://thedailyshow.cc.com/videos/9y5s8l/newt-gingrich-s-poverty-code.

Norton, M., and S. Sommers. (2011) *Whites see racism as a zero-sum game that they are now losing*. Retrieved from: https://www.researchgate.net/publication/2581 79999_Whites_See_Racism_as_a_Zero-sum_Game_that_They_Are_Now_Los ing [accessed Nov 25, 2015].

Outlaw, L. (2007) Social ordering and the systematic production of ignorance. In S. Sullivanand N. Tuana (Eds.), *Race and epistemologies of ignorance*. (pp. 197–212). Albany: State University of New York Press.

Rivas, J. (2012, November 2). *Staten Island residents refused to help black mom as Sandy swept sons away*. Retrieved from http://www.colorlines.com/articles/ staten-island-residents-refused-help-black-mom-sandy-swept-sons-away.

Robinson, E. (2010). *Disintegration*. New York: Doubleday.

Scott, J. (2000, June 11). Who gets to tell a black story? *New York Times*. Retrieved from http://www.nytimes.com/2000/06/11/us/who-gets-to-tell-a-black-story. html?module=Search&mabReward=relbias percent3As&pagewanted=all.

Shelley, J. (2005). Jim Shelley: Call the cops. *The Guardian*. Retrieved 30 November 2015, from http://www.theguardian.com/media/2005/aug/06/tvandradio.guide2.

Sherman, M. (2014, June 20). *Why we don't give each other a break*. Retrieved from https://www.psychologytoday.com/blog/real-men-dont-write-blogs/201406/ why-we-dont-give-each-other-break.

Smooth, J. (2011, November) How I stopped worrying and learned to love discussing race. TedX Talk. Retrieved from http://www.illdoctrine.com/2011/11/my_tedx_ talk_how_i_stopped_wor.html.

Sondervan, S., and A. Lack (Producers), and D. Martin (Director). (2008) *Cadillac records* [Motion Picture]. United States: Sony Pictures.

Spade, J., and C. Valentine. (2008). *The kaleidoscope of gender*. Los Angeles: Sage Publications.

Sullivan, S., and N. Tuana. (2007). *Race and epistemologies of ignorance*. Albany: State University of New York Press.

Thurler, K. (2011, May 23) Whites believe they are victims of racism more often than blacks. Retrieved from http://now.tufts.edu/news-releases/whites-believe-they-are-victims-racism-more-o#sthash.tRLX6pWS.dp.

The United States Census Bureau, State & County QuickFacts, Nebraska. (2015) Retrieved from http://quickfacts.census.gov/qfd/states/31000.html.

The University of Kansas Online Catalog. Department of Women, Gender, and Sexuality Studies Web page. (2010) Retrieved http://www2.ku.edu/~distinction/cgi-bin/6479.

Woodson, C. (1933). *The mis-education of the Negro*. Trenton, NJ: Africa World Press.

"Soft Eyes"

Pragmatic Considerations and Strategies for Teaching The Wire

Jocelyn DeVance Taliaferro

How to Teach The Wire

A course on *The Wire* can be a rewarding experience for both students and instructors. In the words of a student "What could be more fun than watching television and learning at the same time?" That is exactly the "selling point" of teaching a class on *The Wire*. Many students enroll in the class because they are excited about the television series. Either they have heard about it and have seen a few episodes, or they have seen the signs all over campus advertising the class. The television show is the hook. The well designed course is the anchor. As other essays in the volume have discussed, teaching using *The Wire*, comes with its own set of special considerations and challenges as part of creation and implementation of the course. Some of these considerations are extremely pragmatic, and some are quite conceptual. To this point, essays in this volume have addressed the conceptual and theoretical decisions of teaching the course. Frameworks such as bourgeois theory, critical race theory, queer theory, intersectionality, and feminist theory, have been used to explore the rich content of the series. This essay pivots and discusses some of the salient pragmatic issues in creating a class on *The Wire*. We look at *The Wire* with "soft eyes"[1] (Mills, 2006). After earning tenure at a large research intensive university, I had the opportunity to teach a Critical Social Policy elective course in the Department of Social Work using *The Wire*. The discussion that follows is a result of my own considerations as well as those of other faculty members who have either taught the course (some are included in this volume) or are in the process of trying to advocate for, implement, or prepare to teach a class on *The Wire*.

146

Pragmatic Considerations for Teaching The Wire

Teaching any course requires that the instructor consider issues of time, content, and the manner in which to divide the course content for optimal consumption and learning. Some courses also require instructors to consider the implications of presenting sensitive material that may challenge dominant hegemonic narratives. This is especially true of developing and implementing a course on *The Wire*.

Instructors using *The Wire* have a unique opportunity, but it does come with costs and challenges. Depending on the institution, the value of teaching *The Wire* is different and should be considered carefully. As an example, at teaching institutions, teaching a course on *The Wire* may be of high value as it is an opportunity for innovative instruction and connection with students. However, at research intensive institutions, innovative teaching is of relatively low value (Nacoste, 2010). Unless research can be attached and some dimension of teaching the course can contribute to the research mission of the university, the course may not be appreciated by university administrators; reappointment, promotion and tenure committees; or boards of trustees that approve permanent courses. Creating a class on *The Wire*, like creating any new course is time, labor, and resource intensive.

It Is Television, Good Television, but Still Sixty Hours of Television

Time is a major consideration for teaching a course on *The Wire*. In 2010, the average American adult watched 2.7 hours of television per day or approximately 19 hours per week (Ford, 2012). A course on *The Wire* obviously would require students to view the series or portions of it. Instructors must consider how much of the show to use in the course and on what schedule students should be expected to have viewed the episodes. As a scholar who teaches social work from a macro systems perspective, all five seasons, but particularly the first four seasons, are relevant and useful to my course that critically explores urban problems and solutions. Therefore, consideration must been given to how much time students will have to watch the show, consume the material, integrate it with other sources of information, and complete assignments. The course, offered over a traditional 16 week semester,[2] provides adequate time for students to watch the series as well as reflect on the course content and objectives. The traditional assumption is that credit hours are determined using a 2:1 ratio of time outside the class for each hour of face-to-face instruction (Ochoa, 2015). Given this ratio, a 3-credit course would be approximately 96 hours for students to watch the show, read ancillary materials, and complete assignments outside of classroom.

When using *The Wire* in the classroom it is difficult to use an episode or single season, particularly seasons beyond Season One. Although instructors do it, because the characters are slowly and carefully developed and each story line scaffolds, to begin in the middle of a season or to select a few episodes provides an acontextual picture of the issues addressed by the series. Teaching a single episode tends to negate much of the unique nature of the show. It is virtually impossible to "drop into" *The Wire* as one would a sitcom or even a network television drama. Characters are routinely introduced to the show's plotline in one season and not fully developed until several episodes or seasons later. For instance, by Season Four Lester Freamon and Prop Joe are very different characters than their initial introduction would suggest. One aspect of the potency of the show is its lack of sitcom and formulaic processes of character and storyline development. It is difficult to *not* use the entire series. Otherwise, determining how to parse the information and episodes for student viewing is a challenge. Several instructors, many in this volume (Baggett, Simmons, Eggleton & DeCuir-Gunby; Stern) and others (Trier, 2010) focus on Season Four to discuss how young people engage with the education system—or are failed by the education system. However, using only Season Four provides a lack of context to be able to understand both Baltimore and the lived experiences of the youth highlighted during the season. Having seen the drug culture promoted in Season One; economic deprivation and decline presented in Season Two, and the politics that have influenced these interdependent systems in Season Three provide a context to understand Season Four. Without this "backstory," Season Four becomes a bit of a caricature of what happens in central city school systems. Therefore, the ability to either provide context outside of watching *The Wire* or having students watch the entire series becomes a critical decision for instructors. Andrew Moore (2011) provides a discussion of the use of Season Three and James Trier (2010) discusses using only Season Four. Both lament the problems of using only a portion of the drama. Moore (2011) "wondered if watching the third season of The Wire was a bit like asking students to read the middle six chapters of Pride & Prejudice or the second act of Hamlet" (p. 4).

Not only must instructors consider the format of the course and the schedule of television watching for students, instructors must consider the amount of time for television watching during course preparation. The time of teaching and preparing for the course is a significant matter as there are five seasons with each season having 10–13 episodes. By any standard, that is a substantive amount of television watching. Watching *The Wire* in its entirety is approximately 60 hours of television. Most instructors have to read material more than once to adequately plan for the classroom environment. The need to become immersed in *The Wire* is not methodically different than being immersed in the literature for traditional course preparation. That means that if an instructor will use all 60 hours of the series, more than 120 hours will be spent watching television. That far exceeds the 19-hour weekly average television watching estimate. One can only assume that instructors interested in teaching a course like this enjoy television—or at least *The Wire*—but even for those that enjoy television, 120 hours may push the limits.

Teaching, Tenure and the Currency of the Academy

Instructors teaching this type of course must evaluate the support that is provided by his/her university for teaching unorthodox courses. Oftentimes, research-intensive institutions do not have the resources to support creative courses like *The Wire*. It is important to note that there are many research opportunities for teaching with *The Wire*. To be able to measure students' grasp of urban issues and *The Wire*'s ability to support that learning, is a research project in and of itself. A class using *The Wire* can be coupled with service learning, field internships, and a host of other pedagogical strategies. However, all of these strategies may be met with resistance.

To get a class using *The Wire* on the course schedule, instructors may have to persuade program directors, coordinators, or deans to assign the course as part of an existing teaching load in exchange for another course or teach the course as an overload. Teaching a course using *The Wire* may then become a "labor of love" as sometimes instructors are not adequately compensated for teaching "out of load" courses. Faculty members who are creative and excellent teachers are often needed to teach either core courses or required courses and therefore, may not have the time in their workload to be able to teach an elective course using *The Wire*. It took literally 10 years of advocacy and a planning grant to be able to develop my current course on *The Wire*.

With the potentially added teaching responsibility, ultimately, instructors must determine the usefulness of teaching a course using The Wire in their own career trajectories. Instructors must be calculating and realistic in the timing and usefulness of teaching a course using *The Wire* as part of the tenure process. Teaching a new course is time consuming and an arduous task in terms of planning and preparation. Therefore, most tenure track Assistant Professors are given the advice to teach the same courses as much as possible to allow more time to continuously improve delivery of instruction and/or reduce the time needed to develop material and to allocate more time to research and scholarship. Teaching a course on *The Wire* does not lend itself to this advice. As an assistant professor, in an institution where scholarship is highly valued and the currency of tenure, I was counseled on multiple occasions to put teaching a class on *The Wire* on hold until after the tenure process was successfully completed. However, if teaching is the currency of tenure at a given institution, a course using *The Wire* may be exactly the type of product that would show teaching innovation and creativity.

Getting a Course Using *The Wire* Approved

Beyond the personal decision to teach the course, a question of where the course fits into the curriculum must be addressed. The opportunity to teach a course on *The Wire* may not be readily available at a time when university resources are thin. The "good" and "innovative" faculty members are asked, or assigned, to teach core or required courses. This responsibility is especially true in accredited programs[3] like social work and public administration, two disciplines ripe for use of *The Wire* to explore urban issues. Because of accreditation requirements, new courses are often introduced as elective or special topics courses. However, core courses such as policy, human behavior in the social environment or other courses with urban systems related content can be adapted to use *The Wire*. It is important to note that using *The Wire* in a core course may require additional attention to the core competencies and student learning objectives for the course.

Further developing a permanent course may meet territorial complications from other departments, because *The Wire* explores multiple disciplines like communications, sociology, social work, philosophy and possibly a host of others. Due to the interdisciplinary nature of the series, the process of course approval would necessitate consultations from many different departments and colleagues. It is important to have a clear and transparent plan from which discipline or framework the course will be approached. Many institutions desire collaboration but may not have the infrastructure developed for co-teaching and cross-listed courses from multiple departments. It may be a bit of a challenge to have a permanent course using *The Wire* for instruction.

Online Instruction and *The Wire*

Once a course is developed and approved, the pedagogical strategy should be carefully considered. While there may be advocacy for online instruction to accommodate student schedules and learning styles as well as to ease financial constraints in departments, face-to-face instruction remains the traditional and dominant method of course information or knowledge delivery in post-secondary education (Sweeney, O'donoghue & Whitehead, 2004). Nonetheless, the inclination to teach *The Wire* online is quite persuasive. Because there is so much television to be watched during a course using

The Wire, it seems particularly suited for an asynchronous online course and almost inefficient to hold the course face-to-face. While asynchronous online courses offer students flexibility of schedule, there are many instances where a real time or face-to-face interaction is valuable. I and other instructors have delivered the course in both and each has its rewards. The online environment allows students to explore very sensitive topics without having to "see" their classmates and being able to confront hard issues with a certain level of anonymity. There is a degree of safety in the structured "faceless," but not anonymous, environment of an online course that is conducive to having difficult discussions candidly. Students are able to share experiences without being "seen" or having to "face" their classmates. While anonymity in online forums sometimes shields bad behavior because the writer is not known to the readers, in the online classroom experience, the writers are known by name and the instructor is watching and grading. Therefore, the negativity and vitriol that is found in anonymous online chat rooms and forums is largely absent from online class discussion. The opposite occurs in that it is often a quite supportive environment.

An online course using *The Wire* may also appeal to the generation of students currently enrolling in college courses due to their familiarity with technology. While television is not a particularly new technology, the course can be supplemented with other tools such as Youtube© videos (instructor created or curated), online tutorials, quizzes, forums, interactive maps, and other online tools. Online education may be particularly attractive to many students due to their familiarity with the Internet. Currently, traditional students (those coming straight from high school) on college campuses are considered Millennials or the Net Generation (Jones, Ramanau, Cross & Healing, 2010). Researchers suggest that Millennials as learners are digital natives who are characterized as having grown up with technology rather than having to migrate to its use (Prensky, 2001). These individuals were born the same year that the Internet was created (Guy & Lownes-Jackson, 2013).

It may be commonly thought that traditional students' native experiences with technology influences the ways in which they learn (Moody & Bobic, 2011) and their desire to use technology in class. Digital natives are comfortable with a wired (or wireless environment), expect immediate feedback, prefer learning by doing, are comfortable sharing and interacting with others, team oriented, seek structure, prefer interaction, are visual and kinesthetic as well as interested in addressing issues (Oblinger & Oblinger, 2005). However, it is important to avoid making an ecological fallacy in discussing the learning and preferences of Millennials (Margaryan, Littlejohn & Vojt, 2011). Generalizations about their digital acuity can misrepresent many members of the cohort (Jones, Ramanau, Cross & Healing, 2010).

The digital divide, the inequity in access to technology, contributes to an uneven comfort with all things online and digital (van Dijk, 2006). Further, academic discipline influences the use of technology in the classroom (Margaryan, Littlejohn & Vojt, 2011). Margaryan, Littlejohn & Vojt (2011), found that courses that used more technology tended to be more technical classes, such as engineering as opposed to social work or other social sciences. They found that "'Digital Natives' and students of a technical discipline (engineering) used more technology tools when compared to 'digital immigrants' and students of a non-technical discipline (social work)" (Margaryan, Littlejohn & Vojt, 2011 p. 429). Instructors cannot assume that all students will have similar comfort levels with technology. As many more non-traditional students enter colleges and universities (Taliaferro & Ames, 2010), online instruction may provide convenience, but may add a technology learning curve, thereby increasing the complexity of a course. A student who is challenged by the course management system (e.g., Moodle, Blackboard, etc.) may not be able to grasp actual course content while spending time on technology proficiency. Therefore, while the online environment may seem like the perfect platform for teaching a class using *The Wire*, there are technological concerns that must be mitigated to foster student success. To assume that students will automatically be comfortable in an online class because they may have an interest in, or are intrigued by, a class that actively uses watching television as a pedagogical tool would be a mistake.

Do No Harm to Students

Beyond insuring there are no additional or superficial barriers to instruction, the implications of exposure to violence must be considered. *The Wire* has multiple scenes that portray violence—violence against children, violence against women, and violence rooted in homophobia. One of the most chilling and remarkable acts of violence includes the shooting of Wallace by his friends Poot and Bodie. This scene is particularly stunning to students as they have come to like Wallace and feel like he has a chance to overcome the obstacles of his environment. Another act of violence that is not displayed on screen but its results are displayed is the torture and subsequent murder of Omar's lover Brandon. While the torture is not witnessed by viewers, the violent nature of his death is evidenced by his badly beaten and grotesquely displayed body. Throughout the series, students are exposed to copious amounts of assault, shootings, beatings, stabbings, and other incidents of violence.

To prepare and warn students about this disturbing imagery, the following warning is posted in red at the top of the first page of the course management system and course syllabus.

Note to ALL students: This course and the DVD contain adult content that may be offensive. Please note that by maintaining your enrollment in the course you understand and recognize that to be the case. You also accept responsibility for any risk this may cause.

While this message does not preclude students from being offended or impacted by the level of violence in the show, it is an attempt to prepare them for the type of information to which they will be exposed. Because *The Wire* was aired on cable television it had the latitude to portray much more graphic images than local television shows with which students are most familiar. As such, instructors must anticipate the impact of the illicit violence and potential trauma triggers.

Violence Against Women and *The Wire*

Illicit violence has been linked to negative outcomes. There is an association between television violence aggression (Miller, Grabell, Thomas, Bermann & Graham-Bermann, 2012) and rape myth beliefs among adult men and women (Kahlor & Eastin, 2011; Lee, Hust, Zhang & Zhang, 2010). Television violence is thought to contribute to the culture of violence that perpetuates violence against women (Yodanis, 2004). Television violence may indirectly promote sexual violence in that it reinforces attitudes and perspectives that diminish women and their power (Malamuth & Check, 1981). Further television violence against women has been found to emotionally desensitize viewers (Linz, Donnerstein, & Adams, 1989) and increase acceptance of rape myths (Weisz & Earls, 1995). Yodanis (2004) suggest that at a macro level, this undermines the status and power of women and on the micro level, it impacts the psyche and normalizes damaging beliefs about women and violence toward them. It is not to say that watching *The Wire* will cause students to act violently or perpetrate violence against women. It is to acknowledge that students may be impacted by the level of violence displayed. As such, instructors will need to not only prepare students for the violence they will see but be cognizant of the impact of the violence on students. While *The Wire* has multiple instances where violence and abuse are perpetrated against women, it provides an opportunity to discuss the origins, types of acts, and implications of violence on the micro, mezzo, and macro levels. Instructors can also use the content of the show to explore the many ways subtle violence and micro aggressions are perpetrated, particularly against women.

Television Violence and Fear

According to Busselle (2003), mass media is particularly powerful at showing the myriad of things to fear in society. There is significant research on the relationship between television violence and fear of crime. Madan, Mrug & Wright (2013) found that exposure to violent media was associated with increased anxiety but was somewhat less for those with prior exposure to media and real life violence. Joanne Cantor (2000) provides a meta-analysis of media violence. She details research that suggests that media violence contributes to aggressive behaviors, leads to desensitization, and creates fear, particularly in children (Cantor, 2000). Violent television, specifically crime drama and reality crime viewing contributes to higher levels of fear of crime (Custers & Van den Bulck, 2011).

Many students are disturbed by the images of killing, sex, illicit drug use that is portrayed in *The Wire*. These scenes may offend students' sensibilities and be considered vulgar, gratuitous, and sometimes unnecessary. However, the life events of poor urban residents is sometimes vulgar and offending to the sensibilities. It is important to prepare students for the vivid images and emotional reactions elicited by the show during the course of the five seasons. Students are particularly impacted by the deaths of D'Angelo and Wallace to the point of experiencing feelings of loss. Students have continued to "mourn" these characters in assignments in later seasons! These two incidences cause significant emotional events in many students because they have had an opportunity to "get to know" the characters.

In addition to witnessing violence, students have to be prepared for "triggers" such as drug use, sexual assault, abandonment, and other problems that students may have faced in their experiences. There is the need to have space within the course as well as private space to be able to process emotions and responses to these triggers and images. Over the last few years, college campuses have seen an increase in violence against individuals that have impacted the entire campus. As a result, instructors must be hypervigilant and prepared for the behaviors that may result from these triggers. It is not to say that engaging in a course that exposes students to violence will result in mass campus violence, but it is important that instructors are equipped with resources for students who may be impacted by the various scenarios found in *The Wire*.

College campuses have mental health services within the student health services. Instructors can ensure students are aware of these often free professional resources. Professional mental health service providers help students explore their responses to sensitive material and provide support for students in need. Beyond counseling centers, Behavioral Intervention Teams (BIT) are becoming more visible on college campuses. BIT "is a multi-disciplinary group whose purpose is meeting regularly to support its target audience (students, employees, faculty, staff) via an established protocol. The team tracks "red flags" over time, detecting patterns, trends, and disturbances in individual or group behavior." (Nabita.org, 2015. para 1). These teams are designed to protect the health and safety of the college campus community by managing situations that may pose a threat, such as school shootings, bullying, campus intolerance, and a host of other risks to campus safety. While it is optimal that these resources are not necessary, making students aware of them may be warranted when teaching using *The Wire*.

Do No Harm to Baltimore and Urban Areas

A significant concern of Baltimore residents regarding *The Wire* is the portrayal of "their city." Even the former Mayor of Baltimore, Kurt Schmoke, has spoken out on what he terms the mis-portrayal of the city in *The Wire* (the guardian, 2008). He suggests in a 2008 Op-Ed that:

> The casual viewer of the show would not know that Baltimore is the home of outstanding museums, fine universities, world-class medical research institutions, inviting tourist attractions, and beautiful, tree-lined residential communities. What the viewer would see and what *The Wire* exposes is the reality of the "other" Baltimore. That is the side of the city that is scarred by vacant houses, hampered by a poor performing public school system, and plagued by a concentration of poverty that leads to high levels of illegal drug abuse and violent crime. These two Baltimores co-exist in a relatively small area only 40 miles from the nations' capital, Washington D.C. (the guardian, 2008, para 2].

Baltimore has been a "character" in contemporary media many times before *The Wire*. There was *Diner* (1982), *Hairspray* (2007), *Homicide: Life on the Streets* (1993), and *The Corner* (2000). Each portrayal of Baltimore was quite different and none elicited the kind of reaction reserved for *The Wire*. In December 2014, HBO rebroadcasted a remastered High Definition (HD) version of *The Wire*. While it once again received much acclaim, not everyone was thrilled about the portrayal of Baltimore City. A recent Facebook discussion elicited visceral reactions from Baltimore residents. A portion of the discussion is below:

> CRYSTAL R. I watched a few episodes of *The Wire* and agree with everyone that the acting and production are amazing. However, I can't get past the terrible damage that series did to MY city. Until you work in public relations for institutions in Baltimore, you just won't understand. That show makes me angry. I will NEVER watch it again!
>
> JOCELYN T. @Crystal, I do not work on public relations but as someone that teaches urban issues, this is a gold mine. I actually teach a class on critical social policy and urban issues. I'm also writing a book on how to use *The Wire* to teach urban issues. I think what needs to be considered is that these things happen in EVERY urban center across America. Not just Baltimore. Baltimore was the perfect backdrop because of its complexity and texture. As you watch, if you choose to, you will see the multitude of

stories, circumstances, and issues. The first season is the surface. Seasons 2–5 provide significant commentary on the true issues of Season 1.

CRYSTAL R. I just wish people would put it in its proper perspective. But they don't! I worked in [area in Prince Georges County Maryland] for more than three years. They thought, and still think Baltimore is *The Wire*. DC is not viewed that way. When they get here, they see something totally different. I've got a really hard job!

TAYLOR G. Maybe the reason people still talk about it is because it's still happening…. the schools are not getting better, instead, they are closing them. The relationship with the politicians, police and the citizens are steady dividing. And those are people who act the same way about ANY city—not just Baltimore. People think all cities are bastions of crime, poverty, and Black thugs. So these people are not taking issue with Baltimore. They are taking issue with urban centers

RYAN H. Yep! That has been my gripe for years with *The Wire*. I have no love for the show and can't get behind something that every tourist refers to as the real Baltimore and their fear of Baltimore.

This discussion on a friend's Facebook page[4] is indicative of the comments from some Baltimoreans regarding the portrayal of the city. There is legitimate concern that students who are not familiar with the city, or any urban area, will be lead to think that all cities, and Baltimore in particular, are bastions of crime and poverty. As Peggy Jones discusses in the previous essay, students' lack or misinformation may have an injurious impact on the perceptions of poor people and communities. Left unchallenged, these conceptions can be damaging. As such, the next section of this essay will discuss strategies for teaching *The Wire* that are congruent with the unique class content and use of *The Wire* as a case example to study urban issues.

Activities and Strategies for Teaching The Wire

In teaching a course on *The Wire* beyond pragmatic decisions for the instructor, there must be consideration of teaching strategies. It would be a missed opportunity if such an edgy and relevant nontraditional course was taught using only a conventional lecture format to deliver content. Teaching a course of this type is also an opportunity to change students' and instructors' paradigms around teaching and learning. In the following section, activities, and strategies for teaching will be discussed. While these strategies may not be completely new, they are a diversion from a simple lecture format.

Context Matters: About Baltimore

The Wire portrays a very real *part* of Baltimore City. However, the show does not portray the entirety of Baltimore City with equal emphasis. It is important that students understand that most central cities deal with problems of crime, drugs, institutional failures, poverty, police brutality, and the host of other reflections of urban problems. But central cities are also complex ecosystems that have multiple layers and divisions. Baltimore City is considered the city of neighborhoods where there are very clearly defined named neighborhoods (e.g., Northwood, Perring Loch, Canton, Gwynn Oak, Park Circle, Edmonson Village, Harlem Park, Sandtown-Winchester etc). The show takes place in some of the more highly concentrated poverty areas of the City.[5]

With a population of 622,793 residents and a median income of $41,385 (Quickfacts.census.gov, 2015), clearly the entire city is not drug infested and impoverished with individuals living in dilapidated housing or high- or low rise public housing. While the poverty rate is quite high, slightly less than 24 percent (Census.gov, 2015), it is important to discuss with students the diversity of income and economic resources in a city like Baltimore. Baltimore's major industries include professional, scientific and technical services; educational services; information technology; cyber security; biohealth and healthcare; government; not-for-profits; higher education, government, and sports (Greaterbaltimore.org, 2015).

Approximately 80 percent of the city's population over the age of 25 has a high school diploma and 26.8 percent hold a Bachelor's degree or higher (Quickfacts.census.gov, 2015). The homeownership rate for the city is 48 percent with approximately three individuals per household (Quickfacts.census.gov, 2015). Baltimore residents are productive citizens. However, it cannot be ignored that between January and October 1, 2015, there were 249 murders in the City of Baltimore, up from 211 in 2014 and 234 in 2013 (The Baltimore Sun, 2015). Not surprisingly, these homicides were concentrated in lower income areas of the city.

To place these figures in context, examining statistics for Oakland, California, Boston, Massachusetts, and Philadelphia, Pennsylvania, are useful. These locations were chosen as the Baltimore Development Corporation (BDC) has identified these "benchmark" cities as comparable to Baltimore and are seeking mirror the economic development of the areas (Baltimore Development Corporation, 2015). These cities were chosen because all are port cities; "have economies that rely on technology centers, health care and higher education; are either majority-minority or have fast growing minority and immigrant populations; and have a blue-collar tradition but are embracing technology and service economies" (Baltimore Development Corporation, 2015, p. 12). Table 1 provides a comparison of the cities.

To illustrate the complexity of context, students are provided information via maps, charts and graphs using census data and other online interactive tools. Students are encouraged to look up crime rates for their hometown;

Table 1: Baltimore, Boston, Philadelphia, Oakland Comparison

	Baltimore	Boston	Philadelphia	Oakland
Population	622,793	655,884	1,560,297	413,775
African American	63.1	24.4%	43.4%	28%
Median Income	$41,385	$53,601	$37,192	$52,583
Poverty	24%	21.4%	26.5%	20.5%
High School Diploma	80%	85.0%	81.2%	80.2%
Bachelor's Degree +	26.8%	43.9%	23.9%	38.1%
Homeownership Rate	48%	34.1%	53.3%	40.4%
Homicides 2014	211	52	248	80
Homicides 2013	234	41	246	91

Sources: *City of Oakland (2015); Newsroom,WBUR (2015); Phillypolice.com (2015); Quick facts.census.gov (2015);* The Baltimore Sun *(2015)*

the city of the university they attend; Washington, D.C.; Baltimore, MD; and one other city of their choosing. Students then provide reflections on the disparity or similarities of the various indicators. Many students are surprised at the results. Some find their city of origin has more crime than they realized. Others have noted that while the city in which their university is located is considered a big city by many students, based on demographic indicators in comparison to other areas suggest it is more suburban than urban.

This discussion, usually in the format of an online forum, is an opportunity to explore issues of cities and urban centers in general. After students have engaged in a scholarly discussion about urban centers, students are then encouraged to reflect on their chosen city in a more light-hearted fashion, using "judgmental maps" that became popular in 2014 (Judgmentalmaps.com, 2015). These visual aids allow students to be able to see how various areas portrayed in *The Wire* do not depict the entirety of Baltimore City. This discussion is particularly relevant as some students who register for these types of course may never have been to urban areas.

Finally, it is important to include discussions with students about the systemic and institutional aspects of urban experiences that make these areas so challenged. Looking at the statistics, some students may be inclined to apportion all of urban problems on residents and their individual decisions. However, there are institutional and systemic reasons for the plight of urban communities. *The Wire* is outstanding in its illumination of institutional issues of nepotism, incompetency, politicking, inadequate resources, economic bifurcation, declining economic industry, and unintended consequences. These issues coalesce to create impediments that are often far too great for individuals to surmount. It is incumbent upon instructors to highlight these structural issues that impact the daily life and reduce the life chances of urban residents.

More Than Just Television Watching

In addition to providing additional geographic context, there are opportunities to provide additional contextual resources. To make this a legitimate course that engages students in urban issues, there must be more than watching and discussing the television show. It is paramount to provide supplemental scholarly resource information to provide the historicity and a paradigm for the issues being discussed. Further, source material can be added to ensure that course objectives are met. Therefore, in addition to the series, a list of readings can be assigned to provide both a historical and contemporary perspective to the examples *The Wire* provides.

In addition to traditional teaching aids such as peer reviewed journal articles and book chapters, tools such as YouTube© and other internet videos, online quizzes, and case studies, discussion groups are used to convey material. Instructors can create videos (or other electronic widgets) to orient students to the information in the coming season. These short videos or lecturettes, as I refer to them in class, can provide new vocabulary, introduction to upcoming concepts, explanation of conflicting perspectives as well as an orientation to the salient themes on which the instructor would like to focus. These videos can serve as an outline or study guide for students. While this information could be conveyed in a written format, which is also recommended in addition to the video, having the video provides a little more interaction and appeals to various types of learners (Klement, Dostál & Marešová, 2014).

Student Engagement Methods

Keeping students engaged beyond watching the television series may be onerous. Discussion boards, blogs, and nontraditional exams are methods of engaging students while assessing student performance and grasp of concepts. These strategies for instruction can and have been used in other types of classes but they are particularly well suited to a course on *The Wire.*

Discussion Boards and Class Sessions

Several types of discussion boards or forums can be used in class, those that are related to course content as well as those that are slightly "off topic." While watching the series, inevitably students will be interested in discussing aspects of the show that are not particularly relevant to the discipline related course content. To address these not as relevant topics, the course has a "First Impressions" board or forum.

FIRST IMPRESSIONS BOARD/FORUM

Students are encouraged to use time in class or online discussion board to process or debrief what they have just "witnessed." This forum is an opportunity for students to talk about everything from cinematography and the theme song to the fact that one of the characters had on a Duke University T-shirt.[6] This is a time for students to free associate *and engage* in discussions that really do not pertain to urban issues or discipline related content. In general, this forum is for students to lead discussions and provide feedback from their peers and engage in peripheral conversations without side tracking the more relevant conversations of urban issues discussed as formal course content. This is also a space where instructors can informally determine students' perspectives and frameworks for viewing the material.

WATER COOLER

In addition to the first impressions forum, the course has an online discussion board called the "water cooler." This space is particularly suited to an online class as students naturally create this atmosphere in a face-to-face course before and after class and during breaks. Because an online environment, particularly if it is asynchronous, does not provide the opportunity for students to talk informally, this space simulates the proverbial office water cooler experience. The water cooler is used in varying degrees by each class. The instructions for the water cooler are as follows:

> Please use this space to chat with your colleagues about non-course related things. Post announcements, achievements, whatever you like. You can discuss just about anything but we will maintain civility and respect here. For the most part, I do not monitor/enter this area unless I am invited in by one of you! This is your space. Please note, this space is for NON-COURSE RELATED information. Do not post information about the course here. It is an optional space and I do not come here so I will not see your post. Use this space for shooting the breeze, talking about other television shows, promoting your activities that you want your colleagues to know about, telling your peers about your dog's latest antics... whatever you like. This is the space where you get to create community.

GENERAL DISCUSSIONS

Other discussion boards or forums and discussion topics are focused on the issues of the course. Students are given prompts online and they are also encouraged to add their own questions. In the face-to-face environment, students are encouraged to list questions before class that can be discussed in class. Rather than have students write out lengthy responses they are encouraged to participate in dialogue during the class period. However, students regularly return to the online discussion forum and continue in-class discussions online. These online forums provide an outlet for students to discuss material that may have been to embarrassing or sensitive in class. For instance, a student used the online forum to discuss her own foster care system experiences when Randy was sent to the group home at the conclusion of Season Four. While she ultimately had to face her peers the next class period after this self-disclosure, she did not have to share this very personal information, in her words "with everyone looking at" her.

Overall students respond positively to these discussion boards. This is by no means an exhaustive list but a few options for how to engage students in the online and face-to-face course delivery.

Exams and Activities

Assessing student learning is an important component of every course. Again, using traditional means of multiple choice exams is less than imaginative for a course with rich content such as *The Wire*. Adding creative and more participatory assessments maintains the *novelty* of teaching a course on *The Wire*. As a component of the online course, an interactive course blog is developed by all of the class participants. Each season of *The Wire* has its own blog to which students contribute. Each student is assigned a role so that not every student is posting at the same time, and furthermore, so that each group of students has a specific task for that season. The roles and responsibilities for the blog are detailed in Table 2.

Table 2: Blog Roles

First Writers	Respondents	Searchers	Breathers
These students are responsible for posting initial questions and insights about the season's material to the class blog by the first Tuesday of the first week of the season.	Students in this group build upon, disagree with, or clarify the first readers' posts.	Students in this group find and share at least one relevant online resource. In addition to linking to the resource, the searchers provide a short evaluation of the resource, highlighting what makes it worthwhile, unusual, or, if appropriate, problematic.	These students do not have to contribute to the blog. They can take the week off if they want to.

The roles for each student are assigned the first season of the series. These rotate with each subsequent season. If students are readily engaged and everyone is actively participating, and the roles are no longer necessary, they are no longer assigned. It is important to note that breathers rarely take the week off. Most of the time, the conversations are so appealing that the students participate. Inevitably, a student will say "Oh Man! I couldn't breathe this week!" Students are not restricted to their assigned role. The following note is added to the instructions of the blog "*Note: You do not have to stay in your role! As long as you fulfill your role you can take on another one too.*"

Although students often exceed the expectation, each student is responsible for posting an approximately 100–300 word response to the season's events based on their role on the blog. There are a number of ways to approach these open-ended posts. Students can consider the season's events in relation to its historical or theoretical context; write about an aspect of the season that they do not understand, or something that is surprising or jarring; formulate an insightful question or two about the season and then attempt to answer those questions; or respond to another student's post, building upon it, disagreeing with it, or re-thinking it. Students are asked to use the reply format so that it is as much of a conversation as possible.

For both the online and face-to-face classes, the final project for the course is a Concept Map. Concept maps are a visual exploration of explaining an issue, in this case social policy. This assignment provides a way for students to demonstrate their understandings of complex related issues and organize the information of the class into patterns, relationships, and connections. Students are expected to utilize visual and spatial thinking to incorporate the major themes of *The Wire* and the major course concepts.

Students are asked to reflect on the course content, think back to the question prompts, discussions, seminar discussion readings, lecturettes, and create a concept map that details the major concepts (ideas, theories, perceptions, solutions, and models) of social policy depicted in *The Wire*. Students are asked to select an organizing concept which serves as the center of the map or unifying theme. Then other dominant themes are expected to be organized on the map and relationships between themes clearly defined. Students are encouraged to do this in (self-determined) groups but allowed to do it individually if they so choose. Other components of the assignment include an abstract and a bibliography for the map.

The products of the map assignment have been of mixed quality and scope. Some student's submissions have been simple MS Word or PowerPoint documents. Others have included multimedia features such as music, video clips, and charts. One of the most creative has used a Prezi presentation that had more than 100 links and modules.[7] The assignments have continued to show creativity and a depth of understanding that is quite impressive.

While this is not an exhaustive list of assignments of activities used in courses using *The Wire*, these are examples of pedagogical tools that can be employed to encourage discussion, foster participation, and encourage student's intellectual curiosity. As with any academic course, the content must be provided in a way that compliments the instructor's personality and delivery style. Further, assessments must be tailored to the course's discipline, level, and enrollment.

Shelf Life of The Wire: Pagers and the Projects

Beyond course development, implementation decisions, and assignments, a final challenge of teaching using *The Wire* is its "shelf life." Instructors have to continually find ways of making the course material relevant. While non-traditional students may find *The Wire* very realistic, many Millennials may find it passé. The show makes mention of things like 9/11 and its impact on policing resources; teaching the test, which alludes to children's educational experiences with No Child Left Behind; budget deficits of cities that were being incurred all over America. All of these instances were particularly relevant during the time *The Wire* aired on HBO. Some of these issues have drifted from the popular culture discourse.

An example of the potential lack of relevance is the use of pagers in *The Wire*. An integral part of *The Wire* is the use of pagers as part of its story and plot line. By most standards, pagers are outdated and many students will never have had any interaction with a pager and not understand the relevance of pagers circa 2005 (Guy & Lownes-Jackson, 2013). Some undergraduate students may never have seen a real pager and only have a recollection of doctors on a show their parents used to watch having pagers. Further, the technology, or lack thereof in the police department is also quite problematic in students' understandings or acceptance of the realism of the crime series. The typewriters and equipment used in the series were outdated in 2005 but antique in the minds of students in 2015. With the advent of the modern day network television crime drama (e.g., the *NCIS*, *CSI*, *Criminal Minds*, and *Law & Order* franchises), the lack of technology of the series may serve to compromise the realism for these students. Irrespective of the fact that the technology of *The Wire* is closer to the true experiences of urban policing, than the technology of the network television crime drama students may find the lack of technology unbelievable and therefore negate the realism of *The Wire*.

Additionally, with changes to housing policy, fewer high rise towers and public housing as depicted in *The Wire* exist. Public housing with low rises that flank high rise towers is slowly being replaced with more mixed income development. While many of today's students may be familiar with low income housing, fewer are familiar with "the projects" as depicted as the territory of D'Angelo [assisted by Bodie, Poot, and Wallace] in Season One. This lack of connection and context also challenges the authentic feel of the series in 2015 as opposed to during its original run in 2005 and the decade since.

As these artifacts of life in early 2000s recede further into history, use of *The Wire* as a "real" depiction of urban life is contested.

And Then There Was Freddie Gray

While technology and the changes to the urban landscape bring the effectiveness of *The Wire* into question, its exploration of police brutality, social injustice, and context of Baltimore's political system make it highly relevant in 2015. The real life tragic death of Freddie Gray that unfolded in Spring 2015 catapulted Baltimore and many of the issues addressed in *The Wire* into the national spotlight. The following account of the incident is according to a timeline created from multiple articles written by staff writers for the *Baltimore Sun* newspaper (Harris, 2015). On April 12, 2015, Freddie Gray a Baltimore City resident was arrested by police after a foot chase. The reason for the pursuit of Mr. Gray and another man remains unclear except that the two men ran, so police chased them. A controversial arrest and transport followed in which Mr. Gray needed medical attention upon arrival at the Western District Police Station, the station prominently portrayed in *The Wire* as the home of Sargent in Charge (SIC) Carver as well as Officer Eddie Walker (the corrupt patrolman and nemesis to Namond and Michael in Season Four).

Mr. Gray was transported to the University of Maryland Medical Center Trauma Center in downtown Baltimore (simply referred to as Shock Trauma by Baltimore residents). One week later on April 19, 2015, Mr. Gray died from injuries, including an 80 percent severed spine, obtained during the transport (Harris, 2015). On April 18th, before his death, protesters begin to demonstrate in front of the real Western District Police Station, these protests started by city residents and later joined by the Leaders from the ACLU, NAACP, Baltimore City chapter of the Southern Christian Leadership Conference, expanded to City Hall and continued peacefully until April 24, 2015, with few arrest (Campbell & Anderson, 2015). On April 25, 2015, a few protesters damaged property and businesses during otherwise peaceful demonstrations. On Monday, April 27, 2015, the day of Freddie Gray's funeral, the demonstrations erupted with clashes between police and demonstrators, damage to property, looting of businesses, multiple arrest and ultimately the engagement of the National Guard and a citywide curfew issued by Stephanie Rawlings-Blake, the Mayor of Baltimore City.[8]

These unfortunate violent protest and unrest in Baltimore sparked by the treatment of Freddy Gray highlighted issues of police brutality, racial profiling, poverty, social inequity and a host of urban problems. It illuminated the "burn behind the burn" as termed by Malik Shabazz a Washington, D.C., lawyer and leader of Black Lawyers for Justice (Pitts, 2015 para 2). The unrest, seen on televisions across America, was a result of the frustration of city residents over social and economic injustice and brought these issues and Baltimore, Maryland, to the forefront of the national discourse and made *The Wire* relevant once more.

This pinpoint in America's history, coupled with other incidents of police brutality and social injustice in Ferguson, New York, Baltimore, are an opportunity for instructors to look at inequity and racial discrimination, racism, and its history. These poignant events can be used to make the incidences depicted in *The Wire* relevant. Not only can instructors use the vivid images of the police brawl as they "crack heads" in a raid and the encouraged cover up of Officer "Prez" Pryzbylewski's pistol-whipping of a teenage boy by Daniels in Season One, or the brutality of Officer Walker as he breaks Donut's fingers in Season Four to exemplify issues of over policing and brutality. Instructors can help students explore the underlying issues of urban communities by unpacking the circumstances and events that led up to these eruptions. Instructors can help students see the agency, decision-making, resourcefulness and resilience of community members and yet still the disadvantage of urban communities.

The Wire can be viewed parallel to the real life incidences of Eddie Gray, Eric Garner, and Michael Brown. Many students may not be able to understand the reasons for the unrest in these cities and across the country. They may feel intimidated by the talk of social justice and White Privilege. They may feel confused by the incongruence of what is said about police behavior and what they experience in their communities. While it must be made clear that *The Wire* is fiction, it is an excellent entree into the discourse of urban problems and their solutions.

In an economic and social environment of intolerance, economic bifurcation, and redacting of the social safety net, it is imperative that students have an awareness of the complexity of social problems and therefore the need for nuanced social welfare policy responses. While many students may think there are silver bullet solutions to problems of urban areas, they simply do not exist. Because most students are not and cannot be exposed to the complexity of social problems in an intimate way, the HBO miniseries *The Wire* can be used as the "fishbowl" in which students can get this exposure. Because students must have an awareness of problems to find reasonable solutions, courses on *The Wire* can be designed to provide a space for reasoned discussion and debate regarding social policy problems, policies, and programs.

NOTES

1. "Soft Eyes" is a reference made in Season Four regarding the need to look at things from a different perspective and deeper than a surface level interpretation.

2. The calendar of a semester is 16 weeks but when accounting for holidays and breaks, the schedule is most likely a 14 week schedule. This is particularly relevant in the graduate level environment when classes often meet once per week.

3. Social Work and Public Administration in particular have program accreditation in addition to university accreditation. For instance Social Work programs are accredited by the Council on Social Work Education and have to be reaffirmed every eight years.

4. While Facebook is to some extent public, the names have been changed and some wording revised to protect confidentiality of the individuals who made comments.

5. Several Google Maps of *The Wire* are available for use in classes. The following link is to a Google Map that depicts location by season's activities https://www.google.com/maps/d/edit?mid=zKqCnkCclaUo.kmL4KEmadkGc&usp=sharing

6. This was a particularly relevant to these particular students as the course was taught at a university located in the state of North Carolina where collegiate sports rivalries are epic.

7. One of the submissions was submitted via a public Prezi. It is quite complex and feedback was given that the only thing that hindered the submission was that it was not guided so it was easy to get lost in the information. A link to it can be found at https://prezi.com/1cdywlyujp5j/the-wire-concept-mapping-project/

8. For a full timeline of the events of the unrest in Baltimore, MD following the injury and death of Freddie Gray, see http://data.baltimoresun.com/news/freddie-gray/

REFERENCES

Baltimore Development Corporation. (2015). *Seizing the momentum, building a brighter future: A comprehensive economic development strategy for baltimore 2014 jobs investment growth.* Baltimore. Retrieved from http://baltimoredevelopment.com/wp-content/uploads/2014/08/CEDS-BDC-Report.pdf.

Baltimore Sun (2015). *Interactive map: Baltimore homicides.* Retrieved 30 September 2015, from http://data.baltimoresun.com/bing-maps/homicides/?.

Busselle, R. (2003). Television Exposure, Parents' Precautionary Warnings, and Young Adults' Perceptions of Crime. *Communicaiton Research,* 30(5), 530–556. http://dx.doi.org/10.1177/0093650203256360.

Campbell, C., and J. Anderson. (2015). Protesters take to Baltimore's streets for a fifth day. *The Baltimore Sun.* Retrieved from http://www.baltimoresun.com/news/maryland/baltimore-city/bs-md-freddie-gray-protests-20150423-story.html.

Cantor, J. (2000). Media violence. *Journal of Adolescent Health, 27,* 30–34.

Census.gov. (2015). *Per capita income in past 12 months (in 2013 dollars), 2009–2013.* Retrieved 30 September 2015, from http://www.census.gov/quickfacts/table/INC910213/00

City of Oakland. (2015). *City of Oakland 2014 shot spotter report.* Oakland: City of Oakland. Retrieved from http://www2.oaklandnet.com/oakca1/groups/police/documents/webcontent/oak050934.pdf.

Custers, K., and J. Van den Bulck. (2011). Mediators of the association between television viewing and fear of crime: Perceived personal risk and perceived ability to cope. *Poetics,* 39(2), 107–124. http://dx.doi.org/10.1016/j.poetic.2011.02.004.

Diner. (1982). Baltimore, MD.

Ford, E. (2012). Combined television viewing and computer use and mortality from all-causes and diseases of the circulatory system among adults in the United States. *BMC Public Health*, *12*(1), 70. http://dx.doi.org/10.1186/1471-2458-12-70.

Greaterbaltimore.org,. (2015). *EAGB > Research > Key Industries*. Retrieved 30 September 2015, from http://www.greaterbaltimore.org/research/key-industries.aspx.

the guardian. (2008). *The wire and the real Baltimore*. Retrieved 30 September 2015, from http://www.theguardian.com/commentisfree/2008/jan/11/thewireandthe realbaltimor.

Guy, R., and M. Lownes-Jackson. (2013). Web-based tutorials and traditional face-to-face lectures: A comparative analysis of student performance. *Issues In Informing Science & Information Technology*, *10*(1), 241–258.

Hairspray. (2007). Baltimore, MD.

Harris, E. (2015). Timeline: Freddie Gray's arrest, death and the aftermath. *Baltimore Sun*. Data.baltimoresunwww. Retrieved 13 November 2015, from http://data.baltimoresun.com/news/freddie-gray/.

Homicide: Life on the street. (1993).

Jones, C., R. Ramanau, S. Cross, and G. Healing. (2010). Net generation or digital natives: Is there a distinct new generation entering university? *Computers & Education*, *54*(3), 722–732. http://dx.doi.org/10.1016/j.compedu.2009.09.022.

Judgmentalmaps.com,. (2015). *JUDGMENTAL MAPS*. Retrieved 30 September 2015, from http://judgmentalmaps.com/.

Kahlor, L., and M. Eastin. (2011). Television's role in the culture of violence toward women: A study of television viewing and the cultivation of rape myth acceptance in the United States. *Journal of Broadcasting & Electronic Media*, *55*(2), 215–231. doi:10.1080/08838151.2011.566085.

Klement, M., Dostál, J., & Marešová, H. (2014). Elements of electronic teaching materials with respect to student's cognitive learning styles. *Procedia—Social and Behavioral Sciences*, *112*, 437–446. doi.org/10.1016/j.sbspro.2014.01.1186.

Lee, M., S. Hust, L. Zhang, and Y. Zhang. (2010). Effects of violence against women in popular crime dramas on viewers' attitudes related to sexual violence. *Mass Communication and Society*, *14*(1), 25–44. doi:10.1080/15205430903531440.

Linz, D., E. Donnerstein, and S. Adams. (1989). Physiological desensitization and judgments about female victims of violence. *Human Communication Research*, *15*(4), 509–522. http://dx.doi.org/10.1111/j.1468-2958.1989.tb00197.x.

Madan, A., S. Mrug, and R. Wright. (2013). The effects of media violence on anxiety in late adolescence. *J Youth Adolescence*, *43*(1), 116–126. doi:10.1007/s10964-013-0017-3.

Malamuth, N., and J. Check. (1981). The effects of mass media exposure on acceptance of violence against women: A field experiment. *Journal of Research in Personality*, *15*(4), 436–446. http://dx.doi.org/10.1016/0092-6566(81)90040-4.

Margaryan, A., A. Littlejohn, and G. Vojt. (2011). Are digital natives a myth or reality? University students' use of digital technologies. *Computers & Education*, *56*(2), 429–440. doi:10.1016/j.compedu.2010.09.004.

Miller, L., A. Grabell, A. Thomas, E. Bermann, and S. Graham-Bermann. (2012). The associations between community violence, television violence, intimate partner violence, parent-child aggression, and aggression in sibling relationships of a sample of preschoolers. *Psychology of Violence*, *2*(2), 165–178. doi:10.1037/a0027254.

Mills, D. (Writer), D. Dimon, and E. Burns (Story), and C. Moore (Director). (2006, September 17). Soft eyes [television series episode]. In Simon, D. (Producer), *The Wire*. Baltimore, MD: Blown Deadline Productions & Home Box Office.

Moody, R., and M. Bobic. (2011). Teaching the net generation without leaving the rest of us behind: How technology in the classroom influences student composition. *Politics & Policy*, 39(2), 169–194. doi:10.1111/j.1747-1346.2011.00287.x.

Moore, A. (2011) Teaching HBO's *the wire*. *Transformative Dialogues: Teaching and Learning Journal* 5(1), pp. 1–14.

Nabita.org,. (2015). *NABITA—National Behavioral Intervention Team Association » Behavioral Intervention Teams*. Retrieved 13 November 2015, from https://nabita.org/behavioral-intervention-teams/.

Nacoste, R. (2010). *Making gumbo in the university*. Austin, TX: Plain View Press.

Newsroom, WBUR. (2015). *Map: 2014 boston homicides*. *WBUR*. Retrieved 13 November 2015, from http://www.wbur.org/2014/01/27/2014-boston-murders.

Oblinger, D., and J. Oblinger. (2005). Introduction. In D. Oblinger and J. Oblinger, *Educating the net generation* (1st ed.). Published Online: EDUCAUSE. Retrieved from http://www.educause.edu/educatingthenetgen/ Accessed on October 12, 2015.

Ochoa, Eduardo (2015) "Dear colleague: GEN-11-06." Online at https://ifap.ed.gov/dpcletters/attachments/GEN1106.pdf Accessed on October 12, 2015.

Phillypolice.com. (2015). Crime maps & stats | Philadelphia police department. Retrieved 13 November 2015, from https://www.phillypolice.com/crime-maps-stats/.

Pitts, J. (2015). Shabazz plans rally for thousands Saturday. Baltimoresunwww. Retrieved 27 October 2015, from http://www.baltimoresun.com/news/breaking/bs-md-shabazz-saturday-20150428-story.html.

Prensky, M. (2001). Digital natives, digital immigrants part 1. *On the Horizon*, 9(5), 1–6. doi:10.1108/10748120110424816.

Quickfacts.census.gov. (2015). Baltimore (city) QuickFacts from the U.S. Census Bureau. Retrieved 30 September 2015, from http://quickfacts.census.gov/qfd/states/24/2404000.html.

Simon, D., and E. Burns. (2000). *The corner*. New York: Home Box Office.

Sweeney, J., T. O'donoghue, and C. Whitehead. (2004). Traditional face-to-face and web-based tutorials: A study of university students' perspectives on the roles of tutorial participants. *Teaching in Higher Education*, 9(3), 311–323. doi:10.1080/1356251042000216633.

Taliaferro, J., and N. Ames. (2010). Implementing an elective BSW community-based evaluation research course. *Journal of Baccalaureate Social Work*, 15(1), 105–119.

Trier, J. (2010). Representations of education in HBO's the wire, season 4. *Teacher Education Quarterly*, 37(2), 179–200.

van Dijk, J. (2006). Digital divide research, achievements and shortcomings. *Poetics*, 34(4–5), 221–235. doi: 10.1016/j.poetic.2006.05.004.

Weisz, M., & Earls, C. (1995). The effects of exposure to filmed sexual violence on attitudes toward rape. *Journal of Interpersonal Violence*, 10(1), 71–84. http://dx.doi.org/10.1177/088626095010001005.

Yodanis, C. (2004). Gender inequality, violence against women, and: A Cross-national test of the feminist theory of violence against women. *Journal of Interpersonal Violence*, 19(6), 655–675. doi:10.1177/0886260504263868.

About the Contributors

Joe **Allen** is a professor of English at Dutchess Community College in Poughkeepsie, New York. He teaches courses in composition, popular culture, and cultural studies and has been teaching full seasons of *The Wire* since 2007. He was also a regular contributor to the music journal *Wax Poetics* from its inception in 2002 to 2008.

Hannah Carson **Baggett** is an assistant professor of education research methods at Auburn University. Her research interrogates how teacher education prepares preservice and practicing teachers to meet the needs of diverse learners. She also uses participatory and community-based research methods to examine inequity.

Brandi **Blessett** is an assistant professor in the Department of Public Policy and Administration at Rutgers University–Camden. Her research examines the role of public administrators as either facilitators or inhibitors of fairness, equity, and justice for historically marginalized groups. She has published several articles and book chapters that explore racial disparities.

Jessica T. **DeCuir-Gunby** is an associate professor of educational psychology and University Faculty Scholar in the Department of Teacher Education and Learning Sciences at North Carolina State University. Her research and theoretical interests include race and racial identity development, critical race theory, mixed methods research, and emotions in education.

Sharonda R. **Eggleton** is a native of Philadelphia and has taught high school science for the past 12 years. A Ph.D. candidate at North Carolina State University, she will complete her degree in curriculum and instruction, educational psychology in the fall of 2016. Her dissertation explores the K–12 STEM messages and experiences of African American women.

Tia Sherèe **Gaynor** is an assistant professor in the Department of Public and Nonprofit Administration at Marist College. Her research focuses on issues related to social (in)justice and equity within the United States and a global context. Her scholarship revolves around participation and engagement; public and social policy analysis and implementation; and pedagogy, learning, and instruction.

Gus P. **Gradinger** is a *Wire* enthusiast and undergraduate business administration student at Chapman University. Relevant experience includes coursework in Humanomics—a self-designed minor—as well as a summer fellowship with the International Foundation for Research in Experimental Economics (IFREE).

Peggy **Jones** is an associate professor of black studies and associate director of the women's and gender studies program at the University of Nebraska–Omaha. Her research interests include intersections between language and identity. She wrote the chapter "My Mother Tongue: A Linguistic Autoethnography" for *African American Women's Language: Discourse, Education and Identity*.

Heather Cherie **Moore** is an assistant professor of community and justice studies at Allegheny College. She conducts research on the diverse representations of Black male students in American film, television, and hip-hop. Her research explores the intersections of Black identity, informal education, social justice, and mass media. She received a doctorate from the American Studies program at Purdue University in 2015.

Crystal G. **Simmons** is an assistant professor of social studies, multicultural, and international education at SUNY Geneseo. Her research interests include the study and curriculum development of Black history and critical race theory.

Mark **Stern** is an assistant professor in the Department of Educational Studies at Colgate University where he teaches classes on education policy and social theory. His current research focuses on the political and cultural economy of public education in the United States. He holds a Ph.D. in cultural foundations of education from Syracuse University and an honorary lectureship at the Centre for Civil Society at the University of KwaZulu–Natal. Recent publications can be found in *Race, Ethnicity and Education, Educational Policy,* and *The Berkeley Review of Education.*

Jocelyn DeVance **Taliaferro** is an associate professor in the North Carolina State University Department of Social Work. Her research interests promote operational citizenship and social justice including nonprofit lobbying, African American student achievement, and parental involvement. Her articles appear in the *Journal of Child and Family Social Work, Journal of Policy Practice,* and *Education and Urban Society.*

Christopher S. **Toenes** is a clinical social worker and writer living in Durham, North Carolina. His work includes being a co-director on the documentary film: *Mission Critical: Ending the School-to-Prison Pipeline in Wake County* (2014), and *A Needs Assessment and Issue Characterization of School "Push-Out" in Wake County, North Carolina.*

Jason P. **Vest** is a professor of English in the University of Guam's Division of English and Applied Linguistics. His publications include *Future Imperfect: Philip K. Dick at the Movies* (2007; 2009); *The Postmodern Humanism of Philip K. Dick* (2009); *"The Wire," "Deadwood," "Homicide," and "NYPD Blue": Violence Is Power* (2010), and *Spike Lee: Finding the Story and Forcing the Issue* (2014).

Bart J. **Wilson** is the Donald P. Kennedy Endowed Chair in Economics and Law at Chapman University's Economic Science Institute. He has published papers in the *American Economic Review*, the *Proceedings of the National Academy of Sciences*, and *Proceedings of the Royal Society B*, and his research has been supported with grants from the National Science Foundation, the Federal Trade Commission, and the Institute for Justice.

Index

adaptive strategies 44, 47–50
Albrecht, Chris 117
Alter, Jonathan 85
Americanization 137
aristocracy 9, 10, 14
At-risk 26–28, 30, 34–35, 37, 44–45, 48, 71–72

Bailey, John 104
Barksdale, Avon 8, 10–11, 13, 19, 100, 103, 109, 126
Barksdale, D'Angelo 7–8, 13
Barksdale organization 7–9, 11, 19, 40, 103–104, 106, 109–110, 142
Bell, Russell "Stringer" 8, 10–20, 100, 103–104, 109–110
Behavioral Intervention Teams 154
bourgeois ethics 2, 6, 7, 10, 13, 21
The Bourgeois Virtues: Ethics for an Age of Commerce 5
The Boys of Baraka 35
Brice, Namond 40, 47, 49–52, 54–58, 80, 164
Brother Mouzone 12–13, 19, 99–100, 110
Brown vs. Board of Education 26
Bubbles 55, 93
Bug 90

Carcetti, Thomas J. "Tommy" 32, 91, 119
Carr, Malik [qm]Poot[qm] 8, 152, 163
Carver, Ellis 2, 95, 105–106, 127, 164
Cheryl 100, 101, 105–106
chess 8, 17, 94, 142; *see also* pawns
class (socioeconomic) 6, 13–14, 17, 25, 27, 30, 32, 33–37, 46–47, 64, 69, 70–71, 77, 81, 83–88, 90–9, 93–94, 119, 121–123, 132–133, 135–136, 140
colorblind 42, 66, 67, 72, 76
Colvin, Major Howard "Bunny" 16, 20–21, 36, 51, 57–58, 119, 129
The Corner 101, 122, 123, 125–126, 143, 155
criminal legal system 69, 73, 76
critical media literacy 24
critical race theory 3, 41–42, 44–45, 64–66, 68, 76–77, 146
Crystal, Billy 101, 112
cultural competency 2–3, 24–26, 33, 37, 77
culturally deprived 26
Cutty 51, 55

Daniels, Cedric 165
Davis, Sen. Clay 18
democracy 2, 64, 66, 80, 81
discourse 2, 27, 29, 64–65, 70, 72, 77, 81, 83–84, 163, 165
diversity 30, 33, 63, 132–133, 143, 157; cultural 24–25
domains of power 136, 139; framework 3, 64, 66, 68, 69, 76, 77
drug sentencing laws 3

Ecological Systems Theory 3, 41, 43
economic bifurcation 158, 165
education 1–4, 11, 20, 24–31, 33–37, 40–43 45–48, 52–53, 65, 67–73, 76, 80–87, 89–90, 92–95, 119, 121–122, 125–126, 128–129, 132, 134, 137, 138, 140, 148, 150–151, 157

Edward Tilghman Middle School 25, 29, 32–33, 70
entrepreneur 26, 28, 82, 94; paradoxical 32–33
epistemologies of ignorance 4, 132–137, 139–140, 143
equal opportunity 43

Fair Housing Act of 1968 45
Freamon, Lester 22, 122, 148

the game 7, 8, 11, 13, 15–19, 50, 52, 74–75, 77, 92, 94, 126
Gates, Bill 85
gender expression 2, 43
giftedness 25, 26, 28–31, 33, 37
Gray, Freddie 164
Greggs, Shakima 3, 98, 100, 113, 126; see also Sohn, Sonja

Hamsterdam 16–18, 20
Hanushek, Eric 85
Hauck, Thomas "Herc" 2, 74, 100, 105–106
hegemony 64, 83
heteronormative 105–106, 113
homeownership 67, 157–158
homophobia 103, 105, 112, 152
hooks, bell 33–34, 129
Humanomics 5, 6, 21

income inequality 3, 116, 120
institutional racism 77
interest convergence 42, 84
intersectionality 25, 42–43, 46, 52, 69, 83, 135, 141, 146

leadership 2, 26, 28–30, 51
Lee, Michael 2, 24–26, 28–31, 36, 40, 46, 48–60, 82, 89–90, 125,164
liberalism 42; neo- 80–83, 89, 94
Lipman, Pauline 82
Little, Omar 2–3, 12–13, 19, 80, 95, 98–101, 103–107, 109–113, 118, 124, 152; see also Williams, Michael K.
lived experience 2, 43, 46–47, 65, 75, 77, 148

marginalization 3, 43, 48, 63–64, 70–71, 75–76
market 6, 9, 16–17, 19, 21, 81, 83; free 14

McCloskey, Deirdre 5, 6, 9–10, 12–15, 17, 20, 21
McNulty, James "Jimmy" 2, 7, 9, 18, 100–101, 104–106, 108–110
Means, Alexander 82
meritocracy 42–43, 84, 88
Michaels, Walter Been 82
Millennial 139, 151
Ms. Anna 32, 56, 74, 95

narrative 26, 34–37, 52, 65, 77, 81–84, 98–99; counter 65; master 25, 33; personal 25, 28
A Nation At-Risk 27
The National Education Policy Center 81
Net Generation 151
New Day Co-Op 15, 19, 20
Ngai, Sianne 87
No Child Left Behind Act 27, 71, 83, 123, 163

objectivity 42, 66
oppression 42, 46, 63–64, 66, 76–77, 99, 133, 138–140
Other 65, 68, 77, 86, 133; historically othered groups 25, 34, 35

pawns 8–9, 75, 142,
Pearlman, Assistant State Attorney Rhonda 104
pedagogy 3–4, 26, 29, 30, 32, 34, 47, 51, 69, 71, 73, 80, 82, 91–95, 99, 102, 113, 117, 125, 128, 129, 132, 135, 138, 149–150, 152, 162
Phenomenological Variant of Ecological Systems Theory 3, 41, 43
pragmatic intellectualism 31
predominantly white institutions 4, 26, 86, 132, 141
price elasticity of demand 11, 19
Proposition Joe 8, 12–13, 15
Proposition 63 71
Proposition 227 71
Pryzbylewski, Roland "Prez" 2, 31, 46, 51, 55–56, 70–71, 73, 125, 127–128, 165

queer theory 3, 98–103, 105–107, 109, 111–113, 146

racial socialization 43
racialized contexts 3, 41, 47–48, 53

racist ideology 42
The Rational Optimist 5
redlining 66
Rethinking Schools 81
Ridley, Matt 5

Sapper 12
Schiavelli, Vincent 101
school-to-prison pipeline 72
sentimentalism 86–87
sexuality 2, 46, 64, 68, 91, 105–107, 109, 112, 135–136, 138,
Shamrock 11
Sharrod 90
Simon, David 7,-9, 17–18, 21, 40, 82, 87–90, 98–102, 111–113, 116, 118–129, 143
snitching 32–34, 74–75
snoop 126
social construction 3, 42, 65, 70
socially disadvantaged 26
Sohn, Sonja 111–113, 129
Stanfield, Marlo 18, 20, 28–29, 40, 100, 104, 109–110, 122, 123
storytelling 42, 65, 89

Teach for America 81
tracking 27, 82
trauma 93, 153, 164

undergraduate 3, 24, 33–37, 98, 101–102, 109, 113, 117, 119–120, 127, 142, 163
University of Maryland 51, 72, 119, 164

violence 7, 15–17, 30, 75, 86, 88–89, 92, 99, 141 152–154

Wagstaff, Randy 24–26, 28, 32, 95, 127
Waiting for Superman 3, 81–88, 90–93
Walker, Officer Eddie 75–77, 164–165
Weems, Duquan 24–26, 28, 30–32, 40–41, 46–52, 54, 56–58, 90, 95, 125, 127
white privilege 133, 135, 165
white supremacy 42
Williams, Michael K. 105
Wright, Brandon 12, 103–105, 152

www.ingramcontent.com/pod-product-compliance
Lightning Source LLC
Chambersburg PA
CBHW031136270326
41929CB00011B/1647